D0451567

THE BANK TELLER

and other essays
on the

POLITICS OF MEANING

The Bank Teller and Other Essays on the Politics of Meaning is copublished by Acada Books and The New College of California Press.

ACADA BOOKS, founded in 1996, is an independent press dedicated to publishing books that inspire personal and social transformation. Acada Books publishes college texts in the social sciences, concentrating on books that combine the scholarship and focus of a college text with the readability and accessibility of a general nonfiction book. For more information, visit Acada Books on the Web at www.acadabooks.com.

NEW COLLEGE OF CALIFORNIA is an accredited, alternative college born in 1971 out of the spirit of idealism that characterized the social movements of the 1960s. Offering graduate and undergraduate degrees, New College seeks to link education with the creation of a just, sacred, and sustainable society. The New College of California Press is a new alternative university press that aspires to publish works of all kinds that reflect the college's transformative spiritual and political vision. For more information, visit New College on the Web at www.newcollege.edu.

Susun Weed

THE BANK TELLER

and other essays

on the

POLITICS OF MEANING

PETER GABEL

 ACADA
BOOKS

 New College of California

Copyeditor: David Sweet
Proofreader: Jill Batistick
Indexer: Debbie Lindblom
Designer: Desktop Miracles

© 2000 Peter Gabel

All rights reserved. No part of the material protected by this copyright notice may be reproduced or utilized in any form or by any means electronic or mechanical, including photocopying, recording, or by any information storage and retrieval system, without the written permission of the publisher.

Acada Books
1850 Union Street, PMB 1236
San Francisco, California 94123-4309
Tel. 415.776.2325
info@acadabooks.com
www.acadabooks.com

All of the essays included in this volume, with the exception of "The New College Manifesto," were originally published in *Tikkun* magazine, 2107 Van Ness Avenue, Suite 302, San Francisco, California 94109, 415-575-1200, www.tikkun.org. Letters to the editor are reprinted with the permission of Eric I. B. Beller, Robert Blauner, Mark Bridger, Barry Bunow, and Joseph Chuman. Alan Dershowitz's contribution to "The Moral Obligation of Criminal Defense Lawyers in the Wake of the O.J. Simpson Trial" is reprinted with his permission and is gratefully acknowledged.

Publisher's Cataloging-in-Publication
(Provided by Quality Books, Inc.)

Gabel, Peter.
   The bank teller : and other essays on the politics of meaning / Peter Gabel. – 1st ed.
      p. cm.
      Includes index.
      ISBN: 0-9655029-6-1 (hardcover)
      ISBN: 0-9655029-7-X (paperback)
      1. Political culture—United States.   2. Political psychology.   3. Political sociology.
4. Meaning (Psychology)   I. Title.

JA75.7.G33   1999   306.2'0973
                                                             QBI99-50062

Printed in the United States of America

1 2 3 4 5 — 04 03 02 01 00

To Sam!
—and to the memory of my father, Martin Gabel

CONTENTS

PART III

The Spiritual Dimension of Public Policy

PART IV

The Law Not as Rules but as a Meaning-Creating Public Culture

PART V

Short Essays on the Nature of Movements, the Media, and Foreign Relations

PART VI

How Can We Build a Parallel Universe?

A PRACTICAL PROTOTYPE

PREFACE

YOU ARE ABOUT TO ENJOY A UNIQUE INTELLECTUAL EXPERIENCE—reading one of the most significant thinkers in the United States as he reveals the deepest realities of daily life in contemporary alienated society. The politics of meaning that Peter Gabel articulates in this powerful collection of essays has the capacity to fundamentally transform our society. The ideas you read here will remain with you for many years—and eventually they will become the major ideas shaping the thinking of all those who wish to heal and transform the world. Peter Gabel has been more than a brilliant theorist—he is someone who has put his whole life behind the ideas herein articulated. For over thirty years, since the time he began his intellectual evolution in the late 1960s, Gabel has courageously sought to embody his beliefs in the real world.

Gabel was among those in the generation of the sixties who continued to hold his ideals for social transformation when they became less popular in the mid-seventies. After graduating from Harvard Law School and then teaching at University of Minnesota Law School, Gabel had a clear path to the kind of success that so many others opted for in despair of seeing the kinds of societal changes for which they had earlier struggled. Instead, Gabel became an intellectual activist, joining with others to create a powerful assault on the privileges and self-deceptions of the legal profession through the formation of the Critical Legal Studies organization. Rather than pursue a career in the elite universities where "critique" might go easily with comfortable tenure and social power, Gabel moved to San Francisco and became an architect of the Law School at New College of California, an accredited alternative progressive institution that continues to perpetuate the revolutionary energy of the 1960s. Gabel's vision and humanity was quickly recognized by his colleagues, and he soon became president of New College of California and with a few close allies shepherded that school for twenty-five years.

But Gabel's restlessly creative mind could not find fulfillment in the categories provided by legal scholarship, so while he was teaching and administering at New College he simultaneously pursued a Ph.D. in clinical psychology at the Wright Institute in Berkeley. We recognized each other almost immediately as brothers who shared a similar commitment to *tikkun olam,* the healing and transformation of the planet, and as people who dared to "go for it" rather than wish we had while wondering why we had not. Out of that friendship sprang a series of ventures together, including the creation of the Institute for Labor and Mental Health, where I developed the empirical foundations of my own thinking about the deprivation of meaning in the lives of middle-income Americans, and in the creation of a graduate school of psychology at New College that Peter and I jointly administered in the first part of the 1980s.

Over and over again, I watched as Peter made choices that sought to embody his own highest ideals, even when that seemed wildly impractical to those around him. He was unwilling to compromise with partial or pretend relationships—he insisted on the deepest honesty. When people around him who had experienced the liberatory possibilities of the sixties began to forget all that they knew, Peter reminded them, insisted on staying true to what he knew, even when doing so was not popular.

After Nan Fink and I founded *Tikkun* magazine, Peter played a decisive role in shaping its direction. Although *Tikkun* came out of the Jewish world, it sought to address the failure of the liberal and progressive world to understand the hunger for meaning and purpose and loving connection that is so central to the lives of most people. Peter became our most articulate and consistent theorist of how these issues play out in daily life, and what you are about to read is largely a collection of the insights he developed in *Tikkun.*

In the mid-1990s Peter and I founded an organization called the Foundation for Ethics and Meaning, and in a large gathering of some eighteen hundred people in Washington, D.C., in 1996 we found confirmation of our perception that the ideas of the politics of meaning were the most powerful way to get to the heart of the contemporary realities of American politics and society. Peter took the lead in forming a "law task force" that continues to push forward some of these ideas within the sphere of law.

Although my own work as editor of *Tikkun* and as author of the book *The Politics of Meaning: Restoring Hope and Possibility in an Age of Cynicism* has given me greater public visibility, I've always tried to remind people that the fundamental conceptual framework of the politics of meaning was a joint product of the two of us. It's often hard to say which of us generated which part of the framework—we brainstormed, argued, and struggled together on many parts of this analysis, and to some extent that process enabled us to overcome some of the sickening egotism that leads many intellectuals to treat their ideas as some private preserve that they need to bank and protect from use by others.

Nothing would make us happier than for you to take the ideas in this book and make them your own.

I feel blessed by creation that it placed me on the earth at this particular moment, and gave me the opportunity to think and grow with Peter Gabel. I believe that the world needs his ideas and needs his leadership. My hope is that as this book becomes widely read, others will come to recognize Peter as the unique treasure he is, and begin to assimilate the importance of his work and the continuing power of his life.

—Rabbi Michael Lerner
July 1999

INTRODUCTION

IT IS IMPOSSIBLE TO BE ALIVE TODAY WITHOUT FEELING at a distance from one's own life, without *being* at a distance from one's own life. We are present in an absent world. Within ourselves, we feel each day and across all our days a longing for the promised land, a longing to fully realize the impacted Someone who we know we are through a meaningful coming-into-connection with the presence of the Other. By "the Other" I mean both actual other persons who hold in their presence both the desire and the capacity to bless us with the recognition that would allow us to emerge into authentic community, and I also mean the Divine Other that authentic community necessarily exists in relation to. For when we emerge from our isolation and become fully present to each other through the blessing and power of mutual recognition, we experience a spiritual elevation that inherently points us in an ethical and transcendental direction. We know immediately, self-evidently, that realizing ourselves through becoming present in community is but a moment on the path toward Being realizing itself through the healing and transformation of all that it is not yet. That is why the experience of authentic community always leads to the struggle for social justice and toward affirming the sacredness of the natural world—my becoming-present to the other, and to myself through the other, is not a completed state to be contemplated but a movement toward something beyond the present moment of which the present moment is an incarnation. The ethical imperative that emerges from the experience of becoming present through mutual recognition is thus not some burden or externally imposed duty, but a spontaneous discovery of where we want to go and must go if our life is to be meaningful. Out of the pain and disconnection of drifty isolation, we thus enter the world and discover the significance of the relationship of the present to the future—that is what meaning is.

Today this experience of authentic social connection and consequent sense of higher meaning and purpose is largely denied to us. We are surrounded by an empty outer world that purports to be real and full of energy and direction. This is the world of the Internet and the stock market, the world of the impeachment of the president and the Academy Awards and this month's holiday and so-and-so's wedding. Each day we wake up and try to take part in this world, try to "catch up to" its purported reality and make it our own.

But we can't. We can't catch up to it because it has no spiritual center. It is not really there, and we are really here. The fact that there is now free e-mail on Yahoo! *means* absolutely nothing to us. Monica Lewinsky is a "story" that she herself cannot catch up to before the story of herself vanishes into the War in Yugoslavia and no one shows up at her book signings. We take a vacation, but the pleasant sensations cannot support the vacation's attempt to *mean* something. Each day millions of vacations come to an end and dissolve into mere "time off" that happened and is now over. Time off from nothing, from a succession of meetings and errands that don't quite ever add up to anything because they do not emanate from and do not return to the spiritual center of who one is. The result is a crisis of meaninglessness—a disconnect between our very substantial, felt longings to realize the spirit that we are through an embodied communal life within which our spirit is recognized and engaged in the making of meaning toward externalizing and realizing communal life's own highest development, and an actual surrounding life-world that is strangely antisubstantial and absent to itself, that is impossible to grab onto while requiring of us that we go through the motions of participating in it.

This book is about how we construct and reconstruct this alienated world in spite of our desire for authentic social connection and higher meaning and purpose. It is also about the new link that is needed between spirituality and politics if we are to lead ourselves out of this paradoxical situation. I say the situation is paradoxical because although every human being on the planet seeks the communal redemption and sense of mutual recognition that I speak of—just as every baby seeks out eye contact with mother—our collective effort to express and realize this desire at present keeps taking a form that can only lead to this desire's imprisonment, to what I call the "the circle of collective denial" that results from a "rotating lack of confidence in the desire of the other" (p. 87). Our desire to fully recognize and be recognized by the other engenders a vulnerability to the other that keeps appearing to threaten us with a kind of spiritual annihilation that in turn leads us to deny our authentic desire and hide behind a congerie of images and masks, both personal and collective, which in turn keeps creating and re-creating the very alienated world that we long to transcend. The fear of annihilation by the other in turn keeps creating and re-creating the increasingly real risk of annihilation, the actual extinction of human life on earth.

Consider the following two news stories reported on the front pages of this week's newspapers in the United States (May 26–June 2, 1999):

1. This year's American corn crop has been genetically engineered to produce worm-resistant kernels of corn. But this corn also, as a result of the genetic manipulation, has produced a toxin that is accidentally killing off the beautiful Monarch butterfly.

2. During the last years of the Soviet Union, Soviet leaders sought to dispose of hundreds of tons of anthrax bacteria—enough to kill everyone on the planet many times over—by pouring bleach into the canisters of pink powder containing the anthrax and dumping the thus decontaminated anthrax onto a remote island in the Aral Sea. However, the Aral Sea has since been shrinking as a result of Soviet irrigation policies, and the remote island has grown from 77 square miles to 770 and will soon be connected to the mainland. In addition, live anthrax spores have recently been discovered in the island's soil and can easily be spread by rodents, lizards, and birds. Uzbekistan and Kazakhstan are now calling on the United States for help.

The essays in this book seek to provide a description, at once spiritual and political, of the alienation of self from other that has produced these awe-inspiring stories. Each point of divorce from our spiritual center in the stories— for example, hallucinatory nationalism and the demonization of the other, the severing of scientific knowledge and its use from the spiritual being of natural phenomena, the way that a television commercial for cornflakes would unknowingly reinforce our inability to experience the being of the butterfly and its wonder for us, the despiritualization of public policy that could have led the experts who approved the decisions to mutate the corn or breed the anthrax to believe that their decisions were entirely rational, the alienated assumptions underlying existing conceptions of law that could make the creation of the genetically engineered corn and the production of the anthrax entirely legal, the "perfectly normal" organizational consciousness of the humans who produced, say, the genetic material in the first story and the canisters of pink powder in the second—each of these points of divorce from the soul are taken up in one or another of the essays in the book and are brought into connection with the essential divorce of self from other, and from the Divine Other, that is the book's central theme.

But self and other are not actually divorced, and that is why we are still here, and why a "great turning," as Joanna Macy has called it, may still occur. The problem is rather that our connection is denied. Our task is therefore to figure out how this connection that always subtends our reciprocity can be affirmed. The carrying out of this task requires that we develop a new connection between spirituality and politics that Michael Lerner and I have called the politics of meaning.

The politics of meaning is both a way of understanding the world and a strategy for how to change it. We begin with the cry (we could call it a claim or an assertion, but it is really a cry) that our collective Spirit is in crisis because the economic, political, and social institutions that envelop us fail to speak to our common longing to connect with one another and with the natural world in a sacred and life-giving way. This alienating (distancing, isolating) cultural envelopment frustrates our longing to participate in a spiritually meaningful communal life that would aspire to the fullest realization of our social being. Instead, social-economic institutions, such as the competitive marketplace, foster a climate of materialism, individualism, and mutual suspicion that denies this common longing, drives our loving and caring impulses underground, and seeks to prevent their expression through the threat of humiliation posed by our culture's main social defense mechanism—cynicism.

Reinforcing these social and economic institutions is a dominant political culture that uncritically accepts the view that economic self-interest is the key to understanding what motivates people and therefore ultimately shapes social reality. Locked in a two-hundred-year-old individualistic paradigm that treats spiritual longings as a private matter to be dealt with by each person in isolation rather than as an inherently social matter of great public importance, most American thinkers, politicians, and pundits from all political spectrums present narrow money-centered or economy-centered explanations of what people want from their political leaders—high-wage jobs; the legal right to equality of opportunity to compete in the marketplace; early computer literacy in public education; health care defined as impersonal insurance coverage; Social Security and Medicare as comprising the sum total of what older people want and need. That people have a need for social connection, meaning, and community that they desperately want addressed in our public social and political life is rendered invisible by this prevailing discourse. That the frustration of these needs influences and explains much of what happens in mainstream politics—explains, for example, why so few people are motivated to vote, or why those who do so often support conservative initiatives that provide them with at least a distorted sense of community ("English Only" laws, for example), or why people so often vote against their economic self-interest when their hope and idealism is spoken to (consider the broad working-class support for Ronald Reagan or the willingness of early Bill Clinton supporters to pay higher taxes for health care and for the participation of young people in a government-supported National and Community Service Program) . . . these are meaning-centered aspects of our political life that those trapped in the dominant economic paradigm cannot see or understand.

The politics of meaning insists that people's subjective longings for love, caring, meaning, and connection to a spiritual/ethical community larger than the self are as fundamental as the need for food and shelter in the purely physical or economic realm. We wholeheartedly support the struggle for economic justice and security, but we insist that people are fundamentally motivated by more than sheer physical survival, that we are social beings who long to be confirmed by others and to give to others, to emerge from our painful isolation and fully recognize one another in an experience of relationship that Martin Buber called "I and Thou." In Michael Lerner's formulation, each of us deserves to be recognized as created in the image of God, understood not as a supernatural being but as the ethical force in the universe of which we are each a unique manifestation. And each of us deserves to live in a social world in which fostering the spirit of empathy, affirmation, and compassion that accompanies such a recognition would be the very centerpiece of public life.

The strategic aspect of the politics of meaning calls for developing a new kind of politics that actually seeks to create a spiritually alive public sphere, that aims at awakening and speaking to the longing for participation in meaningful community as a central goal of politics itself. In part, this means creating a safe and affirming political movement that embodies the compassion and spiritual aliveness to each other that we seek in the larger society. A politics of meaning must be one that spreads hope infectiously, by example, in order to successfully counter the way our ideas are likely to be caricatured by the cynicism of a media defended against the very longings we are naming. Our strategy also requires developing broad public policies and concrete political initiatives that are meaning-creating in the sense that they evoke, at the rhetorical level, and point toward, at the practical level, the creation of the lived experience of connection, compassion, and community.

It is this emphasis on the creation of meaning that distinguishes the politics of meaning from other liberal and progressive approaches. For the past one hundred fifty years, the politics of both liberals and the Left has been based primarily on the achievement of objective, material goals—more jobs, improved wage levels, health benefits, Social Security, expanded economic opportunity unimpeded by discrimination, or, at the more radical end of this liberal-Left spectrum, worker ownership and control of the means of production. Although we support these objective goals, they have historically been based on a vision of politics that fails to address the social alienation, the alienation of "I" from "Thou," that we see as the principal source of the inequality and injustice that these goals seek to rectify. For liberals and the Left, politics has been understood as an effort to acquire State power to change external aspects of reality, rather than a spiritual effort to manifest our collective presence in public space in a way that can heal the alienation of I from Thou. Yet it is just such an effort that is needed to overcome the fear of one another that keeps us sealed in our individual boxes and unable to experience the longing for connection with the other that dwells within each of us. People long for the opportunity to give and be given to, to care and be cared for, to see and to be seen in a relation of truly being present to each other; and if given that opportunity in a safe context that is unlikely to backfire on them, they will choose the meaningfulness of empathic community over the isolation of individual self-interest. A political movement that is able to make the eradication of objective inequality and injustice a meaningful expression of the subjective longing for participation in an empathic community can gradually create a revolution. But a politics that seeks only to alter the externals of the current distribution of wealth and power while leaving people in the passive isolation of their "individualism" will inevitably provoke bitterness and resentment and will have difficulty sustaining even modest liberal reforms, much less inspire a more fundamental social transformation.

So, for example, a policy that seeks to discourage teenagers from joining violent gangs must address the meaning and the sense of pride that young people get from gang membership—there is no use expecting a jobs program drawn from the economic paradigm to counter the communal appeal of gangs;

so any such policy that we develop must link its job-training or skills-training features to meaning-creating activity (such as the opportunity to give, and to be recognized as generous, that is often provided by participation in community service activities if they are designed with this "subjective" goal in mind). Universal health care should have our support, but within a rhetoric and a practical framework that gives people the opportunity to feel that they are taking care of others and are being cared for by others, rather than in a form that conceives of health care as simply insuring physical bodies by raising taxes on isolated and alienated individuals to fund an impersonal bureaucracy designed to appease the economic self-interest of doctors and insurance companies (and that fails to speak to *their* respective meaning-centered aspirations to care for the sick and provide security for those who suffer unforeseen losses). Teaching empathy in public schools and deepening each student's sense of awe and wonder in the presence of birth, death, and the miracle of the universe itself should take priority over standardized tests emphasizing high-pressure competition to demonstrate proficiency in mechanistic skills (for example, number calculation) disconnected from any meaningful context. Corporations should be expected to file what Michael Lerner has called an Ethical Impact Report demonstrating their record of caring for their workers and the wider social and natural environment as part of the process of applying for public contracts, rather than being rewarded by the public only for submitting the lowest bid.

Such a perspective would revolutionize politics and have immense popular appeal. It is precisely the lack of such a progressive politics of meaning that accounts for the present weakness of a progressive movement that remains wedded to the economistic legacies of Marxism and the New Deal and to a rights-based approach to law that can only re-create rather than begin to heal the painful disconnection from each other that reinforces and is reinforced by our competitive, adversarial economic and legal institutions. The result has been the ceding of the longing for meaning and purpose to the Right, to the Christian Coalition, the Promise Keepers, the family values movement, and the Republican Party in general, which puts itself forward as the party of moral and ethical community (as expressed through defense of the patriotic nation in public life, and the ethical and loving family in private life).

For a progressive politics-of-meaning movement to succeed in really achieving national political influence, it must be a movement that challenges, in its being and its words, the current level of social alienation and isolation—in workplaces, professions, unions, schools, family and friendship circles, churches and synagogues, and in the conduct of politics itself. As I argue in one of the essays in this book ("The Relationship between Community and True Democracy: On the Need to Create a 'Parallel Universe' as the Lesson of the Republican Revival"), it is the creation of this kind of "parallel universe" within both civil society and the culture of government, coexisting alongside the alienating routines of the status quo, that will draw people, especially the younger generation, to become part of us. One goal of this book is to show in a practical way how such an effort can be attempted in our approach to everyday issues of public policy, such as health care or affirmative action, and in actual interventions we can make in our workplaces and professions (for an example of a workplace intervention, see "Generating Meaning and Connection in Workplace Culture: The New College Manifesto"; for a profession, see "The Politics-of-Meaning Platform Plank on Law"). But an equally important goal is to advocate for a way of being in politics that learns the lessons of the collapse of Marxism as well as the failings of the social movements of the sixties and the New Left. I present my highly personal version of what those lessons are in this volume's "How the Left Was Lost: A Eulogy for the Sixties." It is clear to me from my own experience that a politics of meaning must learn how to embrace rather than traumatize those who tentatively dare to resist their cynicism and take the risk of opening themselves up to a hopeful and idealistic vision of what the world and their own lives could be.

The resurgence of an interest in spirituality in the United States in recent years is a testament to the widespread dissatisfaction and emptiness that the politics of meaning is naming and addressing. But many of these spiritual movements are aimed at the pursuit of individual solutions to a social alienation that can only be healed socially. Individual solutions cannot work because the purely personal search for transcendence does not challenge the social isolation, the alienation of "I" from "Thou," that creates the disconnection from the soul in both self and other, which is what needs to be transcended. Transforming ourselves as individuals is a part of what a spiritually transformative social movement requires, but even individual efforts toward transcendence require the support of the other because we are inherently social beings. From our first breath—from conception—we exist only in relation to the other, and as I emphasize throughout this book in a phrase borrowed from R. D. Laing, we are each the other to each other. This means that we cannot transform ourselves without seeking with others to transform the alienating public culture that envelops us, and it is this social or reciprocal effort that is what the politics of meaning means by "politics." It is the link between spirituality and politics, in this sense of generating reciprocal affirmation through meaningful public action, that we must discover and invent, and it is this aspiration that distinguishes the politics of meaning from many of the other spiritual movements in America today.

I have organized the essays in this book to provide the reader with a thorough grasp of the philosophical foundations of the politics of meaning and then move toward ever more practical examples of how the theory can be "applied." I put the word "applied" in quotes because the ideas that animate the politics of meaning are not a set of analytical concepts that one can learn and then apply to particular aspects of reality in a logical, deductive fashion. These ideas are based on an intuitive knowledge that is intended to reveal the meaning of social experience, at both a general and a particular level, so that the reader can recognize this meaning through a felt experience of comprehension. As the essay on "passionate reason" in the book's first section explains, this felt experience can be achieved only through the internal revelatory power of illuminating description, rather than through the kind of "hard analysis" that is so characteristic of economics, the natural sciences, and even the dominant paradigms in political science, sociology, and public policy. Thus while this book in one sense begins with more abstract and theoretical essays and moves toward more concrete and practical ones, the aim of each essay is meant to reveal different aspects of the same experiential truth, the truth of our desire for meaning-giving social connection and also the painfulness of the reality of our current alienation. As such, the essays can be read in any order depending on the personal interest of the reader. At the suggestion of my editors, I have written separate introductions to each section of the book—designed both to provide a unifying frame for the essays within each section and to connect the book's parts so that the reader can more easily follow the book's development across its divergent subject matters. However, if at first you have trouble connecting with some of the more philosophical essays in part 1 ("The Meaning of the Holocaust," for example, is a difficult essay on an extremely difficult subject), I encourage you to first read "What Moves in a Movement" in part 5.

The writers from previous generations who most influenced the development of my thinking were Jean-Paul Sartre and the radical psychiatrist R. D. Laing. It was through them, and through the classroom teaching of philosopher and literary critic Frederic Jameson at Harvard in the late 1960s, that I first came to be able to see that the "alienness" that I felt within myself was more the result of the world than the result of some missing part in me. Encountering the ideas of these teachers at the same time that I was encountering the opening up of desire that was the 1960s decisively shifted my entire adult development and gave birth to a kind of explosion of insight that later gave rise to these essays. Along the way my thinking was profoundly deepened by a several-year study of both Marxist and psychoanalytic traditions—by the works of Marx and Freud themselves and by the many followers of those writers who modified and deepened their thought. During my years in graduate school in the late 1970s at the Wright Institute in Berkeley, I had the good fortune to spend several years studying Marx and Engels, Antonio Gramsci, Herbert Marcuse and other writers in the Frankfurt School, and the entire canon of Western Marxism that has been in hibernation since the collapse of the Soviet Union. At the same time in pursuit of my doctorate in social-clinical psychology I read and was influenced by Freud and his followers in the object-relations school, most notably by the writing of British psychoanalyst Ronald Fairbairn, by Harry Stack Sullivan's interpersonal theory, and then by the important insights of Jacques Lacan, who helped to bring my thinking about the origins of alienation in childhood to a new level. Today, I no longer agree in a direct way with the thinking of any of these writers with the exception of Laing and Sartre because I see both the Marxist and the Freudian traditions as too joyless in their thinking—their rationalism and materialism seems to me to have kept them from actually grasping the liberating and hopeful spirit of Being itself, which is at the center of Being's spiritual development and its struggle against its own alienation. For me today it is much more important to grasp the truth of "All You Need Is Love" and to go from there than it is to master the analytics of Freudian or Marxian conceptual schemes that want to explain the present "from the outside" by going backward from the outside into the past. Nevertheless, the ideas in these traditions had a big impact on my understanding of what Love is up against.

Among my own generation, I owe the most thanks to my friends in the critical legal studies movement and the politics-of-meaning movement—especially Duncan Kennedy, Karl Klare, Alan Freeman, Morty Horwitz, Mark Tushnet, David Trubek, and Gary Peller from the critical legal studies days, and Michael Lerner and Michael Bader from the present days of the politics of meaning. Apart from specific insights about the world that I have learned from these lifetime comrades, all of them have continually strengthened my belief in hope and vitality itself, which as I have just suggested is the main thing for me in understanding what is wrong with the world and how perhaps to lean into the situation and change it for the better. The same thanks is owed for the same transmission of confidence to my great friends and coworkers at New College of California, where I have spent virtually my whole adult life trying and failing and trying again to build a loving and less alienated world in my own everyday existence. Martin Hamilton, Milly Henry, Kathy Voutyras, Bob Brown, Michael McAvoy, Chris Kanios, Paul Harris, Colleen O'Neal, Diana Bullock, and Bill Bloodgood have been the mainstays of my everyday life for over twenty years and the mainstays of my belief in the possibility of utopia, without which it is hard to make even small radical transformations of the present moment.

Special thanks are reserved, however, for Michael Lerner. With the exception of the New College Manifesto that concludes the book, all the essays in this book were first published in *Tikkun* magazine over roughly the last fifteen years and were improved by the wisdom of Michael's suggestions and support. But my collaboration with Michael began long before *Tikkun*'s birth in 1985: we met in graduate school at the Wright Institute in 1975 and began there the series of conversations, joint projects, and public conferences that enabled both of us to develop our thinking about the need for a new theoretical framework for those who wished to transform the world in a more humane, egalitarian, and loving direction. The ideas that Michael has put forward in *Tikkun* and in his books—especially in *Jewish Renewal* and *The Politics of Meaning*—have greatly influenced my thinking, as much as his solidarity and steadfastness have strengthened my confidence. The overall vision that we call the politics of meaning is very much the product of each of us and both of us, the result of two quite different individuals together deepening their understanding of the world by deepening their connection to each other through intellectual work, political activism, and permanent friendship.

Finally, thank you to Paul Garber for his editorial assistance with earlier drafts of the manuscript; to Gary Peller for flying out to San Francisco and spending a week with me helping to organize the essays in the most compelling way; to Matthew Wilkes for his careful reading and improvement of the final manuscript; to my publishers, Brian and Robin Romer, for linking the work of creating the book itself with a genuine belief in the importance of its ideas; and to my partner, Lisa Jaicks, for her love and encouragement.

PART ONE

PHILOSOPHICAL FOUNDATIONS
The Desire for Mutual Recognition

THESE ESSAYS PRESENT THIS BOOK'S CENTRAL ideas in philosophical form, but with the exception of "On Passionate Reason," they do so through descriptions of important concrete examples drawn from everyday life (corporate life and culture), history (the Holocaust), and the prevailing secular-liberal worldview (the theory of evolution). My main ideas can be roughly stated in the abstract as follows: We all are animated by a desire for mutual recognition and affirmation that is as fundamental as the need for food and shelter. We have inherited a world in which that desire is routinely denied, by each of us as well as the others around us, not through any fault of our own but through the legacy of centuries of conditioning that lead us to alienate ourselves from ourselves, from one another, and from the natural world. The conflict between our desire and our envelopment in a social environment that denies this desire (through a process that I call "misrecognition"), and the distortions in human relations and in our ways of seeing and thinking resulting from this conflict, provide the key to understanding what is wrong with our existing social reality and how to change it. Perceiving the centrality of the desire for mutual recognition and the ubiquitous social alienation produced by the denial of this desire requires a new way of seeing and a new way of thinking, one based on the passionate, empathic illumination of our shared lived experience rather than a detached "analysis" of an externally conceived "society" seen as an "entity." This new method of thinking is the way to bring out the link between the spiritual nature of our longings as social and natural beings and a new approach to politics as a kind of spiritual activism that emerges from an understanding of these longings. Such a spiritual politics, or politics of meaning, must pursue the goal of a progressive social transformation—including such objective goals as the redistribution of wealth and the creation of a just, cooperative, and ecologically sustainable economy, as well as such subjective goals as the creation of community and the recovery of the sacredness of all human and natural life—by healing the legacy of alienation that is the principal source of the world's objective and subjective wrongs.

Yet this kind of abstract presentation of the book's ideas, while perhaps being helpful as a sort of skeletal framework for tying these essays together, is of limited value for a philosophy that makes *illumination* the basis for its claim to being true. Illumination requires concrete examples, descriptions of aspects of social reality that reveal that reality in a new way. That is why I have chosen in the opening section to take three disparate phenomena of major social importance and attempt not to "explain" them with abstract concepts, but to *reveal* the social meaning of these phenomena through the concrete use of these concepts in a way that enriches the description of these phenomena, that makes their social meaning more visible. Thus in this opening section, I describe first the world of banks and bank tellers, in a new way that is meant to illuminate the nature and meaning of corporate hierarchies. Then I seek to capture the experiential meaning of the Holocaust, in a way that is meant to illuminate the link between the terror of humiliation that underlies our social alienation and the infliction of human suffering. Finally, following a theoretical chapter that places the method of illumination you have just encountered in the first two essays in the context of (and in opposition to) this century's dominant critical approaches of Marxism and deconstruction, I give another example of my descriptive approach in addressing the distortions imposed by science upon the creationism-evolution debate. My aim here is to show that the approach advocated in this book can make visible the meaning not only of institutional structures like corporate hierarchies and otherwise incomprehensible social evils like the Holocaust, but also the meaning of alienated knowledge, or knowledge cut off from the spiritual foundations of our social being and the being of nature.

Thus the idea of part 1 is to present a philosophical vision of the nature of social reality as a whole by showing how that vision illuminates the meaning of three concrete significant aspects of that reality.

THE BANK TELLER

The Experiential Origins of Hierarchy

IMAGINE A ROW OF BANK TELLERS SERVING CUSTOMERS in a typical American bank. Although all of them appear to be performing competently, taking and giving paper, opening and closing drawers, showing for the most part efficient politeness and a good mood to each person who approaches the window, we know that they are under a great deal of stress. We know this not primarily because we know the objective conditions that define their respective situations—that they must perform a repetitive series of manual operations very rapidly in order to keep their jobs, earn a subsistence wage, and so forth—but because we detect in each of them, simply from the vantage point of an onlooker, a continual artificiality. Each reveals in every word and gesture what we might call the attitude of being a bank teller. Each feels compelled to *enact* an "efficient politeness" and a "good mood." They feel this politeness and good mood not as spontaneous expression, but as a kind of role that is somehow superimposed on their being from an experiential "outside."

Thus we can detect that they feel somehow "outside" themselves and "inside" the enacted role of being-a-bank-teller. And we can detect that this is stressful to each of them precisely to the degree that it is artificial, that through being compelled to feel artificial in this way they feel at the same time unable to express themselves spontaneously. Neither we nor they can know what this spontaneous expression would look like exactly because both we and they feel it only as an absence.

A good way of measuring this absence is to notice that each gesture is a moment "behind" or "too late," and it is this fraction of delay time that reveals to us the gesture's enacted quality. We can see that they are perpetually acting *as if* they were bank tellers, and one way of measuring the gap between these as-if performances and the absent spontaneity that is somehow buried inside them is in the felt sense that if spontaneity were to somehow "break through" (as sometimes happens), the delay time would vanish, absorbed in the plenitude of total presence. A whole person would have momentarily erupted through the split being of the "bank teller"; through the split "between" the as-if performance and the absence that is immanently bound within it. In a milieu of as-if performances like those of the row of bank tellers, the absent spontaneity cannot be described positively, but only negatively as something "not there," although we would immediately recognize its positive incarnation if it were suddenly to appear—we would feel that *that* is what was missing or "not there" a moment before.

This feeling of being perpetually trapped within an as-if performance that seems to come from the outside is an experience of ontological passivity. By this I mean that in their very being these bank tellers feel a loss of agency in relation to their own movements. They feel compelled to enact a "self" that is somehow not *their* self but another self that seems to move through them in the form of a role and that leaves them feeling "other" to themselves and "other" to each of the others with whom they interact. Yet this feeling of "otherness" is not a feeling that descends on the tellers individually; it is rather a collective phenomenon that unites the tellers to one another in a perverse way. Thus a new teller, when she first arrives at the bank, will proceed to indoctrinate herself into her own passivity by taking cues from all the others in discovering how to act (or how to enact herself), and in so doing she will gradually come to feel "with" the others in an as-if way, in the sense that she will come to feel, as do each of the others, that they are all undergoing the same passive experience which establishes among them a social bond. But since this social bond is constituted as a feeling of being other-than-themselves-together, of being collectively trapped within the same role, it is simultaneously pervaded by a collective sense of universal isolation, since no one is capable of really making contact with any of the others spontaneously without violating the norms of being-a-bank-teller.

Ontological passivity is, therefore, a collective experience that simultaneously divides a group of people by an infinite distance and unites them in the false communion of being-other-than-themselves-together. The source of this collective passivity and impotence is to be found in the relation of the tellers to the bank as an institution. This "bank" has a double reality, or rather its singular reality must be understood simultaneously from two points of view. On the one hand, the bank is a functional organization of human labor that has a determinate relation to economic production, in that it serves to reproduce finance capital in what economists call an "efficient" way. There is a certain division of labor that corresponds to a certain level of technological development, and the functional organization of work that derives from this correspondence bears a definite relationship to a system of economic pressures (this bank must compete with other banks, and so forth). But this approach to defining what the bank is can tell us nothing about why the tellers behave and feel as they do, because it is an approach that turns the bank into a thing.

To understand the bank as a living milieu, we must attempt to grasp "the bank" from the inside, as it is experienced by the people who dwell "within it" and who thereby create it as a collective Gestalt. In this subjective sense, the institution of "the bank" is, as we shall see, an imaginary entity to which the tellers (as well as the other "bank personnel," the customers, and so forth) have given over their being by believing in "its" existence as a determining power. Precisely to the degree that the tellers feel a loss of agency in relation to themselves, they feel themselves to be agents of "the bank" as an imaginary entity, and they feel themselves to be united with one another or socially bonded in relation to this imaginary entity. It is not an economic method of explanation but rather a sociophenomenological method of description that can make "the bank" intelligible as a lived experience for the people who create and then "inhabit" it.

The first step in gaining access to this lived experience is to detach ourselves in a radical way from the social milieu that is generated through the communication of signs (spoken language, tone of voice, gestures, and so forth) within the bank. If we can manage to attain this hyperobjective viewpoint, we can observe something that is at once perfectly obvious and normally very difficult to see or "remember"—namely, that "the bank," for all of its pretense and style, consists of nothing more than a group of people in a room. From this position of hyperobjectivity through which the social interactions before us are stripped of their symbolic and signifying content, we do not experience "the bank" at all except perhaps as a kind of random fact about what they call this type of social gathering ("this is what they call 'a bank'"). Yet to the people immersed within the socially communicated reality within the room, "the bank" has a ubiquitous presence—in fact, they cannot, except in very private and quasi-unconscious moments of distraction, escape from their absorption in "the bank" and see before them simply a roomful of people. This person who approaches the window is first of all a "customer," that person on the left is first of all a "teller like me," those velvet ropes are first of all not merely ropes but signs that "the bank" uses to "line up the customers," just as the adjacent machine with the green lights is first of all a "computer" that "the bank" uses to retrieve information about "customer accounts." Every object and person within the room, in other words, is always already layered over with a relatively impenetrable symbolic coating that seems to derive from this "bank," this entity that appears to allocate to each person a role and to each object a signifying power.

Yet from this subjective point of view, "the bank" *is* nowhere. It does not reside in the Board of Directors or in the President's office, or anywhere else except in the minds of those who believe in its existence as a kind of phantom presence that has vampirized their being and made them agents of its imaginary power. How does this collective internalization of "the bank" take place?

The answer to this question is to be found in a complex reciprocal relationship between the role of collective anxiety and the role of the bank hierarchy in shaping the internal experience of each of the bank's members. At a very deep and basic level, every person in the room feels that she is subject to both the physical and psychological power of other people, that if she fails to conform to the norms of expected behavior within the bank, she will be thrown out of the bank by force or be subject to psychological humiliation. If a "customer" fails to act like a "customer," he will be thrown out by a man with a gun; if a "teller" fails to act like a "teller," she will be fired or at least risk being socially ostracized; the same or similar sanctions are available for the "President" and even the "Chairman of the Board." This fear of dismissal in both the physical and the psychological sense is ever present at what we might call "the base" of everyone's experience, and it establishes the experiential ground for the transmutation of people's being that occurs through the internalization of the "bank," in the sense that if these conditions were not present, people might refuse to conform to what was expected of them and recover their spontaneity.

What is the source of this shared anxiety among the bank's members that each of them is in danger of being "dismissed" or humiliated by a dominant other? In part, this fear is a rational response to real inequalities of power in the bank, to the fact that many of the bank's workers must depend for their survival on owners who may be indifferent to them except as factors of production and who have the power to deprive them of both their income and their sense of social identity. But a deeper reason for the anxiety, and one that may even account for the persistence of the inequalities of economic power, is a contradiction that exists at the heart of everyone's experience. On the one hand, each person wants to connect with the others in a life-giving way, to make contact in a way that would produce a feeling of genuine recognition and mutual confirmation. This desire is fundamental to being a social person, and it animates all of us in every moment of our existence. Yet at the same time, everyone has learned to fear this very desire because its realization implies an openness to the other that leaves the self essentially vulnerable and risks a kind of total humiliation should the other respond with "disconfirmation," domination, or rejection. Since the experience of genuine connection and confirmation has been very rare for all the bank's members owing to the alienation and mistrust that pervades our social world, and since their desire for it is therefore associated with the anticipation of pain and loss, the very existence of others has become a source of ontological anxiety for them. Each person has learned to expect to be "dismissed," and so each seeks to avoid being fully present to the other by mediating his presence through a distancing persona and by making himself unconscious that this mediation has occurred.

The transmutation of each person's authentic being into a false or as-if self, therefore, occurs through a process of collective and reciprocal flight on the part of everyone from experiencing his or her own desire for real contact and the vulnerability this desire implies. By absorbing themselves in their role-performances and implicitly asserting (to themselves and others) that these performances constitute who they really are, the bank's members try to withdraw the immediacy of their social presence from their outward appearance, becoming anonymous "bank tellers," "customers," "Vice Presidents," and so on, whose artificiality makes them inaccessible to the threat of the other's gaze. The lack of agency that we earlier observed in the tellers' relationship to their own movements can now be understood as the outcome of an intentional effort to "empty" their role-performances of any signs of authorship or personal identity, and the delay time we observed in their gestures can now be seen as reflective of a chronic self-consciousness through which their outward expression is repeatedly uncoupled from its generative foundation. Yet we must ask ourselves why, if the desire for genuine connection is really a basic aspect of our being, do these tellers not find a way of resisting this perpetual flight that can only leave them continually threatened and isolated? The answer is that while they all feel the same unrealized desire, no one can ordinarily gain the confidence that the desire she feels within herself is also felt by those around her. From the point of view of her isolated position, each person always already experiences all the others as other-than-themselves, as participants in collective flight. And since the possibility of recovering one's authentic being can come only through being recognized as fully human by another, no one can normally find the strength to resist in a milieu where the possibility of such a recovery is reciprocally denied. Instead, each person feels compelled to become "one of the others" and participate in the collective flight that holds everyone's alienation in place.

The medium through which this collective flight is carried out is commonly called a hierarchy. The bank hierarchy, as I am using the term here, is a purely imaginary entity that is generated by the felt need of everyone to "identify" with "the bank," to establish the ontological basis for one's passivity as a false self by constituting an "other" before whom one can be recognized as false. This hierarchy bears no relation to the direct interpersonal relations through which real power is exercised in the bank, since real power is exercised not "from above" (there is no "above") but by one person acting directly upon another, by the subordination of one to another's will. The hierarchy is rather conjured up imaginatively as a way of escaping the universal sense of danger that I have described: it provides what we might call the imaginary vehicle through which everyone becomes able to find an imaginary and passive station in relation to everyone else. The hierarchy allows each person to substitute a legitimate authority, which is "the bank" itself as a subjectively constituted institution and which can serve as the relational agent for each person's self-falsification, for the illegitimate sense of humiliation that haunts each person's true being and true sense of what is going on in the room.

To see how the hierarchy comes into being, we need only look carefully at the reciprocal interaction that commonly takes place among two tellers and their so-called "supervisor." Let us suppose that the two tellers are called Jane and John, and that the supervisor is called Harold. Jane and John work side by side at their windows. Harold, who is otherwise engaged in a variety of lower-management clerical tasks, walks back and forth behind Jane and John and occasionally looks at them to see not only what they are doing, but who they are being. Jane discovers the contours of her as-if performance through watching John, as John does through watching Jane, and in this sense Jane and John "recognize" one another as "bank tellers." Both, in other words, take the position of "other" to the other and in so doing discover the way of becoming other to themselves. Yet because this relation of reciprocal otherness involves a loss of agency in relation to themselves and a sinking into ontological passivity that is measured by this loss of agency, both of them require an agent to ground their impoverished "identities." They must project into a third party the active power to establish the ontological basis for the series of performances that they experience as passive and lacking in any self-generated agency. Without such a third party, they could not "exist" as "bank tellers" because there would be no source for their being. This role is allocated to Harold, whom they perceive to be their authority (author-ity). And in together perceiving Harold as the source of their being, they also discover their own unification as "tellers-together," which is to say that they discover a social bond through their perception of how they believe Harold perceives them, and this bond reassures them to the degree that it compensates for the feeling of actual isolation that dwells within each of them. Harold allows them to feel the illusion of being "with" one another to the degree that each, in being "other" to each other and "other" to themselves, are "other-together" before Harold, as they perceive him. And because Harold must always remain with them as their relational "authority figure" in order for them to exist as tellers-together, they internalize him and "identify" with him as the one to whom they owe their own identities. Even in his absence, they know how to act because they have internalized his authoritative image and made it part of themselves.

Harold knows how to play his part through his empathic understanding of how tellers are supposed to be, and in fact he enacts his authority in all his relations with them, in his way of approaching them, advising them, and in criticizing their performances. Yet it is evident that this "Harold" we are describing is no more an actual person than are Jane and John. Harold merely plays the part of "supervisor," in that however "active" and "authoritative" he appears for John and Jane, he remains passive in relation to himself. He discovers his being-as-a-supervisor only through the reciprocal internalization of themselves-as-supervisors that characterizes the relations among the supervisors at his level in "the bank," relations that are pervaded by the same passivity that pervades the interrelations among the tellers. The supervisors, in enacting their authority in relation to the tellers, are also "other" to each other and "other" to themselves, and as a result they also require an agency outside themselves to activate and ground their own passivity. Harold finds this agency through his own supervisor, who is perhaps a "Vice President" and who performs for all of the supervisors at Harold's level the same ontological function that Harold performs for the tellers. Thus Harold discovers how to become a supervisor through watching and internalizing how the others at his level enact themselves as as-if authorities, while their actual experience of collective passivity is grounded for them by a superior whom they project and then internalize as the agent of their as-if selves. Thus, in the teller-supervisor-Vice-President relation we discover the ontological foundation of the hierarchy as a form of collective being, a form that I am calling imaginary because it creates the appearance, among people who are in fact simply people, of a top-down ordering that serves to establish each person's sense of his or her imaginary social place.

The paradox of the hierarchy, however, is that no one actually feels in command because the authority that the hierarchy distributes throughout itself is never more than the active role-complement of the universal passivity out of which the hierarchy is born as a projected-internalized, imaginary entity. If, for example, we reach the "top" of the hierarchy, we find a President who does not feel himself to be his own "author," because his authority is merely the as-if authority of a "President" in a "bank." He receives his authority, in other words, from the subjects who constitute him, and this requires of him that he find the basis of his own being outside himself in precisely the same fashion as the others. Yet there is no *one* "above" him; his ontological recourse is the Board of Directors, who are constituted as the "fiduciaries" of "the bank." In the realm of the imaginary, the "Board of Directors" is comparable to the modern "State," in that just as the State serves as the imaginary basis for the political unification of the "United States" and so establishes for each of us our imaginary identity as "Americans," so the Board of Directors is the incarnate representation of "the bank's" existence as a political organization (and this Board is itself enfranchised by the State, which establishes the political legitimacy of "the bank" as an entity that derives its existence ultimately from the democratic constitution of "the nation"). Thus the "President," like all the other bank personnel, finds his agency outside himself and shapes his being to the set of performances required of him by "the bank" as it is embodied for him through the Board to which he is "accountable" in an imaginary way. And since the Board members experience themselves as fiduciaries in the service of "the bank," we find that the ultimate source of authority within the hierarchy is "the bank" itself, as a phantom "other" to whom everyone "within the bank" owes their as-if existence. In this milieu of universal otherness, "the bank" is believed in as a kind of "God," an object of belief that is invested with authorship or authority for the group as a whole.

The relationship of "the bank" as an imaginary entity to the hierarchy as an imaginary ordering is, therefore, that the hierarchy is the vehicle that the group uses to bring "the bank" to themselves through a series of embodied human gazes. The underlying fear of domination and humiliation from which everyone flees is transmuted, through the constitution of "the bank" and the hierarchy through which it is concretely and intersubjectively mediated, into the shared submission of being-"other"-together before an imaginary object with whom everyone identifies as the active foundation of their passive and false selves. In and through this process, they recover an imaginary sense of being "with" one another as "of the bank," even as they are utterly lost and isolated from one another as real people who would know themselves as agents of their own collective activity.

The self that is produced within this hierarchical environment is, to borrow R. D. Laing's phrase, an ontologically divided one that has a rather complex organization. Each person experiences his or her authentic being as a privatized nonself that is denied recognition and that is therefore "invisible" or unconscious: it is known or comprehended only through the experienced bodily tension that derives from not being oneself and through a continual obsessive and preconscious fantasy life that reaches a dim awareness in moments of distraction (as in being vaguely aware of wanting to sleep with a customer, or in vaguely noticing that a shape on a wall resembles a wild dog). The "visible" or conscious self that is enacted in behavior is experienced as a "public" or "outer" synthesis of as-if performances, which is at once lived as passively undergone to the degree that it lacks any sense of its own agency and yet is "owned" to the degree that each person feels this self as "I." And corresponding to this ontologically passive public self is a projected-internalized active or authoritative "other" that serves as the passive self's agency and that generates within everyone the feeling that one's being is fashioned from the outside. This ontologically divided self-organization is the internalized residue of all forms of social organization within which people lack the actual power to express themselves freely in their practical activity together, which is to say virtually all forms of social life that have existed in human history and that exist today on earth.

Yet because each person's privatized and authentic being continually clamors for recognition in order to realize its desire and explode the false "outer" self that contains this desire, we must look more carefully at the interpersonal dynamic through which everyone's true needs are perpetually subdued in order to see how the clamoring of desire for genuine recognition by the other perpetually checks itself through being held in check by the other. The way to do this is to observe what happens in the event of a disturbance that reaches visibility, as when John begins to complain to the other tellers that he really hates his job, that it somehow makes him feel unreal and like an automaton. If John makes this complaint to Jane alone over a cup of coffee, there is no threat posed to the collective belief in "the bank" because coffee with a quasi friend (they work at adjacent windows) is sanctioned as a private space appropriate for passive commiseration, or in other words, the complaint remains sufficiently private to elicit a restorative concern.

But if John begins to "go public" with his dissatisfaction, he threatens to expose the imaginary nature of "the bank" as the vehicle of collective flight, producing within everyone an anxiety that the humiliation that everyone is fleeing from will be drawn to the surface and will *occur* for each of them. As a result, to the degree that John reveals himself publicly as being in pain, everyone will adopt toward him the position of the authoritative other through which their passive selves are secured. They will see themselves in John, see their own alienation from themselves and one another *recognized* through his affirmation of its existence, and so they will secure their own "otherness" to themselves and to one another by taking the position of the agent through whom their passivity is founded. They will act toward him, in other words, as if he is "crazy" and indicate to him that he ought not to be *being this way.* But in addressing him, they will actually be addressing themselves as they are revealed through him, simultaneously quelling their own anxiety and reestablishing their imaginary connection with one another as depersonalized "personnel," as "of the bank." In taking the position of the authoritative other, they secure a collective reassurance that is also a collective denial. And through this collective denial they perpetually suppress their true desire to recognize one another as fully human beings.

The clamoring for authentic recognition of which I speak is therefore held in check by the perpetual anticipation of this "reversal of voice" whereby the others adopt the attitude of the Other toward each other and themselves. And it is the perpetual conflict between the clamoring for recognition and the anticipation of rejection (for each person knows that he, too, would join the others in rejecting another) that produces collective despair and adaptation. But in order to guarantee that this reciprocal holding-in-check will not unravel, the "lines of authority" through which "the bank" is sustained as a totemic source of unification are usually externalized and represented in a "flowchart," which may appear in an office manual or may even be posted on a wall. This "flowchart" is nothing other than a "constitution" of the imaginary ordering in the hierarchy, and it is the institutional analogue to "the law" insofar as it attempts to legalize in an authoritative document the alienated relations that comprise "the bank" as an imaginary entity. Its image resides within the consciousness of everyone as something that can be pointed to in the event of a disruption, and its effect is to reify these alienated relations, to represent the collective experience of passivity and otherness as a timeless "fact" or "bank life." To the degree that the flowchart is internalized by everyone in this way, it establishes for everyone the basis of their abstract integration with all of the others, or in other words, it generates an appearance of social unification that contradicts the felt sense of isolation and disconnectedness that pervades each person's private experience of being in the room. As such it is both reassuring and compensatory insofar as it signifies to each person that she is "of the group" (that she is "part of something"), and repressive insofar as its abstract image of social integration is a denial of each person's concrete sense of the truth.

As a sign that is "pointed to" in the event of a disruption, the flowchart becomes an interpretive document that inscribes the necessity for both the passivity of the self, which is signified as an abstract "role" within each box, and the inevitability of reversal, which is represented in the lines linking the flowchart boxes from top to bottom. The chart is therefore a spatial representation of the temporal experience (for everyone) of being-in-the-bank, and because the spatial inscription appears as something fixed (instead of being merely the drawing that it actually is) it functions, insofar as it is internalized, as a social defense mechanism. It becomes, in other words, a shared internalized representation of "the group" that simultaneously inhibits everyone's genuine impulses for connection and recognition and partially gratifies these impulses in an imaginary way.

This, then, is a "bank" as it appears to the people who "inhabit" it. As a social institution, or an institutionalization of a particular way of being social, it is obviously not unique, but rather typical of virtually every social formation in contemporary society. Changing such institutions requires overcoming the alienation and fear that give rise to them. And this will not happen until we find a way of collectively gaining confidence that the desire we each secretly feel within ourselves exists with equal intensity in those around us, no matter how remote, threatening, or unreal they feel compelled to make themselves appear.

The Meaning of the Holocaust

Social Alienation and the Infliction of Human Suffering

CAN THE POLITICS OF MEANING HELP US to understand the Holocaust? The recent articles in *Tikkun* by Daniel Goldhagen and Zygmunt Bauman demonstrate such a need because both of these articles make assertions about the meaning of the Holocaust that the authors themselves cannot account for. Goldhagen's now famous claim that the German people as a whole were willing executioners wants to locate the meaning of the Holocaust in a relentless, culturally pervasive anti-Semitism. He argues that this anti-Semitism was literally a historical constituent of German consciousness that through cultural conditioning long preceding Nazism came to, in part, define Germanness itself. But even if this were true (and I do not believe that it is), it would only lead us to the question of what this type of nationalism built on dehumanization means for those who are taken over by it. Unless we are to assume that newborn children are blank slates upon which any conditioning can simply be imprinted in a way that then "fills up" their consciousness, we are pushed to ask deeper questions about the meaning of that conditioning process itself, about whether it is an expression of some distortion, denial, repression, humiliation that would inherently transcend the formation of German identity as such and point toward a more universal problem.

Bauman's thought-provoking counterposition is that analyses like Goldhagen's are actually expressions of a "hereditary victimhood" on the part of post-Holocaust Jews—that these Jews want to find meaning in a martyrdom borrowed from a holocaust that they did not themselves experience, leading them to elevate "survival" above all ethical values and to color the world as being comprised of one-dimensional persecutors capable of providing them with the victim-centered meaning that they seek. He shows how Goldhagen's version of the Holocaust as primarily the story of the voluntary actions of Hitler's Jew-hating helpers involves a distortion of the evidence Goldhagen uses to support his own position and a blindness to the very substantial evidence that contradicts it. According to Bauman, Goldhagen distorts his evidence in this way because he, and people like him, are reassured by the sense of meaning gained from their hereditary victimhood and so cannot be fulfilled unless the world continually reveals open hostility, violent conspiracies, and the ever-present possibility of another holocaust. Yet in reading Bauman's piece, too, we are simply pushed to the deeper question of what this paranoid sense of meaning itself means.

If this Jewish survivalism is counterrational and even potentially dangerous to Jewish survival itself (since it is arguably an aspect of Jewish consciousness in Israel that makes another war in the Middle East more likely), then the sense of meaning provided by this preoccupation with survival and victimhood must itself be accounted for by some deeper meaning, some immanent distortion and self-deception, that would make it "worth it" for these post-Holocaust Jews to pursue such a contradictory and potentially self-destructive course of conduct. Understanding that deeper meaning requires going beyond the particular form of Jewish identity characteristic of post-Holocaust Jews toward revealing that universal underlying meaning of which it is but a particular manifestation.

The politics of meaning aims exactly at understandings of this type. We seek to illuminate distortions of the longing for meaning as manifestations of that very longing, as pathological particular incarnations of a fundamental universal need. That need for meaning itself emerges from a desire that is at the heart of our very social existence—the desire for a mutual recognition through which we become fully present to each other as social beings in connection, fully confirmed in the relation Martin Buber called "I and Thou." In the unalienated social existence to which we aspire, meaningfulness is the realization, through a potentially infinite number of particular cultural embodiments, of the I and

Thou of mutual recognition. That is why movements for social justice are inherently meaningful—as they "rise up," these movements generate the very experience of becoming-present-to-each-other through a confirming recognition that grounds the call for the correction of injustice, which is always manifested as a denial of this I-Thou relation, in a particular social-historical context. At the same time, it is the emergent awareness of injustice as a denial of the I-Thou relation that exerts an ethical pull on the wider culture and in turn pulls the movement, as realization of the desire for mutual recognition, into existence.

The great problem that we face, and here we begin to reach the question of the meaning of the Holocaust, is that the aspiration toward the affirmation of mutual recognition that exists within all of us remains subordinated to the legacy of alienation that makes the other appear to us as a threat. Rather than ascribe the source of this problem to, say, the distrust fostered by the competitive capitalist market, I think it is more accurate to understand this problem as located in the spiritual evolution of being itself, and in the as yet incomplete struggle of being to know itself as Love that realizes itself through the affirmation of the other, through the I-Thou relation. The achievement of this relation in its full social manifestation—that is, in a manifestation that is able to attain a confidence that can surpass the doubt of alienation and become the foundation of a fully human social history—requires a movement of social development that is at once spiritual, political, and material, and we may well be in an ecological race against time to succeed in building such a movement.

But insofar as we have not yet achieved it, the other remains to us a threat to whom we must deny our desire for full relation, since the revelation of that desire requires a letting-go of the withdrawn ego that would leave us vulnerable to an unthinkable humiliation. And insofar as we retain the withdrawn ego, we appear to the other as threatening also—as "one of the others" like the other whom we ourselves perceive as threatening us with the humiliation of nonrecognition.

The entire process of acculturation that each of us has gone through in the formation of our present social selves has carried the weight—across many generations—of the threatening nature of the other. It has led us to develop a painful social split between the artificial self of the outer persona and the concealed inner self full of the hidden longing for recognition that the outer self, in its very artificiality, denies and renders inaccessible to the other's gaze. And in its paranoia, the withdrawn inner self must constantly monitor its outer presentation of self through a perpetual unconscious self-observation, simultaneously enacting the outer persona and scanning that enactment, which is always at risk of being seen through because of the inherent contingency—or if you like, uncontrollableness—of every actual encounter with the other. Think of the television newscaster's pseudofamiliarity and the panicky quickness with which he or she instantly corrects any slight slip of the tongue or misstatement, or the occasional completely incoherent "jokes" exchanged on these local news shows that the newscasters instantly "cover" with laughter as if the jokes made sense. These behaviors reveal—in both their artificial enacted quality and the near-instantaneous corrections of any "role-mistakes"—the threat of humiliation posed by the surrounding others. And we are all newscaster-like to some degree, claiming to the other to "really" be the outer persona we appear to be while concealing, individually and together, the fragile inner self that both longs for and fears being seen.

I am saying that this is the general social climate that envelops us, the human race, across nationalities and across our cultural particularities. There is, of course, a much more hopeful and positive way of representing the situation that would emphasize the beauty and joy of being alive, the love and recognition that we have been able as individuals and as cultures to achieve, and the upward spiritual and political movement toward each other that we may be able to discern. But my aim in writing this article is to try to understand the dark side of our present social existence, and especially the paranoia in the face of the other and the terror of humiliation that still haunts our every interaction.

Faced with the painful contradiction between our desire to realize ourselves through the other in the I-Thou relation and the prohibition against doing so that appears to be the lesson of our conditioning, the withdrawn self is driven to imaginary solutions—that is, to solutions that are withdrawn from the actual, concrete terrain of embodied self-other interactions and are lived out in the withdrawn security of the mind. To the extent that the outward persona enacted for the other retains the characteristics of an artificial role (the newscaster, "Dad," the president's need to "look presidential," and so forth), the withdrawn self seeks the protection of anonymity, presenting a performance without actual ontological presence. To maintain this inaccessibility while still seeking to satisfy our longing for the completion of authentic social connection drives us to collude in creating imaginary communities "in our heads," in an inner existential space that is literally behind the bodily enactments of our personae. There are many examples of these imaginary communities and the immense social power they acquire because of the essential longing for social connection that they address: Ronald Reagan's beatific invocation of "Morning in America"; the conservative appeals to "family values"; the sense of belonging and acceptance offered by the God and religious embrace of the Christian Right; the sense of connection to community elicited by inflated or hortatory patriotism and accompanying invocations of our bond with the Founding Fathers.

These communities are imaginary in the sense that they are not enriched by the mutual presence of the I-Thou relation. Though they purport to constitute a "We," they do not manifest the presence to each other in concrete lived experience that characterizes the reciprocity of a real "We." Instead they reflect a disembodied shared allegiance to an image cathected "in the mind" and literally withdrawn back from the real relation to the other, an allegiance that is then incorporated into the artificiality of the outer persona through such signifiers as uniforms, pledges, narrative clichés (for example, the American history taught in civics classes to young teenagers), clubs, marching bands, and the like. Assisted by the passing on of intergenerational authority to those who coordinate the intergenerational transmission of these images, they provide us with fantasies of connection in the service of protecting us from the threat of humiliation posed by the real other. That is why belief in these images is directly or indirectly compulsory, not just in the normally coercive rituals of the Pledge of Allegiance and the Lord's Prayer (at least in their schoolroom versions), but in the covert prohibition against challenging the purported "reality" of the social facade, the "reality," say, of the claim that "we" are Americans living in a land of freedom, opportunity, and happiness. The cultural fascination with the post-1960s remake of the movie *Invasion of the Body Snatchers* (the Donald Sutherland version rather than the 1950s, anticommunist Peter Lawford version) resulted precisely from how well it conveyed this prohibition against revealing the truth of our alienation: the alien Pods seek to take over the world by replacing actual humans with identical fake replicas who in turn organize to ferret out those remaining humans who cannot conceal the signs of their actual humanity.

The Nazis were an imaginary community, a special intensification of the imaginary unity of "the German People." When I say "the German People" are imaginary, I am not denying that there are elements of actual relation and mutual recognition in the common language, culture, and history that really does connect them, that makes them feel German together. I am saying that this connection retains the spiritual impoverishment of the centuries of alienation we have yet to surpass. Whether we understand the origins of this alienation from the other in the material struggle for survival or as the consequence of sin and a fall from grace or as an expression of our evolutionary lack of spiritual development that has made God-consciousness and the awareness that Love is the realization of Being only primitively available to us, nationalistic communities like "the German People" are not characterized by the mutual presence and recognition that imbues the I-Thou relation. Forged out of violence and war, pervaded by hierarchical images of status and divisions of class, race, and gender that contradict the capacity to fully experience the other as a "Thou" in a true relation of recognition, "the German People" with its "Fatherland" and its patriotic songs are a connected unity only as an image in the mind—in the existential reality of each present moment's social interspace, this imaginary unity remains corroded by the fear of each person in the face of each actual other, just as is true of "the American People" in this country. And this was the case also in post–World War I Germany.

Now we come to the crucial point. For insofar as communities are imaginary, they are unconsciously haunted by the very absence of connection that they have been constructed to deny. The threat of humiliation and nonrecognition posed by the mere existence of the actual other toward whom we are at the same time inherently pulled by the desire for mutual recognition that constitutes us as reciprocal, social beings—this threat is what has led to the protective divisions in the self that I described earlier. And just as the artificial persona enacted toward the other must claim to be real in order to deny the other access to the longing of the withdrawn self within, so the imaginary community that purports to satisfy our socially inherent need for connectedness and recognition must be outwardly manifested as real in order to seal off the pain of our actual isolation and the desire for and fear of the other that accompany it. Yet the collusion that allows and even forces these false appearances of self and community to be taken as real cannot actually make them so. It only renders what is real socially invisible or what we call "unconscious," but it does not get rid of what is real—this longing to be seen and confirmed through relation with the actual other, the conditioned terror of disconfirmation and humiliation, and the volatility and passion of these conflicting impulsions that constitute the energy field of real social life in its concrete existential dimension. And this reality haunts the collective allegiance to the imaginary communities that are intended to cover it up through the reciprocal collusion that denies it.

In present-day America, the emptiness of both mass culture and political life reveals the way that social alienation can at times achieve a relative stability.

The general absence of authentic connection, of the presence to each other that characterizes the profound transparency of the I-Thou relation, the bland rotation of the outer-role systems, and the imaginary communities that purport to unite us that today are transmitted mainly by television ("we" all supposedly watched the final episode of *Seinfeld;* according to "our" spokesperson, "we Americans" have more opportunity today than ever before; etc.)—all of these aspects of our contemporary culture sometimes seem so natural that their alienated character becomes almost invisible. Indeed, the very success with which social emptiness is managed today suggests that liberal late capitalism may aspire to solve the threat posed by a direct encounter with the other by trying to postpone it forever: by ironizing all seriousness, assimilating social existence itself to its televised representation, and disseminating legal drugs like Prozac that really do make meaninglessness feel better. That Francis Fukuyama could seriously suggest that the current period of moral void and spiritual and political disengagement is "The End of History" is an indication that this idea of infinite postponement is not so far-fetched.

But the situation in Germany in the 1920s and early 1930s was very different from our own. World War I had been a war of imaginary communities—nothing quite validates my description of the nonrational psychodynamics underlying social alienation than the absurd irrationality of that war's origins and the utterly predictable catastrophic suffering that it would cause. Like the Vietnam War in which, as Tom Hayden has so eloquently put it, fathers sacrificed the lives of their real sons in order not to lose their connection to the image of America that they had gained in World War II, World War I revealed our capacity to disattend to easily foreseeable real consequences in order to preserve our allegiance to imaginary community. And as I have indicated, the reason for this is the real terror of the negation of our very social being, as yet so underconfirmed in history, that makes the dissociation from reality "worth it." In this context, the defeat of "the German People," coupled with the further humiliations of the reparations, the accelerating "worthlessness" of "the German currency," and the challenge to the very existence of a "German community" by Marxists intent on revealing it as epiphenomenal in relation to the underlying reality of the international class struggle, all of these forces threatened to disintegrate the imaginary recognition that each German experienced as "national pride."

When the world achieves the spiritual development that will, when it is achieved, permit a self-evident confidence in the confirmatory nature of the

I-Thou relation, the type of recognition associated with pride and humiliation will be surpassed or significantly altered in its meaning. But in a world still addicted to imaginary communities as a defense against the threat posed by the actual other, the "belief" in the imaginary community uses the inflating character of pride as a means of keeping out of awareness the fear of humiliation that this "belief" is meant to deny. In the absence of a spiritual-political social movement that might have addressed the alienation that produced World War I and the mourning and healing needed to truly recover from it (and neither the League of Nations nor Marxism was capable of this kind of analysis and response), no social base existed that could soften the psychological effects of the Germans' loss of pride in their national identity. To desire in your being the recognition of the other and the blessed grace and completion of the I-Thou relation, and then to feel as a result of your conditioning that you are actually nobody in the face of a dominant other who will use the vulnerability of your desire to humiliate you—that is not a tolerable option, not even an option we can bear to become fully conscious of. And as a result, the degraded "German People" were drawn to a Nazi Party capable of reinspiring a sense of national pride powerful enough, at the imaginary level, to reexpel the threat of the other's nonrecognition and humiliation from their conscious experience.

But while the grandiosity of Nazism was able to restore each underrecognized "little man's" sense of pride, worth, and self-recognition as "a German," as "one of the German people," the Nazi community remained an imaginary unity whose special character consisted in having been virulently infected by the humiliation that gave rise to it. Its violence, its megalomania, its preoccupation with purification, its desire to assert a world dominance that would last forever—all of these elements of Nazi culture so clearly reveal a drivenness to get rid of some haunting inner demon—that sense of ontological inadequacy that is in fact a universal feature of social alienation but that had broken through into consciousness sufficiently to traumatize the Germans of the Weimar Republic. It had to be gotten rid of, this threat of humiliation; and yet—and here is the crucial point—it could not be gotten rid of because it was itself a constituent element of Nazi consciousness. Glassy-eyed, goose-stepping, and inflated into a prideful rage, the SS officers, like the young women feeling an erotic thrill as they watched the spectacle of the rally, were enacting themselves as if they were part of an upsurge of authentic affirmation and recognition. But they were deceiving themselves. The Nazis were an imaginary community, haunted by the same fear of humiliation and lack of true affirming reciprocity as other such communities, but the necessity of their grandiosity made the denial of their vulnerability to the threat of the actual other more urgent and more difficult to achieve.

Psychoanalysis has long recognized that one way to reconcile incompatible parts of the self is to engage in splitting and projection. In her book *For Your Own Good,* Alice Miller presents a thoughtful application of these concepts to the Nazi personality structure, but remains within the boundaries of conventional psychoanalysis. In the framework that I am presenting, we shall see that the Nazis did indeed engage in splitting and projection, but in order to deny the existence of the absence that haunted them—haunted their inflated outer personae and the imaginary nature of their grandiose unity as a master race. Let me repeat, because this is very important: to be absent in this way is to seek not to be present to the actual other, to withdraw one's innocent longing for the actual other's affirmation of one's authentic being and to seal off that longing behind the glassy eyes and rigid musculature of the external persona, so that in spite of the choreographed external unity of those enormous Nuremberg rallies, the core of each person's actual social presence remained pulled back into his or her head and removed from the inherent vulnerability of the truly embodied relation. And since this "outerness" of the Nazi movement was infected with the breakthrough of the humiliation that had given rise to it, it faced a perpetual threat that had to be warded off with great urgency.

This warding off the threat of humiliation by the actual other took many forms, such as the disciplinary rigidification of the internal hierarchies of the Nazi Party with its compulsory and decisive salutes and the internal use of the Gestapo, the SA, and the SS, all of which facilitated the maintenance of what might be called "disciplinary hegemony"—that is, the effective use of terror to monitor and secure the outer collusion of the German people as a whole in maintaining the appearance of unquestioned allegiance and "belief." These Germans were themselves actual others in the sense that I have been using the term—that is, each was an "existent," an inherently relational being with a consciousness capable of dissolving by withdrawal of belief (in social combination, accidental or intentional) the false outer unity of the Nazi's pseudocommunity. Warding off the threat of humiliation consisted first, therefore, of assuring—through real organization—the absolute allegiance among the Germans themselves to belief in the reality of the hallucination of their connection—the realness, for example, of Hitler's hallucinatory invocation of "the Blood" that incarnated Nazi-German unity.

But the most important method of warding off the inner demon that so infected and threatened to dissolve this imaginary unity was to try to split off the threat of being revealed as false (an ever-present threat emerging from the fear posed by the ever-present pull toward authentic recognition that can arise only through the letting-go of our withdrawnness and the becoming-present-to the-other in full relation) and to project this split-off threat onto other imaginary communities that were defined as the source of the threat to "the German People." To those of you who are familiar with the idea of splitting as a psychological defense, this may sound straightforward and even simple, but it actually involves a subtle transposition that is of great social importance. For in splitting off the internal demon and projecting its threat onto an external, demonized other, the Nazi transposes the haunting internal threat of humiliation of the fragile and withdrawn inner self (by its exposure, through the transparency of relation, to the actual other) into an external threat to the Nazi's "outer" imaginary community itself. This has the effect of not simply denying the inner absence that threatens the heart of Nazi identity, but rather of acknowledging the felt presence of the threat and then externalizing it and changing its object to fully remove it from the concrete domain of real social existence. In place of the ever-present threat to the actual withdrawn self by the actual other that haunts and therefore divides the Nazi's being and that therefore can neither be acknowledged nor eliminated, the process of splitting off and projection allows the Nazi first to secure the undivided "reality" of the Nazi's outer imaginary community and second to make this imaginary community the threatened object in place of the vulnerable and frightened soul within. Through this ingenious, hallucinatory transposition, the Nazi can attempt to actively master a fear of humiliation that he must otherwise passively suffer and that he is otherwise helpless to affect: through it, he "unifies" himself, enables himself to actively acknowledge the threat that would otherwise have to be denied by expelling that threat from the self and projecting it in the form of a contemptible infection into the demonized other outside the self, and he gains the capacity to actively mobilize his energy, in the form of a truly "blind rage," against a threat that has now been transformed from a threat to the soul of exposure and authentic humiliation into a threat to the pseudo-integrity of the Nazi's outer persona and the imaginary community itself to which it belongs. Acknowledging the threat and transposing it in this way strengthens the Nazi's self-deception: it allows him or her to say, "We are perfect, real, and pure, and we will stamp out the 'them' who are external to us and impure and seek to infect us with an alien presence that is not in us."

As Bauman points out in his critique of Goldhagen, there were many groups who served as carriers of the Nazis' split-off projections, including those deemed mentally deficient, physically disabled, or sexually deviant, but the Jews were the primary demonized others. And certainly the selection of the Jews for this purpose has everything to do with the history of German anti-Semitism, which is to say with the history of the Jews having to absorb these same split-off projections in times of "normal" alienation, which did not produce a holocaust however much violence German Jews had to routinely endure. But one of the main points I wish to make here is that whatever the scope of the historical anti-Semitism that made the Jewish people the most likely object of Nazi demonization, within the distortions and conflicts of the Nazi mind the Jews were imaginary, as imaginary as the Nazi's master race of Germans themselves were. By this I mean that Nazism, as a catastrophic manifestation of alienated consciousness whose recurrence remains a possibility so long as the ubiquitous pain of social alienation and the longing for mutual recognition remain so poorly understood and so little responded to, produced a consciousness sufficiently cut off, through denial, from even the impoverished relational empathy that characterizes our experience of the actual other here in the real world that the Jewish people became an "It" to them, to again use Buber's terminology.

Or to state this still more precisely, insofar as the Jews functioned as the externalized carriers of the Germans' own inner demons in the service of denying these demons, the Jews' existence as Thou had to be denied as well. Any felt relation to the Jews' actual humanity would have inevitably entailed some resonance of the mutual recognition that is constitutive of the true relation and so would have revealed the underlying humiliation that had already been the traumatic source of the hyperinflation of the Nazi's artificial persona. Thus the Nazis needed to try to convert the Jews from actual others (and here I mean not "Jewish" others as such but simply vessels of social humanity) into It-Jews, the imaginary demonic community described in *Mein Kampf.*

This effort at total dehumanization was, of course, impossible, based as it was on a denial of reality, and it was this impossibility that makes intelligible the development from the anti-Semitism of the 1930s to the Holocaust itself. For while the process of splitting off and projection allowed the Nazis to enact a stamping out of the impurities that threatened to expose the unreality of their communal identity, it was only an enactment, an imaginary "cleansing" that not only could not "work" but necessarily revealed itself as not working every step of the way. If you foster a spirit of generalized anti-Semitism or even a

Kristalnacht in the service of the denial of your internal demons, and if these attempts at mastery change nothing, the psychological defense itself requires that more be done to eradicate the infection. Thus the "Final Solution" comes to seem like the only thing that will work—actual extermination of the substitute object that has been designated as the threat to the Nazi and to the community of Nazi Germany. It is probable that unconscious guilt also plays a part in this inevitable acceleration of expulsive measures: the construction of the Jews, through splitting off and projection, into an imaginary, dehumanized collective being with whom one is not in relation as a community of actual others is also impossible in any real ontological sense—the projection of the It-identity is simply a denial of the Thou relation, of the human presence of the Jews as actual others. The more violence that is done to them without "eliminating the problem" haunting the Nazi's grandiosity, a problem that includes the guilty unconscious knowledge of the humanity of the actual others being degraded and brutalized, the greater the future violence required to maintain the continuing denial of that humanity and the greater the wish to exterminate that humanity altogether.

But what then of the "average German," some of whom are today the seemingly normal parents and grandparents of German friends of my generation? In my opinion, it is precisely the passive-active, knowing-unknowing compliance of the average German that should dispel the notion that the Holocaust was a uniquely German phenomenon, the product of a uniquely distorted or evil culture. Precisely what I have been trying to show is that the Holocaust is an intelligible manifestation of an alienated world in which the desire for mutual recognition and affirmation is systematically denied, in which the fear of the other as an agent of humiliation rather than the source of completion of our relational being envelops each of us in "misrecognition"—that is, in an artificial social environment that coerces each new generation to seek to remove its full social presence from the reality of social existence.

The true social presence within each of us, withdrawn into our heads and concealed from revelation through the body, rendered unconscious by being denied the blessing of recognition that it deserves, forced to deny its own longings by a preceding generation imprisoned in its own alienated conditioning and condemned to reproduce this denial in the next generation, destined to blindly navigate its way from birth to death through the opaque distortions of a visible world that is driven by the contradictory imperative of seeking to empty itself of the very transparency to the other the desire for which impels it forward—that is the "existent" that is lost and frightened and volatilely conflicted behind the armor of our embodied social manifestations. It would not only be perfectly possible but even typical of the alienated consciousness I am describing for the "average German," only loosely anchored to reality, to go-along-at-a-distance with a dimly understood dehumanization that could be producing an actual mass murder. If at that historical moment Nazism was ontologically reassuring and even "exciting" in its restoration of "national pride," and if in any case the Nazis were in charge and seemed to establish the conditions for ordinary Germans' alienated security as withdrawn observers not having to be present, and if these ordinary Germans were accustomed to regarding the public world as an irreal and largely imaginary spectacle, is it so surprising that they would collude unconsciously—in a perfectly normal way—in the dehumanization of the Jews? Wouldn't it have been more remarkable if they had been able to overcome their withdrawn state so coercively reinforced by the dynamics of that historical moment and actually experience the immensity of the suffering and horror for which their "normal" collusion was in part to blame?

The Germans are not absolved from moral responsibility by this analysis. On the contrary, the ethical call that the future makes upon the present, that God's universe makes upon its current manifestation, is to strive to become present to the other as a Thou and to make visible the unity and sacredness of all Being. The Germans' continuing failure to heed this call and to take responsibility for the Holocaust is revealed by their incapacity to engage in a true period of national mourning for the Holocaust, a serious collective spiritual encounter with an awareness of their sin as a lived reality of suffering that actually took place. This has nothing to do with public officials "apologizing for the Holocaust," but calls instead for a stark spiritual break with the reproduction of an alienated everyday life that made the Holocaust possible.

But for us to believe that we could not have done what the Germans did is to ignore our own everyday participation in the failure to recognize the other, the failure to truly seek to affirm against the mistake of our cultural conditioning our longing to achieve a lived relation to the other as a Thou. When during the Gulf War the media replayed again and again the technical proficiency of "our" cross-haired bomb sights and laughed each time with one of "our" generals at the Iraqi bus driver who narrowly missed extermination, we revealed to ourselves Hannah Arendt's banality of evil and participated in it as "average Americans." Whatever the difference between a war and the Holocaust, that bus driver was not "our" enemy. He was an actual other, a vessel of sacred humanity, dehumanized by a spiritual impoverishment for which we are all responsible and which we all must try to heal.

ON PASSIONATE REASON

Beyond Marxism and Deconstruction

IN THE CURRENT HISTORICAL PERIOD, progressive forces in the United States and actually throughout the world find themselves without any coherent vision that could articulate either what is wrong with the way things are or what kind of world we want to bring into being. We are caught between two points of view, both of which are inadequate to grasp the true problems of social existence. One point of view I will simply call Marxism, which is the most developed form of progressive thought to emerge from "objectivity"—the separation of subject and object—characteristic of the Enlightenment. The problem with Marxism is not simply that it "hasn't worked," but that it was always based on a mistaken and overly objectified view of the nature of human desire and need itself. Its tendency to explain social phenomena by reference to economic dynamics, however plausible in light of the brute facts of nineteenth-century life and the mystifications that justified the economic oppression characteristic of feudalism and earlier forms of society, reflected a positivism that eclipsed the most distinctively social aspect of existence itself—namely, the desire of every living being to be recognized and confirmed by others and the attendant desire to create a vital world of social meaning and purpose based upon this social connection. Marxism was "smart" in the sense that it could plausibly correlate actual social and historical processes with apparently "objective" processes beyond the will or conscious control of any human being or group of human beings. It nevertheless misunderstood this very correlation, failing to see that it was social alienation, an alienation and distortion of social desire, that underlay the very "objective" and involuntary character of economic dynamics or of the so-called economic system itself.

There has as yet been no theoretical account of this social alienation that has gone beyond the psychoanalytic theory of the family and enabled us to understand the social-psychological dynamics that actually constitute and reproduce large-scale social processes and institutions. The legacy of Marxism still dominates progressive thought. People on the Left still talk primarily in economic terms about the nature of and solution to fundamental social problems because they do not yet have any other way to talk. As a result, conservative forces, which have a better instinctive understanding of the centrality of social connection and meaning to people's lives, have gained ascendancy in the West through their affirmation of religion, the "free" world and market, and traditional family values; and through appeals to the imaginary or "substitute" social connection symbolized by, for example, the flag. This conservative ascendancy cannot be effectively challenged by the Left's prevailing economistic worldview, because that worldview simply fails to address the desire for a community of meaning that is the very heart of the Right's message. As Michael Lerner and I have long argued, you can't fight the passionate appeal of the conservative vision with a laundry list of economic programs.

The failure of progressive forces to develop a social theory based on an understanding of alienation can be traced in part to the effects of the second point of view currently enveloping the Left—the one associated with poststructuralism and deconstruction, with the work of Jacques Derrida and Michel Foucault and their followers. This point of view has reacted against the horrors associated with Marxism and other totalizing social theories by rejecting the project of social theory altogether. Poststructuralists find in such theories an intrinsic tendency toward domination (Foucault's famous link between Power and Knowledge), which makes social theory itself part of the problem rather than part of the solution.

The poststructuralist line of criticism has many virtues, including its modesty, its emphasis on pluralism and "different voices," its emphasis on the importance of particularity and context in interpreting the meaning of social phenomena, and its capacity to disarm the sort of Big Theorizing that has been used for centuries to oppress and to justify the oppression of women and minorities. Yet, ironically, poststructuralist criticism remains as dependent upon the limitations of the Enlightenment as the type of social theory it criticizes. The specific error of poststructuralism is that it unjustly equates social theory with the explanatory conceptual schemes that have followed upon the rationalistic project of the Enlightenment; then it declares these grand conceptual schemes to be false on their own terms as well as socially repressive (Derrida's attack on "phallologocentrism"); and, finally, it rejects *any* universalist theory of social interpretation that could tie disparate social phenomena together and help make the problems of the world intelligible as a whole to people. The poststructuralists do not allow for the possibility that there is a kind of reason and general knowledge that can emerge from passionate understanding, and that this kind of reason is precisely what is needed for the illumination of the meaning of social phenomena expressive of the movement of social desire.

The poststructuralist's "ban" on social theory has weakened the Left's ability to develop a moral critique of the existing society and to articulate a compelling vision of the kind of society we want to create. The goal of both philosophy and social theory traditionally has been to establish a true link between being and knowledge, or to make what is as yet unrevealed to consciousness about the meaning of its own existence accessible to critical reflection. For those who have sought to transform the world in a more emancipatory and humane direction, this intellectual activity was meant to provide people with a common reflective knowledge that could, through the experience of shared insight, inspire people to act to change things. The current left-wing academic and intellectual climate in the United States, increasingly influenced by post-structuralism and deconstruction, is impeding the continuation of this project by making a fetish of the notion of "different voices," by failing to tie the particularistic knowledge it values so highly to any common, general insight into the truth of social life *as a whole*. The goal of wrenching away the distinctive experience of women and minorities from the oppressive, universalizing categories of dominant culture has certainly been a laudable one. But the denial, in the name of cultural uniqueness, that there is any way to reunite and illuminate the meaning of these diverse experiences through the development of a more supple and experiential social theory grounded in our common humanity makes it difficult for us to challenge the Allan Blooms and William Bennetts of our society. The effect of essentializing our differences and, therefore, of relativizing social knowledge has been to leave progressive forces open to conservative and neoconservative charges of "nihilism." It deprives us of any common intellectual language with which we might criticize the existing society as a whole, or discover our common social objectives.

The methodology that would take us beyond Marxism and deconstruction must involve an explicit attempt to overcome the separation of passion and reason characteristic of Enlightenment "objectivity" as well as what might be called the irrationalism implicit in the poststructuralist rejection of the possibility of social theory altogether. It must be a method based on what I earlier called "passionate understanding"; its epistemology has its roots in the phenomenological tradition of philosophy—in the work of Husserl, Heidegger, Merleau-Ponty, and Sartre—and is implicit in much feminist writing. Such a method proceeds on the assumption that all human reality shares a common ground and is expressive of a common social being, even though this common reality is manifested in a potentially infinite number of distinct and unique social forms; that every person has the capacity (under supportive social circumstances) to transcend the particularity of cultural conditioning so as to understand, on the basis of one's own being, the meaning of the experience of others; and, finally, that the validity of this understanding is based not on any logical "proof" characteristic of detached scientific analysis, but on the persuasiveness of one's evocative and critical "comprehension" of the phenomena that one is describing.

This way of linking being and knowledge has really always been at the heart of the true elements in psychoanalytic thought, although in Freud's day it was dressed up in a sort of metaphorical scientific vocabulary. Today, there are few psychoanalytic writers who do not, at least implicitly, acknowledge the centrality of engaged, intuitive comprehension to the construction of psychoanalytic knowledge. But this point of view has yet to really make its way into critical social theory, in part because the tradition of philosophical phenomenology (with the exception of Sartre) consists largely of individualistic introspection by abstruse German and French thinkers whom almost no one understands. The kind of critical social thought that I'm talking about here demands that people passionately throw themselves forward into the lived experience of the social phenomena that surround them and attempt to illuminate through evocative description, rather than detached analysis or "explanation," the universal realizations and distortions of social desire that these diverse phenomena share across the cultural richness of their differences.

One central point about the link between this new social theory and politics is that transcendent social knowledge can emerge only from transcendent social experience. True social change can occur only through the building of social movements that allow us to recover our awareness of the desire for mutual confirmation and to gain the confidence that this desire also exists in the heart of the other. This implies a rejection of the simplistic notion of "revolution," although not of the radicalism that the notion of revolution has traditionally symbolized. Instead, we should think of social movements as more or less spontaneous outbreaks of social desire that must become vehicles for the gradual building of a true historical confidence in the possibility of genuine reciprocity. The success of any such effort requires an awareness that this process of confidence building will be continually undermined by the history of our alienation and mutual distrust. True social change requires a kind of collective strength and compassion that progressive forces have yet to demonstrate in the social movements that have arisen thus far, and it requires the building of forms of culture that enable us to internalize the conviction that the kind of change I am speaking of really can occur beyond exhilarating outbursts—in the face of the media's caricatures of previous social movements and the many other anxious public attempts to suppress our memory of what we can still become, it is important to affirm the silent knowledge shared by millions of us that the sixties were among the most wonderful times that have blessed our existence together on this earth. It is only by retaining our memory of that experience, as well as other perhaps more partial ones like it, that the kind of expressive theory I am speaking for can come into being and allow us to communicate about how to move forward.

CREATIONISM AND THE SPIRIT OF NATURE

The Critique of Science and Darwinian Evolution

We are led to Believe a Lie
When we see With not Thro the Eye

—WILLIAM BLAKE

I

I GREW UP IN NEW YORK CITY DURING THE 1950s, and most of my friends from that period regard the creationists as a bunch of nut cases who are for some reason being taken seriously by a significant percentage of the American population and even by the mainstream media. Their attitude is not surprising to me because my friends and I all received a normal, northeastern liberal education, and we all were taught that Darwin's theory of evolution, which was based upon science, had long since put to rest theories about Divine Creation, which were based upon superstition and fantasy. Darwin's theory was presented to us not as "just a theory" or as one view among others, but rather as the discovery of a new truth, very much like the discovery that the earth was round rather than flat. So to my generation of middle- to upper-class white New Yorkers, the resurgence of creationism seems a little like a resurgence of the Flat Earth Society—something one might expect to occur in the hills of Appalachia but not something to be taken seriously in the courts of the United States or on the evening news.

I now see the attitude of my upbringing as a tragic expression of being unable to fully experience existence, or what might be called the "inside" of the world. To understand what I mean by this, think of a green plant near a window that leans toward the sun. We have all seen this many times—the upper leaves and branches seem to stretch in a sensual way up toward the warmth and light, while the lower leaves and branches do the best they can and curl around toward the sun with the same apparent desire and intention. A scientist would tell us that it is mere sentimentality or personification to think that the plant is leaning toward anything, that what is "really" going on is "phototropism," the first phase of something called "photosynthesis," a process by which the chlorophyll in the plant combines with light to produce oxygen. Within the scientific paradigm, the plant is drawn to the light not because of any sensual desire for warmth and light of the sun, not, in other words, because of any intentional movement of the plant as an embodiment of life, but simply because plants, in the words of a leading biology text, "capture light energy and use it to form carbohydrates and free oxygen from carbon dioxide and water" as part of their natural functioning. Ascribing intention or desire to the plant's movement attributes an immanence or inner life to the plant that is not observable by objective, impartial methods, and therefore cannot qualify as "knowledge" according to science.

Although most people I know would be inclined, if asked, to explain the plant's movements by using this kind of scientific model, there are a number of things about it that are unconvincing. For example, anyone who has actually watched a houseplant grow toward the window over a period of time can't help noticing how *unified* the plant's movements are—how much it seems to move toward the sun as a whole organism. Science undoubtedly has an explanation for this ("efficient conservation of energy" or the like), but this kind of explanation cannot capture the sensual unity that one senses in the plant, the sense of pleasure that seems so manifest in the bend of the upper stem and the stretch of the highest leaves and that seems to contrast so strikingly with the droop of plants denied access to the same sunlight. To the scientist, this may sound "merely subjective" and like a species-centered projection, but this sense that I have (and that I claim *we* have) that the meaning of the plant's living movement exceeds the photosynthesis explanation is a very strong one.

Can this intuitive "sense" of the plant's life be the basis of a kind of knowledge of the plant, a kind of knowledge that may correspond more closely to the plant's actual existence than the scientist's knowledge can possibly do?

To answer this question, we must look more carefully at the method of gaining knowledge used by the scientist and notice how this method may serve to limit what the scientist is able to see. First of all, the scientist begins his or her inquiry by taking the position of a detached observer who treats the plant as an object. From this position of detachment, the scientist cannot "sense" anything about the meaning of the plant's movements because to "sense" something this way requires the opposite of detachment—it requires engagement with the plant's life through a kind of empathy or intuition. Instead, the scientist sees only light rays, green goo in the plant tissue (named "chlorophyll" by the scientist), chemical transformations resulting for some unknowable reason from their interaction, and the production of a new chemical substance (called "oxygen" by the scientist). What the scientist finally calls photosynthesis is most certainly a kind of knowledge about what occurs chemically in green plants exposed to sunlight, but it is a kind of knowledge that derives from the objectification of the plant, from treating the plant as a kind of "thing," albeit a "living thing."

But if the plant isn't a thing, there is no way that the scientist could know it, because the scientist's way of looking can see only things and properties of things. Objectification of phenomena allows one to see these phenomena only from the outside, and if they have an inside, we can know of it only through the use of some other method—that is, through empathy and intuition.

There would be no problem with the theory of photosynthesis if scientists were content to show some humility and limit themselves to the claim that green plants, when observed like objects, reveal regular chemical changes that lead to the production of oxygen. But most natural scientists have long since abandoned this kind of humility, assuming instead that *the knowledge of phenomena gathered by the use of the scientific method corresponds to the nature or "being" of the phenomena themselves.* This is reflected in the notion that the plant leans toward the window in order to fulfill its natural function of producing oxygen through photosynthesis. There is nothing in the scientist's observation of the plant that could give him or her access to why the plant moves as it does—on the contrary, as we have just seen, the methodological constraints imposed by the twin processes of detachment and objectification preclude the acquisition of any knowledge of the meaning of the plant's movements as a living organism.

The "nature" of the plant, its capacity to sprout from a buried seed and to produce the green life of "chlorophyll" and to lean toward the sun and, for that matter, its capacity to wilt and die—all of these things are inaccessible to science, and science can never hope to explain them. What we might call the *existence* of the plant, the unique presence that animates the branches and leaves, can only be grasped by embracing the plant in an intuitive movement of comprehension from one living being to another.

It is by opening up this channel of intuition that we can recover and begin to develop a kind of knowledge of life that corresponds to the nature of life as something existing rather than something dead, like the scientist's world of objects. You may have thought that I was slightly crazy in talking about the plant's sensual stretching as an expression of its desire for warmth and light. But from a point of view that is capable of affirming the truth of intuitive knowledge, it is the scientist who appears slightly crazy for suppressing all of the perceptions of the plant's movements that could make sense of the plant as a form of life and for treating the plant as a kind of "photosynthesis machine." It is the scientist who must suppress the most immediate reactions to the plant's movement that spring from his or her humanity—that the plant is beautiful in its reaching toward the sun, that it looks and smells healthy, that its presence adds vitality to an otherwise sterile room—and who must convert the plant into a mass of chemicals before feeling he or she can know anything legitimate about it. But doesn't it make more sense for these initial reactions to be credited as giving us direct knowledge of the plant's existence, leaving to science the task of using its distinctive instrumental methods—detachment, objectification, the examination of chemical transformations—to analyze (but not account for) how oxygen is produced? This approach would accord to the plant its ontological status as an existing form of life, and yet allow science to give us useful knowledge about plant biochemistry not accessible to intuition. From this point of view, we could free ourselves to see the plant as a presence like ourselves, desiring the nourishment of the sun's warmth and light and undergoing vibrant physical transformations as this desire is realized. We could free ourselves to see the unity of spirit and matter that characterizes the plant's and our own existence, and without which this existence is not even conceivable. And we could also envelop the use of science within a qualitative and moral surround that is given by natural life itself in the immanent relation we feel toward the plant as beautiful and good—as miraculously alive and "here," no less than we are.

Wouldn't it be better for our children to learn something like this in elementary school before being sent into labs to dissect frogs or to memorize chemical formulas about photosynthesis? Wouldn't we have "liked school" better and perhaps even appreciated science more if we had been allowed to see the world in a way that requires love and natural empathy rather than a detached and manipulative "smartness" in order to "do well"?

II

This brings me to the debate between evolution and creationism, a debate that is influenced in every way by the failure of either side to grasp the truths that I have just sketched out. (It may seem arrogant to put it this way, but I honestly regard these as simple truths, self-evident to children before they are pressured into believing in Science or God as a condition of being accepted and loved.)

The theory of evolution as developed by Darwin and his followers is roughly as follows: We do not know how life began, but once living species appeared on earth and life began to proliferate, their evolution was guided by the law of survival of the fittest. Every species has been subject to the threat of extinction by natural disasters, climatic changes, or being killed and eaten by other species, and those that have survived have been those most capable of adapting to their then-existing natural environment. The "motor" of adaptation, according to Darwinian theory, has been a process of genetic mutation—accidental changes within the gene pool of particular species caused alterations in the physical characteristics of those species that enabled them to adapt most effectively to the natural dangers confronting them, and therefore to survive where others were wiped out. Thus the extraordinary capacity of a chameleon, for example, to change its color and hide from predators by blending into the background environment is the result of a genetic mutation occurring long ago that enabled the chameleon to survive while other similar lizards perished—and all the species that we see surviving on earth in some way owe their survival to this same process, which Darwin called "natural selection." The existence of human beings, in whom consciousness has evolved in the service of adaptation and survival, must be understood as an outcome of this natural historical process.

The short answer to all this is that *my* existence is not explained by any of it because my *existence,* my sense of being an existing someone here typing on a computer cannot be explained by anything at all. To the degree that I feel present to myself as me, nothing could possibly have "caused" me because there is no way to get from something not me to me without something entirely original coming into existence—namely, me. And the same goes for you. In other words, although it may sound good to say "human beings evolved from the lower species through adaptation via natural selection," if we remember that every particular so-called "human being" is actually an existing someone whose sense of being there as a me *must* be entirely original, then the theory of evolution seems at a minimum to be leaving out something—namely, the actual existence of everyone. And once we try to insert the reality of actually existing into the theory, we run into another basic problem: If I actually exist as a me present to myself here as an original someone, and if I am descended from the apes and so on down the evolutionary line, then each one of those prior beings must have existed also, since you can't get to me from something not me, and we are all me's from our own point of view. The more we think about reality "from the inside," in other words, the more it becomes clear that the theory of evolution can be true only if earlier beings existed as we exist. We must have some interior relation, presence to presence, to that green plant in the window.

Like the theory of photosynthesis as an explanation for the plant's leaning toward the window, Darwin's theory of evolution was constructed by using the scientific method with its twin first principles of detachment and objectification. During his famous *Beagle* voyage, Darwin observed the species sealed in the fossil record as well as the immense variety of species around him as "living things," and he saw what you can see when you look at things that way—transformations of the bone structure of armadillos, peculiar variations in the beaks of finches or in the size of tortoises depending on their islands of residence—in other words alterations in the physical appearances of life-forms as they appear to a detached observer "from the outside." In this respect, his research may or may not have been accurate, but it was certainly a legitimate attempt to amass the kind of knowledge that can be learned by using the methods he employed. But to say that the fact of adaptive physical transformations over time demonstrates that nature "follows the law of survival of the fittest" and that adaptive changes result from genetic mutations is to assume that the methods of the natural sciences are adequate to understand how and why life develops as it does. This could only be true if the existence and development of living things could be understood by a method that objectifies them and studies them "from the outside" when as we have just seen, neither my presence as an existing someone nor the fact of evolution itself is even conceivable from this vantage point. *The method of knowing the phenomena does not correspond to the nature or "being" of the phenomena observed.*

This problem of there being a disjuncture between science's way of looking at the life-world and the nature of the life-world itself has begun to cause some serious problems for contemporary theorists of evolution, who have continued Darwin's quest with great earnestness and good faith and have been trying to improve upon Darwin's original theory while using the same objectifying methods that they believe to be the only way you can really "know" something. (I use "objectifying" rather than "objective" because the scientific method is in fact as subjective as any other—that is, it proceeds via the *subjective* act of objectifying the phenomena observed.) Recent analysis of the fossil evidence, for example, has suggested that Darwin's theory may have been wrong even on its own terms, that survival of the fittest through gradual and progressively more adaptive inherited characteristics cannot explain why some species have survived and others have not. Two of the most prominent modern researchers, Stephen Jay Gould and Niles Eldredge, have argued that the fossil record indicates new species do not arise gradually as a result of a steady evolution from their ancestors, but rather seem to appear fully formed in sudden bursts, after which they exhibit little or no change for millions of years. They have argued that this theory, which they call "punctuated equilibrium," is consistent with Darwin's notion of natural selection, since the periods of rapid speciation seem to occur in the context of small local populations where new adaptive mutations are likely to flourish, while the long periods of equilibrium or stasis seem to result from the homogenizing influence of large, centralized populations in which new and favorable mutations are likely to be diffused by the sheer bulk of the populations through which they must be spread. Nonetheless, the theory of punctuated equilibrium does seem to suggest that for vast periods of geological time, plants and animals have coexisted in a more benign fashion than that implied by Darwin's images of "struggle" and "fitness," and some biologists like Richard Lewontin have argued for a much more complex approach to evolution than that offered by either Darwin or Gould and Eldredge, emphasizing that life-forms do not simply respond to their environments in the passive way implied by the idea of adaptation, but rather constitute this environment as well through a whole range of active interventions emerging from their own historically specific needs. Thus the theory of evolution is now many theories, each with its own proponents, and with each proponent trying to show that "the data" support his or her own point of view.

When I say that this new diversity of perspectives has caused serious problems for contemporary scientists, I do not mean that the scientists themselves consider the disagreement to be problematical. To them, as Gould has argued, evolution itself is a fact, but Darwin's account of evolution was never more than a hypothesis always subject to revision to accommodate new data. And in fact the true scientific method can never really claim to *know* anything for certain about the world precisely because it can see only the "outside" of things—it can never penetrate to the heart of any matter, so to speak, but must limit itself to the perpetual correlation and recorrelation of so-called "objective" facts as they are manifested at the surface of the world. Every hypothesis, no matter how well documented by recurrent observation, might be proved false by some new piece of evidence. Indeed the absolute skepticism and doubt that haunts the scientific method has been enshrined as a kind of absolute virtue by the high priest of the philosophers of science, Karl Popper, who conceived the now generally accepted (but untrue) proposition that no theory can even count as a theory unless it is "falsifiable" by science's own methods for recognizing "evidence." In an environment dominated by these kinds of assumptions, robust differences of opinion regarding how to interpret the data are cause for celebration rather than concern.

The problem has come rather from the creationists, who share none of the scientists' assumptions about what we might call "knowability" and who have been trying to exploit the evolutionists' internal disagreements as providing perfect evidence of the squabbling that results when people lack faith and therefore cannot grasp the nature of things. My aim is certainly not to defend the creationist credo that the Bible must be taken as literally true, that God created life on earth six thousand years ago, that the species existing today are those that survived the great flood and emerged from Noah's Ark, and so forth. But the creationists have been able to touch that dimension of people's ordinary experience that sees life in all its forms as expressive of some indwelling and miraculous beauty and goodness, and that knows with a certain intuition that this indwelling presence must be at the heart of any true knowledge of the world. However absurd the strict content of their views may be, and however evil may be the association of these views with right-wing militarism and anticommunism and with a servile dependency on fundamentalist preachers who purport to speak for an authoritarian God, there is something correct and admirable in their refusal to accept the hegemony of science as a privileged source of truth. And as is the case with many other public issues facing the

American people (like the human need for deep and lasting emotional commitments embodied for most people in the idea of the family, and like the human need for continuous forms of community rooted in an ethical vision of a good and decent way of life, which today is spoken to more by the church than by any secular institution), it is the apparent inability of liberals and the Left to address the deepest questions of reality and existence that is partly responsible for the appeal of right-wing movements who do address them, although often in profoundly distorted and destructive forms. If the theory of evolution equates itself with the denial or marginalization of the spiritual dimension of existence, asserting that people's intuited perceptions of a spiritual presence and meaning in nature are either pure superstition or at best a private matter, incapable of the kind of verification that science requires before something can be said to be "known," then people are going to turn elsewhere to search for a community where their most fundamental insights are validated and respected.

III

You cannot reach 1 by adding 9s to 0.999, and even if evolutionists keep studying the fossil record and revising their hypotheses until infinity, they will never understand what they are looking at until they change their way of seeing to encompass what the paleontologist and theologian Pierre Teilhard de Chardin called "the within of things." This requires not some new scientific instrument but rather an inward letting-go that allows the scientist to overcome his or her detachment in relation to natural phenomena in favor of an immersion in the life-world of these phenomena as they exist "from the inside." The method of knowing that emerges from such an immersion is not the correlation and analysis of objectified bits of data characteristic of the traditional scientific method, but rather the *comprehension* that results from intuition and empathy, a comprehension whose objectivity derives from the natural affinity or likeness that unites the scientist as a living being with the life-forms whose truth he or she is trying to "get to know." It is only as *me* as an existing someone and not as a depersonalized "observer" that I am able to comprehend the meaning of your movements and gestures, and even if I misunderstand you, it is only by intensifying my immersion in your world, refining my intuitive judgment through an empathic reevaluation of the "data" manifested as the living unity of your movements, that I can possibly correct myself. And my "knowledge" that I have done so is founded entirely on the comprehension that results from my capacity *to put myself in your place*—it is a kind of knowledge whose validity rests not on "proof" but on the self-evident insight that emerges across the differentiation of our presences out of the commonality of our being. Since our relation to earlier forms of life could only have been an "evolution" if they also in some way share our being, we can gain access to the development of these life-forms and our relation to them only by founding our research on these same methods—that is, by approaching them as differentiated presences like ourselves and putting ourselves in their place in order to comprehend them. If you want to understand a spider, for example, you cannot get very far by examining its behavior "objectively"—to grasp the intricate unity of its movements, you must try (and this often takes a great deal of empathic watching with constant self-correction for anthropocentrism or "projection") to put yourself in the spider's place—that is, to imagine yourself existing inside a spider's body, living in its unique social-historical and morphological situation.

From this point of view, evolution must be seen as a continuity of existence manifesting itself through embodied beings who are interiorly related intergenerationally and across the alteration of their physical forms. And as existing beings, the various species must be understood as engaged not in despiritualized and quasi-mechanical "behavior" animated by "instincts" (a made-up explanatory scheme deriving from the objectification imposed upon life-forms by biologists) but as engaged in intentional action given direction and meaning by the same desire that animates us: the desire to live (or to put it more negatively, to survive), the desire to realize their spirit in the world through the creation of meaning, and the desire for social confirmation and inclusion through recognition and love. It is perhaps worth emphasizing again that there is nothing species-centered about this way of looking at other life if we can let go of the specialness that we have too long reserved for ourselves and allow ourselves to see that the various species "exist their worlds" as much as we do. The ant carrying a leaf and the spider dropping backward down from the ceiling to anchor a web give a perpetual unity to their organization of dispersed matter that both manifests their presence as existing someones who are "in there" doing the unifying and reveals our commonality of being by virtue of our capacity to comprehend the meaning of what they are up to.

Admittedly, it is one thing to "comprehend" the world of a group of spiders in the way that I am describing and quite another to extend this comprehension to understanding intuitively and from the inside the transformation of physical forms and probably also of consciousness itself that constitutes evolution.

Such a task would require that it be possible to reconstruct the life-world of species who have left few artifactual indications of their social-historical, material, and morphological "situations" (the latter referring to what it's like to live out a particular experience from within a given body type). But however the limits of our access to the "interiority" of the fossil record may inhibit our gaining knowledge of specific evolutionary transformations, there is no reason why we cannot begin to develop some preliminary post-Darwinian notions of how evolution must occur in light of the spirituality manifested in every life-form as both presence (or existence) and desire. If we seek to comprehend the transformations of life-forms through immersion and intuitive description, we must first of all abandon the idea that such transformations can be explained entirely or even primarily by chance genetic mutations. This idea, deriving as it does from the objectification of the physical body of a living organism, has always imposed a dualism of body and spirit on living beings, implying that one thinglike entity, called a "gene," causes a change in another thinglike entity, called a "physical characteristic," without any involvement of the spiritual wholeness or life force that unifies every organism's actual development. But if we let go of the holding-back or detachment that allows us to convert the body into an object and instead bring our life into relation with the life around us, we cannot but see every organism as a unity of body and spirit existing in (or toward) its world. My genes, in other words, are not things inside me; they *are* me insofar as my body is "where I am."

From within this holistic perspective, it may be that what traditional evolutionary science thinks of as an adaptive physical change resulting from a chance mutation is actually a gradual intergenerational transformation in the bodily form of like beings who commune and reproduce (so-called "species"), emerging originally from some individual or collective "sense" of how to overcome a morphological limitation on the realization of desire under specific material and social-historical constraints. Instead of Steven Jay Gould's Darwinian account of how pandas have developed a prehensile digit resembling a thumb, imagine the following scenario: Some pandas who have inherited large wrist bones from their closest relatives, the bears, get the idea of using these wrist bones to hold and strip bamboo shoots by grasping the shoots between the bone and "thumb" that is the first digit of their paw. This will enable them to more easily munch the bamboo that surrounds them in their obscure forest habitat and also "dis-alienate" them by cooling out some of the internal antagonisms that have resulted from fighting over currently scarce food supplies (by making the bamboo shoots easier to eat). This first generation begins to try to use their wrists in this way, but with very limited success because they lack a wrist muscle to give them the needed control and in any case the wrist and paw muscles they do have stiffen up due to age. But their children pick up on the idea empathically—they "identify" with their parents out of love and take up the same project at an early age, sure that it will lead to something good, and eventually they actually understand it in its full social and gastronomical complexity. Starting so early in life to try to manipulate their wrist bones to act as an extra thumb, they are marginally more dexterous than their parents, though still significantly inhibited by the missing muscle. Over the next several generations, the project becomes deeply internalized in the group, perhaps partly through socially constitutive bamboo-munching rituals, until the idea of the new thumb and the developing practical sense embodying this idea becomes *part of what it is to be a panda*. In other words, the very being of the panda is partly constituted by the social-cultural rhythms of panda life, including the intentional organization and coordination of "sense" that animate the panda's bodily movements. Eventually and after many more generations, this "sense" of being-toward-grasping-things-with-our-paws is passed on empathically to the prenatal embryo before its body has formed, and when coupled with the internalized tradition among the pandas (as well as their esteemed ancestors, the bears and the raccoons) of possessing exceptional coordination for using their forelegs in feeding, the desire for the thumb generates a transformation of the panda's musculature—one of the tendons that normally attaches to the panda's "real" thumb becomes attached instead to the embryo's wrist bone. And this "trait" now becomes part of the bodily form that pandas reproduce through lovemaking; it becomes part of their embodied "pandaness," or if it is really necessary to keep the concept of "genes," the trait is now "in" the panda's genes insofar as genes are living carriers of the panda's morphological essence as opposed to being purely physical "things" that cause changes in a despiritualized physical body.

This particular reinterpretation of Gould's well-known defense of Darwin (see *The Panda's Thumb,* in which he purports to explain the same phenomenon through adaptation via genetic mutation) may be incomplete in various ways, but I offer it only as an example of how one could go about trying to conceive of evolutionary change while remaining true to the being or nature of living phenomena. It is a testament to their fear of moving beyond the limitations of scientific "objectivity" that so many people have been willing to believe for so long in a theory of evolution that posits such a spiritually empty vision of natural history (life-forms "adapt" in the service of mere "survival"), which is in turn explained by such implausible mechanisms as chance mutations. This is not to deny that unexplained mutations occasionally do occur and have profound effects on the life-world of every species, nor is it to deny that sometimes evolutionary developments result primarily from the survival-value of given physical characteristics (like, for example, the black-winged "peppered moths" who out-survived white-winged moths when soot from nineteenth-century factories blackened surrounding trees, making the white-winged moths easy prey for predators). But to be able to think that these accidental events furthering the banal, and in itself, essentially meaningless objective of survival could be sufficient to account for the development of existence itself requires a repression of our relation to the "within of things" that suggests a terror of being sucked into a vortex if we dare to abandon the terrain of exteriority as the only legitimate locus of objective knowledge. To gain a true comprehension of panda life and development would require a long immersion in their world and history that I haven't yet done (maybe it was their cultural domination by the larger bears that played a key role in propelling the pandas to seek the autonomy provided by a paw that could grasp), but I couldn't begin to do it without taking the risk of opening my heart to theirs, or in other words without trying to *understand* them. Only then could I begin to see "the data" in a way that could reveal its vital meaning.

IV

The implications of what I am saying here go much deeper than the debate between evolution and creationism because if we could succeed in freeing knowledge from the grip of science and affirm the objectivity of intuitive comprehension as the only route to understanding and communicating about the *being* of things, we could also begin to transform the way people think about politics and ethics, about the meaning of their own lives and the lives of others and about what kind of world we should be trying to create. The success of the proponents of science in linking knowledge of the truth with a method requiring that one look "at" things from a detached and "unbiased" standpoint, while relegating intuitive comprehension to the private realm of personal belief, has had the effect of introducing doubt into the soul of the universe and destroying people's confidence that their own instinctive perceptions and needs could possibly be the basis for deciding what it is that everyone wants and needs. The core of the ideology of science is that you can only know something if you erase yourself, and this leads precisely to a society of erased selves in which people experience each other largely as anonymous strangers without any common anchorage, passing each other with blank gazes on the street and purporting (in order to guard their inaccessibility in the name of privacy) to have no idea what anyone else feels or thinks. We are so preoccupied with being detached observers peering out at an "outside world" created by others that when a pollster tries to use scientific methods to determine public opinion on any given issue, each person nervously tries to guess what he or she thinks others would say. As a result, public opinion turns out to be the opinion of no one, and with everyone feverishly reading the papers or listening to friends or watching TV to try to figure out what to think, democracy turns out to be mainly drifts of "rotating otherness" in a world where no one feels empowered to affirm his or her own existence.

Obviously, this is somewhat of an exaggeration—if things were really this bad we would have had a nuclear war by now—but the belief that scientific methods are "hard" and therefore yield knowledge while intuitive methods are "soft" and therefore yield only opinions both expresses and reinforces an underlying feeling that there can be no objective basis for political or ethical judgments, that "no one has the right to speak for anyone else," and so forth. The denial, implicit in the scientific method, that one can achieve direct intuitive knowledge of the "within of things," and the ethical relativism that springs from it may help to explain the creationists' insistence that the Bible must be read as literally true in every respect. Their rigidity may be an example of what psychoanalysis calls a "reaction-formation"—they need to believe that the Bible reveals absolute spiritual truth to the faithful in order to defend themselves against an underlying insecurity, fostered by centuries of the dominance of scientific ideology, that they do actually have the capacity to claim any direct knowledge of spiritual truth that would reveal in some nonrelative sense what is good for human beings or how people ought to live their lives. Of course, it would be absurd to blame this underlying doubt and "detachment" on the ideology of science alone—at the deepest level, it results from our alienation from one another and our anxiety that if we made ourselves present to each other with the full openness required to feel certain of our spiritual commonality, we would be too vulnerable to rejection, humiliation, and pain. The effects of science have been not so much to cause our "holding back" as to reinforce its legitimacy by allowing us to deny that this kind of intuitive, spiritual certainty is possible.

Overcoming our fear of each other requires much more than launching an assault on the scientific method, but I think it would be an unqualified step in the right direction if we abandoned the illusion that analytical detachment provides us with a privileged form of knowledge and validated the objectivity of what we learn from our passionate immersion in the life-world into which we have miraculously been thrown. No one will ever be able to "prove" the objectivity of intuitive knowledge by scientific methods because these methods proceed via an objectification designed to make intuitive feeling invisible—but it is equally true that the distinctive vitality that characterizes the immediacy and "pull" of being alive is accessible to us through the engagement of intuitive comprehension alone. What establishes the potential objectivity of intuitive knowledge is neither the so-called "neutrality" of science nor the blindness of faith, but the experiential recognition that the passion and need animating each of us animates all of us; that we can rely on our own fundamental need for the confirmation and love of others, for example, as the basis for knowing with certainty that this need fundamentally motivates all living things.

The reason that this kind of spiritual knowledge has political and ethical importance is that unlike scientific knowledge, spiritual knowledge reveals itself only in ethical form. Scientific knowledge, like physics or chemistry or, for that matter, evolutionary biology, is incapable of pointing in any ethical direction because it limits itself to what I have been calling the "outside" of the world. By objectifying phenomena and examining their physical properties from a detached standpoint, the scientist turns the world into a mass of thingified information and processes, yielding a kind of "object knowledge" that may be useful but cannot be good or bad. Adopting this scientific attitude requires at least a temporary repression of any relationship one might have to the phenomena being investigated, and if this repression becomes permanent (which is what occurs when the scientist confuses his or her own act of objectification with the belief that the phenomenon under investigation *is* an object), one can engage in torture without being aware, at least consciously, that one is doing anything wrong. This or something like it is what permits scientists who work for cosmetics companies and the executives who employ them to maim and kill animals with a clear conscience while testing the toxicity of lipsticks—either they think that the animals are thinglike (perhaps "instinctual organisms") or they are able to ignore the issue altogether because they have been educated to believe that only scientific knowledge is "real" while spiritual knowledge is "just a matter of opinion."

If, on the other hand, the cosmetics scientists (or their employers or coworkers) were to let go of their detachment and open themselves to the being of these animals, and if they were educated to understand that the knowledge gained by this immersion in the animals' experience is no less real than the knowledge gained by testing lipsticks on animals conceived as physico-chemical organisms, they would be unable to avoid an ethical crisis. This is because their comprehension of the truth of the animals' suffering would be a kind of knowing that points in a definite ethical direction—their capacity to grasp this suffering would derive from their own identical capacity to suffer, and so they would know that it should end. To put this another way, intuitive comprehension always reveals qualities of experience in the other that impel us in some moral direction through our own experience or revulsion or longing or exhilaration—we can only know suffering in the other through the pain it engenders in ourselves. The scientist who is capable of knowing his or her laboratory animals in this sense cannot avoid deciding objectively, on this basis of what is good for life, whether it is right to torture animals to improve the ornamentation of human lips.

The point here is not to emphasize animal rights in particular, but to suggest that the validation of intuitive comprehension can have a profound ethical impact on every aspect of life because the very nature of intuitive knowledge makes you want to free desire and vitality from the various forms of repression that contain it. Once you "get" that hierarchy and inequality are dehumanizing and that this isn't just a matter of opinion, arguments in favor of these ways of living based on "efficiency" or some other objectifying slogan lose all of their force: instead of feeling inadequate and anxious about whether you really have grasped the intricacy of the argument, you can comprehend the arguer's alienation just from the sound of his voice and the blank stare in his eyes, and the only question is whether it's worth it to try to unbury him so that he can come out and actually experience what he's talking about. Similarly, taking action against the existence of nuclear weapons no longer requires that you know a lot (or anything) about systems of bilateral verification or the percentage of missiles that can penetrate a star-wars' defense shield or any other "object knowledge" of that kind because you don't have to know these things to move away from extinction and toward vitality and love.

Finally, it seems clear to me that the ecology movement would increase its social power if it placed greater emphasis on the validity of intuitive knowledge as a source of direct insight into the nature of being (and therefore into how we ought to *be* being) than it has so far done. Instead of speaking only or even primarily about "balancing the eco-system" or "protecting the ozone layer" in a way that still relies too much upon scientific knowledge to guide ethical action, ecologists should speak directly to people's souls and help them to trust that what they see with their souls (through the experience of beauty or disgust, for example) is actually there. Gaining confidence in this kind of sight is essential to being able to transcend the deadening objectivity of media policy experts and other scientized professional knowers, and to feel at once empowered and compelled to do what you always knew was right.

❖   ❖   ❖

Exchange on Creationism

To the Editor:

I am writing to criticize *Tikkun's* decision to publish Peter Gabel's "Creationism and the Spirit of Nature" (*Tikkun*, Nov./Dec. 1987). In my opinion, it is a glaringly inept piece of pseudoscience, pseudotheology, and pseudophilosophy.

ERIC I. B. BELLER
NEW HAVEN, CONNECTICUT

To the Editor:

The series on creationism was magnificent. I thought Peter Gabel's article was one of the most impressive, profound essays I've read in years.

PROFESSOR ROBERT BLAUNER
DEPARTMENT OF SOCIOLOGY
UNIVERSITY OF CALIFORNIA, BERKELEY

To the Editor:

I am saddened to find that Peter Gabel, with whose basic proposition I substantially agree, must resort to scientist bashing in order to present his radical perspective on spirit and science. Revolutions in science have *not* been terribly bloody except, of course, in those cases where the church (lowercase "c") has intervened, and animosity toward even radically new notions rarely festers longer than a generation. Thus, unlike fundamentalism, science is not *inherently* reactionary. Not that anyone is selling fundamentalism on the pages of *Tikkun*. But the *apologia* for fundamentalist reaction on the grounds of scientific dogmatism rings singularly hollow in view of a reactionary history dating back long before anyone could have perceived science as any sort of threat to church dogma . . .

Scientists talking to scientists go out of their way to stress the provisional and nondogmatic nature of their propositions in a manner I cannot imagine fundamentalists doing. As I write this letter, I happen to have at hand a scientific text by Steven Weinberg, which allows me to quote a *typical* scientific sentiment: "Of course, the standard model may be partly or wholly wrong. However, its importance lies not in its certain truth but in the common meeting ground it provides for an enormous variety of observational data. In the context of a standard cosmological model, we can begin to appreciate their cosmological significance, whatever model ultimately proves correct . . . " (*Gravitation and Cosmology*). This sentiment is typical, as well, of biologists.

We all strive to foster empathy. Indeed, the epistemological enterprise of identifying the limits of scientific knowledge is one in which practicing scientists have played not a small part. I happen to know few more empathetic individuals than acquaintances who study animals, not to mention ecologists who train their disciples to view the world in a holistic way that can well serve as a general model even if one doesn't subscribe to the tenets of a particular discipline. Science, in short, is not nearly so medieval as the rest of society . . .

SAMUEL J. PETUCHOWSKI
BETHESDA, MARYLAND

To the Editor:

Peter Gabel's article "Creationism and the Spirit of Nature" is disturbing, to say the least. It is one thing to promote intuition as a mode of apprehension and a way of subjectively deepening our spiritual rapport with the web of reality. It is quite another to claim intuition as the basis for an explanatory theory of the external world. To suggest a common cause with creationists in this regard is disastrous for not only science and religion, but for politics and ethics as well.

No doubt, the world would be a more humane place if our empathetic and intuitive faculties were more sensitively developed. But it is sad to see many intellectuals, in the name of an ill-defined progressivism, fiercely attack modernity and its finest fruits.

JOSEPH CHUMAN
HACKENSACK, NEW JERSEY

Peter Gabel responds:

There are two main criticisms of my creationism/evolution article expressed in these letters—one that I presented an unfair and overly dogmatic view of the scientific method, blaming science for cultural evils that are not the fault of science but of people who misuse it; the other that the claims I make for the validity of intuitive insight and understanding are dangerous and can lead to fascism.

The first point misunderstands the basic thrust of my critique of science. The problem with science is not that it is inherently rigid or dogmatic; all good scientists recognize that their hypotheses are provisional and are subject to revision based on the discovery of new information. The problem with science, rather, is that the detached objectifying outlook characteristic of the scientific method is inconsistent with the engagement, compassion, and empathy required to understand the spiritual meaning of life in all its forms. These two kinds of knowledge could coexist in a proper relation to one another, but only if the pursuit of quantitative, objectified knowledge were guided by a comprehension of the qualitative, spiritual nature of all living things. Instead, exactly the reverse has occurred over the last several hundred years. The relationship between scientific knowledge and intuitive or spiritual knowledge has been severed; scientific knowledge has been accepted as the only kind of knowledge that can be considered "objective," while intuitive knowledge has been relegated to the realm of mere personal opinion or belief. As a result, scientific research and the technologies spawned by it now run wild without any ethical anchor because they have been crazily liberated from any relationship to the spiritual knowledge—to the knowledge of what is objectively good and bad for human and other living beings—which should guide their use and development.

One of the consequences of this severing of the scientific method from any underlying spiritual understanding is that science becomes capable of producing authoritative but false theories whenever it is applied to living or spiritual phenomena. This is what I claim has occurred in the case of the theory of evolution—from Darwin's theory of natural selection right down through the contemporary ideas of Stephen Jay Gould. Darwin and Gould were/are great naturalists, and I in no way mean to impugn the significance of their contributions as insightful observers of plant and animal life. But because Darwin and Gould limit what they think they can know to what can be "objectively observed," they rely exclusively on factual notions like survival, genetic mutations, climatic conditions, the size and location of particular species, and the like, in generating their hypotheses about how the physical forms of plants and animals have developed over the course of historical time. Suppose I wish to claim as I try to do in my article—not on the basis of logical argument but by a kind of intuitive appeal—that so-called lower forms of life are animated by qualities of spirit, such as intention, desire, the need for love and connection, and the pursuit of sensual grounding and meaning; and that these qualities also must shape the physical development and transformation of the life-forms that constitute the natural world. Evolutionary biologists would respond that while this is legitimate philosophical speculation, it is "not science"—that is, that it is not hard knowledge of "the rules by which nature seems to operate." But, I respond, the presence of spirit in plant and animal life means that nature does not "operate" at all, that it is not a mechanism functioning according to objective laws, and that the theories of the evolutionists that create a dualism between indwelling spirit and the transformation of physical forms—attributing the latter to genetic mutations and a purely "physical" quest for survival—are in contradiction with the ontology of all animate life. The answer of these biologists to this claim would be that the hypotheses of Darwin and his followers remain consistent with the "observed facts" and that they can only be falsified by evidence that is recognized as real by the scientific method.

In this way, the theory of evolution is rendered authoritative via the privileging of detached "objective" analysis over engaged intuitive insight, even though it violates what intuition reveals. It is a mistaken theory, but it cannot be proved to be so by its own criteria, and it will only accept its own criteria as evidence of truth or error.

But I don't want to spend too much time responding to the many scientists who were outraged by my article, because my article was not written primarily for scientists. It was written to try to validate the experience of the many nonscientist readers of *Tikkun* that their emotional, intuitive, spiritual responses to the world provide access to a knowledge of Being in all its forms that is correct, a knowledge that the "scientific method" cannot begin to address. The main point of my article is that the creationist movement is an understandable response to three hundred years of the hegemony of liberal scientific thought, and that the only way to combat the evils of creationism—its fanatical anticommunism, its homophobia and repression of sexuality, its authoritarian use of the Bible and the image of God to enslave the desire and imagination of its followers—is for the Left to stop allowing these people to be the sole spokespersons for the knowledge revealed to the human soul. We cannot overcome the appeal of the Jimmy Swaggarts and Jerry Falwells of the world by declaring that their views are "not science" and are therefore merely subjective, religious opinions. This just leads to an emotional and ethical relativism that people know is the most corrupt aspect of our alienated liberal culture—it affirms that we are ontologically detached from one another and from nature, floating in empty isolation toward a meaningless death. The way to defeat the right-wing creationists is to validate that there is such a thing as intuitive, passionate, ethical knowledge; that this knowledge is grounded in our connection to each other as social and natural beings; and that the right-wing creationists' version of this knowledge is wrong because their understanding of our social and natural existence is distorted and pathological. Why should we let the Assemblies of God run unopposed in the public arena as the spokespeople for God?

This leads directly to the question of whether claiming that there is an objective basis for intuitive knowledge is dangerous and could give legitimacy to fascist movements. This is certainly a serious and legitimate question because fascism acquires its power in part by linking appeals to people's emotions and knowledge of the Truth. The great achievement of liberal culture over the last several hundred years has been its partial protection of the individual from the tyranny of the group, and perhaps the single most important ideological source of this protection has been the idea that people cannot dominate others with truth-claims that are not provable by objective and verifiable methods. This idea has been the basis of the historical link between the claim that science provides the only objective basis for making knowledge-claims about the true nature of reality and the affirmation of the right to freedom of speech and religion. In the realm of feelings and insight into consciousness, no person can silence another in the name of truth because, in the liberal worldview, truth must be demonstrated scientifically and ideas that emerge from feelings or insight into consciousness (roughly, spiritual insight) cannot be demonstrated to be true or false by scientific procedures. To say that spiritual insight is "just a matter of opinion" does, to some degree, protect the individual from being dominated by the spiritual insight of others, and, to some degree, it gives people the courage to think for themselves (since each person's opinion is as good as anyone else's).

Without in any way denying the specific historical importance of the Enlightenment and the rise of science in helping to rid the world of the spiritual persecution that to some extent characterized feudal society, I think we must now recognize that science has become part of the problem rather than part of the solution and that the liberal worldview, at least in its current form, is as likely to be a cause of the rise of fascism (whether religious, racial, or nationalist) as it is to be what prevents it. The reason is not only that liberalism in its current form legitimizes, in the name of individual freedom, an immense amount of completely unnecessary worldwide economic suffering, a fact that certainly plays a part in making large masses of people vulnerable to the promises of redemption and revenge spun out by fascist leaders. It is rather that the liberal worldview, at least when tied to the idea that scientific rationality is the only route to true knowledge, *drives people crazy* because it prevents people from affirming their own felt knowledge that there is a spiritual dimension of existence that is *real* and not just "a matter of opinion," and that this dimension is accessible to all of us through the insight provided by emotional/intuitive understanding. The paradox of liberalism is that in its attempt to protect the individual from the group by insisting on the merely "subjective" nature of spiritual insight as contrasted with rationally provable scientific knowledge, it has made itself into a dogma that drives people toward fascist group movements by denying the reality of the spiritual or feeling world that fascist movements speak to.

There is only one way to combat the power of the religious Right, and that is to recognize that they are addressing something real and valid in people's experience and to challenge them on the merits. If the spiritual/emotional/intuitive dimension of reality is acknowledged as an aspect of the world that can be *known*, then we no longer have to stand idly by and listen to these lunatics tell us that God doesn't want us to sleep together before we're married or that the Bible must be read as literally true. Instead, we can struggle with them over the true meaning of what is revealed to us through passionate intuition and "demonstrate," by the evocative power of our words and the moral direction of our actions, that the religious Right is wrong about virtually everything it speaks to. But to begin to do this, we have to first recognize how wrong we have been to sever the bond between loving and knowing that is the basis for grasping all living truth.

PART TWO

THE MEANING OF
AMERICAN POLITICS

T HE ESSAYS IN THIS AND THE NEXT THREE PARTS of the book are meant to show how the link that I am drawing between the desire for mutual recognition and a politics of meaning can help us grasp the social longings and conflicts that invisibly shape a wide range of social phenomena.

Part 2 focuses on the meaning of American politics by addressing the historical flow of the struggle between desire and alienation as it has been played out from the beginning of the sixties to the present. Although "The Spiritual Truth of JFK (As Movie and Reality)" was written in response to Oliver Stone's 1991 movie, it is very much about the Kennedy era itself as well as the assassination. My goal in this opening essay is to express in words what I believe Stone was at least in part trying to express visually—the effect of the opening up of desire that began the sixties and the forces of fear that sought to shut down that opening in the service of the denial of desire that is at the heart of social alienation. In my view, it is this conflict that has played the central role in shaping the politics of the last four decades. The remaining essays in part 2 are meant to illuminate the many forms that the struggle between desire and alienation has taken by following the chronological development of this struggle, from Kennedy through Clinton, as a historically specific, collective, conflicted energy flow, a flow of the movement of disalienating desire in conflict with the antimovement of alienation's effort to deny that desire.

My views are obviously at odds with dominant materialist or economic explanations of the meaning of politics. Although material needs like the need for food and shelter influence politics, they do so only to the degree that politics actually affects our physical survival as bodily organisms. These material needs, so central to both liberal and Marxist accounts of what is "really" behind politics, are relevant only to one aspect of social existence, the need for the individual to physically survive and to alleviate physical suffering in the face of the objective deprivation of food and shelter or the fear of that deprivation. Without denying that these needs exert some independent influence on political life and conflict, they exert nowhere near the role attributed to them by Marx or by the conventional wisdom reiterated repeatedly ("It's the economy, stupid") in the media, in academia, and by political candidates and their parties across the political spectrum. It is true that facilitating, say, the maximization of profits is an important part of the agenda of both major political parties, and "underlying" material needs play some part in people's commitment to this capitalist objective, but it is also true that the satisfaction of each person's long-term need for food and shelter, even that of the wealthiest capitalist, would be better served by a mutually supportive and cooperative economy founded upon love, recognition, and lasting connection. The individual, competitive pursuit of profit maximization must therefore be explained by something other than material needs alone—namely, by the desire to protect one's physical survival or one's freedom from material suffering *in a social world* characterized by alienation, mistrust, even paranoia. Redefined within the framework I am proposing, the economic meaning of maximizing profits is underlain by a deeper social meaning—the desire to postpone as long as possible (ideally, for eternity) the need to entrust one's physical well-being to the goodwill of other human beings. That is the social meaning of the profit motive. My claim is that this social meaning has a social origin, the failure of love that has emerged from our inability to realize that the other is the completion of our being (through the attainment of the mutual recognition that Martin Buber called the experience of I and Thou) rather than being the threat to our being that our alienated conditioning has mistakenly led us to believe. While material scarcity may have originally contributed to this mis-comprehension of the other's nature, the miscomprehension itself is a spiritual failure of empathy, a failure to allow our consciousness to know that the other is both the same as we are and the source of our salvation from the isolation that separates us from the Community of Being, from a fully present interrela-tion with the other, with nature, and with God.

Since these essays, with the exception of "How the Left Was Lost," were written contemporaneously with the events they describe, parts of them may seem dated if you read them as if they were written today about events in the past. But I would ask you to approach these essays in accordance with my gen-eral aim of developing a descriptive approach to reality that illuminates its social meaning as existential lived experience. From this perspective, the essays ask that you go back in time and identify with the historical moment they seek to capture, moments whose existential specificity we have today all to some extent forgotten. Thus my discussions of the meaning of Bill Clinton's first election in "Clinton and the Id" or that of Newt Gingrich's subsequent Repub-lican revolution in "The Relationship between Community and True Democ-racy" are meant to convey the struggle between desire and alienation as it was uniquely manifested at those moments. That Clinton's presidency turned out quite differently from the spirit of hope that I claim was at the heart of the meaning of his election in 1992, or that Newt Gingrich has now resigned from the House of Representatives rather than being the leader of a revolt against the spirit of hope that I claim was the cultural meaning of his role in 1994—these subsequent developments are not relevant to the purpose of the essays. That purpose is to help us see the meaning and possibilities of the present moment, and of future present moments, by successfully illuminating past present moments—that is, past moments that were present at the time.

THE SPIRITUAL
TRUTH OF JFK

(As Movie and Reality)

OLIVER STONE'S *JFK* IS A GREAT MOVIE, but not because it proved that John F. Kennedy was killed by a conspiracy. Stone himself has acknowledged that the movie is a myth—a countermyth to the myth produced by the Warren Commission—but a myth that contains what Stone calls a spiritual truth. To understand that spiritual truth, we must look deeply into the psychological and social meaning of the assassination—its meaning for American society at the time that it occurred, and for understanding contemporary American politics and culture.

The spiritual problem that the movie speaks to is an underlying truth about life in American society—the truth that we all live in a social world characterized by feelings of alienation, isolation, and a chronic inability to connect with one another in a life-giving and powerful way. In our political and economic institutions, this alienation is lived out as a feeling of being "underneath" and at an infinite distance from an alien external world that seems to determine our lives from the outside. True democracy would require that we be actively engaged in ongoing processes of social interaction that strengthen our bonds of connectedness to one another, while at the same time allowing us to realize our need for a sense of social meaning and ethical purpose through the active remaking of the no-longer "external" world around us. But we do not yet live in such a world, and the isolation and distance from reality that envelops us is a cause of immense psychological and emotional pain, a social starvation that is in fact analogous to physical hunger and other forms of physical suffering.

One of the main psychosocial mechanisms by which this pain, this collective starvation, is denied is through the creation of an imaginary sense of community. Today this imaginary world is generated through a seemingly endless ritualized deference to the Flag, the Nation, the Family—pseudocommunal icons of public discourse projecting mere images of social connection that actually deny our real experience of isolation and distance, of living in sealed cubicles, passing each other blankly on the streets, while managing to relieve our alienation to some extent by making us feel a part of something. Political and cultural elites—presidents and ad agencies—typically generate these images of pseudocommunity, but we also play a part in creating them because, from the vantage point of our isolated positions—if we have not found some alternative community of meaning—we need them to provide what sense of social connection they can. It is a segment of the working class that creates a figure like Rush Limbaugh because of his capacity to recognize and confirm the pain of white working-class people and thereby help them overcome, in an imaginary way, their sense of isolation in a public world that leaves them feeling invisible.

In the 1950s, the alienated environment that I have been describing took the form of an authoritarian, rigidly anticommunist mentality that coexisted with the fantasized image of a "perfect" America—a puffed-up and patriotic America that had won World War II and was now producing a kitchen culture of time-saving appliances, allegedly happy families, and technically proficient organizations and "organization men" who dressed the same and looked the same as they marched in step toward the "great big beautiful tomorrow" hailed in General Electric's advertising jingle of that period. It was a decade of artificial and rigid patriotic unity, sustained in large part by an equally rigid and pathological anticommunism; for communism was the "Other" whose evil we needed to exterminate or at least contain to preserve our illusory sense of connection, meaning, and social purpose. As the sixties were later to make clear, the cultural climate of the fifties was actually a massive denial of the desire for true connection and meaning. But at the time the cultural image-world of the fifties was sternly held in place by a punitive and threatening system of authoritarian male hierarchies, symbolized most graphically by the McCarthy hearings, the House Un-American Activities Committee, and the person of J. Edgar Hoover.

In this context, the election of John F. Kennedy and his three years in office represented what I would call an opening-up of desire. I say this irrespective of his official policies, which are repeatedly criticized by the Left for their initial hawkish character, and irrespective also of the posthumous creation of the Camelot myth, which does exaggerate the magic of that period. The opening-up that I am referring to is a feeling that Kennedy was able to evoke—a feeling of humor, romance, idealism, and youthful energy, and a sense of hope that touched virtually every American alive during that time. It was this feeling— "the rise of a new generation of Americans"—that more than any ideology threatened the system of cultural and erotic control that dominated the fifties and that still dominated the governmental elites of the early sixties—the FBI, the CIA, even elements of Kennedy's own cabinet and staff. Kennedy's evocative power spoke to people's longing for some transcendent community, and in so doing, it allowed people to make themselves vulnerable enough to experience both hope and, indirectly, the legacy of pain and isolation that had been essentially sealed from public awareness since the end of the New Deal.

Everyone alive at the time of the assassination knows exactly where they were when Kennedy was shot because, as it is often said, his assassination "traumatized the nation." But the real trauma, if we move beyond the abstraction of "the nation," was the sudden, violent loss for millions of people of the part of themselves that had been opened up, or had begun to open up during Kennedy's presidency. As a sixteen-year-old in boarding school with no interest in politics, I wrote a long note in my diary asking God to help us through the days ahead, even though I didn't believe in God at the time. And I imagine that you, if you were alive then, no matter how cynical you may have sometimes felt since then about politics or presidents or the "real" Kennedy himself, have a similar memory preciously stored in the region of your being where your longings for a better world still reside.

In his books and essays, Peter Dale Scott has given a persuasive account of the objective consequences of the assassination, of the ways that the nation's anticommunist elites apparently reversed Kennedy's beginning efforts to withdraw from Vietnam and perhaps through his relationship with Khrushchev to thaw out the addiction to blind anticommunist rage—an addiction that, as he saw during the Cuban missile crisis, could well have led to a nuclear war. But for these same elites, the mass-psychological consequences of the assassination posed quite a different problem from that of reversing government policy—namely, the need to find a way to reconstitute the image of benign social connection that could reform the imaginary unity of the country on which the legitimacy of government policy depends. In order to contain the desire released by the Kennedy presidency and the sense of loss and sudden disintegration caused by the assassination, government officials had to create a process that would rapidly "prove"—to the satisfaction of people's emotions—that the assassination and loss were the result of socially innocent causes.

Here we come to the mass-psychological importance of Lee Harvey Oswald and the lone gunman theory of the assassination. As Stone's movie reminds us in a congeries of rapid-fire, postassassination images, Oswald was instantly convicted in the media and in mass consciousness even before he was shot by Jack Ruby two days after the assassination. After an elaborate ritualized process producing twenty-six volumes of testimony, the Warren Commission sanctified Oswald's instant conviction in spite of the extreme implausibility of the magic bullet theory, the apparently contrary evidence of the Zapruder film, and other factual information such as the near impossibility of Oswald's firing even three bullets (assuming the magic bullet theory to be true) with such accuracy so quickly with a manually cocked rifle. You don't have to be a conspiracy theorist, nor do you have to believe any of the evidence marshaled together by conspiracy theorists, to find it odd that Oswald's guilt was immediately taken for granted within two days of the killing, with no witnesses and no legal proceeding of any kind—and that his guilt was later confidently affirmed by a high-level commission whose members had to defy their own common sense in order to do so. The whole process is extraordinary, considering that we are talking about the assassination of an American president.

But it is not so surprising if you accept the mass-psychological perspective I am outlining here—the perspective that Kennedy and the Kennedy years had elicited a lyricism and a desire for transcendent social connection that contradicted the long-institutionalized forces of emotional repression that preceded them. The great advantage of the lone gunman theory is that it gives a *nonsocial* account of the assassination. It takes the experience of trauma and loss and momentary social disintegration, isolates the evil source of the experience in one antisocial individual, and leaves the image of society as a whole—the "imaginary community" that I referred to earlier—untarnished and still "good." From the point of view of those in power, in other words, the lone gunman theory reinstitutes the legitimacy of existing social and political authority as a whole because it silently conveys the idea that our elected officials and the organs of government, among them the CIA and the FBI, share our innocence and continue to express our democratic will. But from a larger psychosocial point of view, the effect was to begin to close up the link between desire and politics that Kennedy had partially elicited, and at the same time to impose a new repression of our painful feelings of isolation and disconnection beneath the facade of our reconstituted but imaginary political unity.

Having said this, I do not want to be understood to be suggesting that there was a conspiracy to set up Oswald in order to achieve the mass-psychological goal. There may well have been a conspiracy to set up Oswald, but no complex theory is required to explain it. And it would be absurd, in my view, to think that the entire media consciously intended to manipulate the American people in the headlong rush to convict Oswald in the press. The point is rather that this headlong rush was something we all—or most of us—participated in because we ourselves, unconsciously, are deeply attached to the status quo, to our legitimating myths of community, and to denying our own alienation and pain. The interest we share with the mainstream media and with government and corporate elites is to maintain, through a kind of unconscious collusion, the alienated structures of power and social identity that protect us from having to risk emerging from our sealed cubicles and allowing our fragile longing for true community to become a public force.

The great achievement of Oliver Stone's movie is that it has used this traumatic, formative event of the Kennedy assassination—an event full of politically important cultural memory and feeling—to assault the mythological version of American society and to make us experience the forces of repression that shape social reality. The movie may or may not have been accurate in its account of what Lyndon Johnson might have known or of the phones in Washington shutting down just before the assassination or of the New Zealand newspaper that mysteriously published Oswald's photographs before he was arrested. But the movie has given us a kinetic and powerful depiction of the real historical forces present at the time of the assassination, forces that were in part released by the challenge to the fanatical anticommunism of the fifties that Kennedy to some extent brought about. Through his crosscutting images of the anti-Castro fringe, the civil rights movement, high and low New Orleans club life, and elites in corporate and government offices who thought they ran the country, Stone has used all his cinematic and political energy to cut through the civics-class version of history and to bring the viewer into sudden contact with the realities of power and alienation that were present at that time and are present in a different form now.

I say this is the great achievement of the movie because no matter who killed Kennedy, it was the conflict between the opening-up of desire that he represented and the alienated need of the forces around him to shut this desire down that brought about his death. This struggle was an important part of the meaning of the 1960s, and it provides the link, which Stone draws openly, between John Kennedy's death and the deaths of Martin Luther King, Jr., and Bobby Kennedy. There is no way for the forces of good to win the struggle between desire and alienation unless people can break through the gauzy images of everything being fine except the lone nuts, a legitimating ideology that is actually supported by our denial of the pain of our isolation and our collective deference to the system of Authority that we use to keep our legitimating myths in place. Oliver Stone's *JFK* brings us face to face with social reality by penetrating the compensatory image-world of mass culture, politics, and journalism. And for that reason it is an important effort by someone whose consciousness was shaped by the sixties to transform and shake free the consciousness of the nineties.

How the Left Was Lost

A Eulogy for the Sixties
Written December 31, 1997

As I sigh in the New Year tonight, adrift with millions of my generation around the world who cannot reconcile their memories of the heightened sense of social connection and moral purpose that emerged from the sixties with the seemingly endless existential social-political desert to which we have been deported in our midlives, I think of Thomas Hardy's famous poem "The Darkling Thrush," written on December 31, 1899. On that profound evening, he looked back upon "the century's corpse outleant," a gray landscape strewn with unfulfilled utopian dreams and the reality of such death, pain, and sorrow that he found himself despairing and incapable of passion or optimism. Suddenly a thrush, impervious to Hardy's solemn presence, began to chirp the most beautiful and hopeful song, momentarily shocking Hardy out of his dismal reflections and forcing him to recognize that this ever-present life force, erupting through the thrush's song, inherently reaffirmed "some blessed Hope" in the universe more powerful than the entropy and failure to which Hardy had been bearing witness.

Though no thrush appears on my horizon tonight, perhaps one will make an appearance two years from now, at the end of this century, if we can create the hopeful social space for him or her to occupy. We can do so by coming to understand how social space has gradually closed around us over the last thirty years, leaving millions of us invisible to each other with our shared but privately experienced secret—that we saw the promised land, we stepped right into it with a sense of great collective discovery that we could indeed "break on through to the other side," and yet we have somehow found ourselves alone at Wal-Mart at the age of fifty.

Of course, many, many of us continue to try to connect the dots every day, to somehow manifest those earlier revelations about the transcendental unity of all being and our potential transparency to each other as loving, mutually affirming beings in whatever good works we continue to do. But it is good and important to face the dark side—that we gradually ebbed away from each other into reciprocal solitude and invisibility, without really grasping how or why it happened.

So on this bleak New Year's Eve, when in spite of all the Times Square hoopla there is so little basis for anticipating the transfiguration that this night so frantically tries to promise, let me try to say what happened, to explain how we lost each other without ever leaving each other's physical presence.

The cultural revolution of the sixties emerged as an outbreak of mutual recognition and intersubjective discovery, an upsurge of social connectedness that—stimulated by compelling social forces from the Vietnam War to the civil rights movement to rock 'n' roll—seemed to ricochet all over this country and across the world in a very brief period of historical time. Certainly, a central precipitating event was the increasingly evident irrationality of the slaughter in Southeast Asia, coupled with a military draft that provided an entire generation and their families with no exit, with no alternative but to try to come to terms with what was happening and to participate in it or to refuse to do so.

But the dawning understanding that emerged in part from this forced encounter with the war was much more comprehensive than anything related to the legitimacy of the war alone. That dawning understanding was that the war was but a horrible manifestation of an insane world, in which we were all trapped in some weird, alienated system of hierarchical roles and unreal collective fantasies. Supported by the felt authenticity of the civil rights movement, by the transcendental insights gained from LSD, and by the emergent joy of the counterculture as an opener of a new social space coexisting with and challenging the artificiality and posturing and seeming unreality of the official culture, we began to "recognize" each other in a new and self-evidently more real way. The collectively felt intimation of a radically more real, more transparent, and more loving way of experiencing and affirming each other revealed, with a sense of profound awe and also amazed laughter, the unreality that was being broken through and also caused this awareness to spread like wildfire, as it touched and liberated in each person his or her latent desire and longing for precisely this kind of breakthrough recognition and connection.

But this movement encountered a terrible problem that it did not understand, that it was actually in denial of. That problem was that the opening-up that fueled both the movement's connectedness and its accompanying insight into the false role-performances that constituted the official social facade was taking place within human beings who had been conditioned for centuries to repress their longing for this connectedness and insight and to believe that the social facade was as real as it claimed to be. This inevitably meant that the hyperexcitement generated by the sudden spread of that desire-realizing breakthrough was fragile, underlain by the legacy of doubt and mistrust that had shaped the formation of our historical personality structures. The opening-up required a vulnerability to the other that offered a great relief from the system of self-protective, artificial roles that had sealed us in our collective isolation. But it also triggered an unconscious fear of being so "out there," so transparent to the other, that it created the risk of a uniquely painful humiliation—the rejection by the other of our extended, unguarded soul. Since we had grown up in a social world that insisted the alienated facade was real, none of us had developed the experiential foundation to enable us to deeply trust that the other would remain out there with us, affirming the reality of our heightened state of reciprocal awareness and connection.

This doubt and its destructive effects began to be felt in every Left meeting that I was a part of, a phenomenon that exists still although there are, of course, very few such meetings today. And it always happened the same way, in thousands of spontaneously emerging counterculture organizations and in the large public meetings that took place almost every night during that time.

The process went something like this: A small group of people would take a leadership role in organizing a political meeting. A large number of people would be drawn to the meeting because of the excitement of being part of the movement, but most of those people would be checking things out with hopeful openness that they could somehow be part of the fusing group while also unconsciously doubting that this fusion, this new reciprocity, could actually be sustained. This collective doubt underlying the collective excitement and hope would be intuitively and unconsciously grasped by a small group of "crazies," who actually (again unconsciously) despised the intimations of openness and hope. These people, so endemic to the Left, were actually unconsciously addicted to conventional authority—they saw the spreading openness and hope as threatening them with seduction and humiliation, and so they sought to destroy the flowering of the group by enacting their authority-dependent victimized rage against the leaders. This they accomplished by opportunistically seizing upon the tentativeness and doubt present in the group as the group's Achilles' heel and then flooding the public space with violent criticisms of the organizers, as well as accusations that the group had been illegitimately constituted.

Often—almost always—these "crazies" were lefter-than-thou, purporting to be the most radical, the most militant, the most authentically committed to the group's political goal. Their attacks usually took the form of "Who gave this group the right to set the agenda?" or "I want to know why there are so few people of color in the room?" or "Before we even get to these issues, we have to recognize the centrality of U.S. imperialism and the fact that some people in this room are still benefiting from it." But their deeper motive was to use their supposed political purity to destroy the movement's transformative potential by capitalizing on the group's own vulnerability and uncertainty as the basis for traumatizing the social space. In instance after instance, from local political groupings in American cities to small radical organizations across the country to the many efforts to create a new national political party in the United States to the dynamics within the Maoist collectives in Western Europe or the dynamics within SDS chapters at U.S. colleges and universities, the process was the same.

And the result was that fewer and fewer "normal" people would come back to future meetings because the evident lack of safety reinforced their existing doubts. This ultimately left the initial organizers with a greater and greater percentage of the crazies, leading ultimately to the dissolution of each group and, eventually, to the sixties as a whole.

The analysis I am offering here is not meant as a bitter attack on the destroyers of a beautiful and potentially transformative historical moment. It is rather meant to show how the residual doubt that all of us inevitably felt about the safety of a radical new openness to each other manifested itself in group processes. Had we understood all this, and had we found the way to build up our confidence that our extension of ourselves toward each other would be met with affirmation by others in a safe environment, the "crazies" would have been marginalized and many of them would have quickly given up and left. Their power then, and their continuing presence in the Left, derives from the fact that we haven't yet figured out how to constitute and confirm a confidence within the group as a whole that a safe path from our existing alienated identities to a more communal and more loving and caring society is possible.

Finally, of course, it is necessary to remember that those who had always rejected the aspirations of the movement and sought to shore up the alienation of the status quo were astutely playing on the same undercurrent of doubt that the destroyers within the Left were exploiting. As millions of hopeful but tentative people drawn to the movement were turned off by the movement dynamics themselves, their doubt about the possibility of success was reinforced by the fact that they could not see the movement's truly hopeful meaning reflected back to them through the media. The sixties generation was gradually transformed back into the politically neutral "baby boom" generation; the meaning of the sixties was increasingly cast as a "troubled time" when everyone did drugs and acted out destructively in the name of a well-meaning but immature idealism; few if any of the successful efforts to extend the transformative efforts begun in the sixties were reported in the news. And so the millions of us that we were ebbed away from each other, increasingly invisible, increasingly finding the old isolating culture reenveloping us and leaving us with our shared secret of disappointment.

But to end on a positive note in this new year 1998, it remains remarkable and hopeful that the sixties lasted as long as they did and permanently changed so many human beings for the better in spite of the forces within us that undermined their most radical transformative aspirations. It is a testament to the power of our desire for genuine mutual recognition and social connection as an unconquerable longing built into our very social being that its temporary containment today can hardly produce an ounce of cultural vitality. In spite of the great cynical "No!" that really seems to enclose today's social universe, the energy of this desire pulses outward toward the other, and makes an appeal to the other, in every human interaction. I hope that our current efforts to build a deep link between spirituality and politics—through the politics of meaning and other related efforts—will provide the next steps in helping us to heal the doubts and fears that have thus far limited our capacity to realize this most basic longing of our common humanity.

DUKAKIS'S DEFEAT AND THE EMPTINESS OF POSTMOVEMENT POLITICS

On the Blockage of Social Desire and the Rotating Lack of Confidence in the Desire of the Other

THE DEFEAT OF MICHAEL DUKAKIS should have been an occasion for progressive people—and by this I mean people who want to create a more humane and socially just society—to fundamentally rethink their ideas about the nature of politics. Although Dukakis might have barely won the election if he had been more charismatic or had "looked more presidential" or had a more experienced staff or had defended the L-word earlier on in the campaign, the deeper truth revealed by the 1988 election is that the Democratic Party and progressive forces generally were unable to articulate a vision of what they (we) stood for that was as compelling as that articulated by the Right. All of us who worked for Dukakis because we had hoped to bring the Reagan era and Republican cultural hegemony to an end, and to rerelease the passion for creating a better world that animated our younger years, could not but feel the same old feeling that we have now come to associate with virtually every Democratic campaign since 1968—that our campaign was somehow hemorrhaging, that our candidate, although a fundamentally decent person, was somehow not able to say what we mean in a way that seemed convincing, while the Republican was able to speak with more confidence and to draw more social support to him, even though the world that he stood for was the wrong world and failed to realize the deepest needs of even his own supporters. Unless we want to spend our old age in either bitterness or pathos, we had better change the way we think about contemporary political and legal culture and come up with a better way of manifesting ourselves and our aspirations for human society in public space.

The basic error in contemporary progressive thought is the failure to fully grasp the social or intersubjective nature of desire, to understand that as social beings, people are animated by the need for mutual recognition and confirmation as much as they are by any physical or biological need like the need for shelter, medical care, or food. A principal truth about human history and about contemporary reality is that this social desire for mutual confirmation is unrealized in people's social existence, leaving them feeling chronically isolated and "underconfirmed" in their everyday family and work lives. I have elsewhere tried to show in some detail how this problem of underconfirmation gives rise to a chronic narcissism in the development of the normal self and how it also accounts for the construction and reproduction of social hierarchies. But what I want to emphasize here are the implications of this unrealized desire for progressive politics and for those seeking to bring about social change through law. The specific point that I want to make is that for progressive forces to succeed today, they must manifest themselves in public space in a way that lifts people out of their sense of isolation and enables them to feel part of a community of meaning within which their desire for social confirmation might be realized. This means that all concrete proposals for the expansion of economic benefits, for the implementation of new social policies, and for the extension of political rights must be framed within an evocative moral vision that "enlivens" these proposals with a sense of social connection and purpose.

In recent years, it is the conservatives who have understood and spoken to the pain and isolation resulting from underconfirmation. However much the Left and the liberal media sought to portray Ronald Reagan as an unintellectual performer who could lure the American people into voting for him by being an experienced actor and a "great communicator," the fact is that Reagan always put forward the conservative economic and social agenda as a way of recovering a sense of social meaning and purpose that could make people feel connected to one another through participation in the nation, the family, and the church group. George Bush also ran a campaign that was successful not primarily because of unanswered negative attacks on Dukakis, but because he focused on the same psychological and ethical needs that Reagan had spoken to. His appeals to the flag and the Pledge of Allegiance linked his candidacy to a commitment to community, loyalty, and solidarity; his repeated call for a kinder, gentler America linked the post-Reagan Republican Party with evocative qualities of social experience that were both corrective of the selfishness and aggressiveness that to some extent characterized the Reagan years and also expressive of some of the better qualities embodied by Bush himself. Although the moral vision of the conservatives has been to a large degree imaginary because it has not been coupled with an economic and social agenda that could realize in practice the longing that people have to live in a real world imbued with love, cooperation, and mutual respect, the Right's symbolic discourse has recognized the centrality of social desire to politics and has offered at least compensatory fantasies to alleviate, at the intrapsychic level, the alienation of everyday life.

In contrast, the Left (including liberals, left-liberals, and radicals) has remained bogged down in a blend of economism, social policy analysis, and process-oriented civil rights consciousness that no longer has a morally compelling, socially constitutive meaning for large masses of the American people. In its original incarnation, the New Deal was much more than a set of economic programs and social policies—it was expressive of a profound, compassionate response by the Democratic Party to the suffering of working people, and its programs and policies were experienced as the embodiment of a new sense of social purpose and direction. In the same sense, the expansion of political rights during the 1960s was understood as a morally redemptive act on the part of the entire country that enabled many middle-class whites as well as minorities and poor people to feel part of a meaning-giving community through which "we" were connected with one another toward the realization of a common vision of a better world. In their respective historical contexts, it was this link, between the creation of new entitlements and rights and the possible realization of what I am calling social desire, that gave the Democrats their evocative appeal.

Today this link no longer exists in any organic, self-evident way, and as a result, the Dukakis campaign's student loan, health care, and child care proposals—although they were good proposals that responded to the objective needs of most Americans—seemed flat and socially meaningless. With the exception of a portion of his acceptance speech at the Democratic convention, Dukakis never articulated a moral vision, drawn from the cultural particularity of that historical moment, which could make these proposals politically compelling to those who would benefit from them economically as well as to those who would not. In fact, slogans like "a good job at good wages" or benefit programs that appear to be mere redistributions of money are actually experienced as psychologically repressive to the degree that they implicitly define politics in a way that treats people's emotional context—their sense of unconnectedness and underconfirmation—as fixed and inevitable. By making the State appear to be a neutral conduit of material resources, rather than a potential locus of transcendent collective meaning, Dukakis ironically made the Democrats appear to be the party of psychological and ethical individualism while allowing Bush to be the spokesperson for the creation of community. Dukakis's programmatic proposals could have been put forward as concrete expressions of a vision of a more humane community that would have been practical and realizable in contrast to the pseudocommunity offered by Bush's appeals to patriotism, and Dukakis could have challenged Bush on precisely that issue. But as it was, Dukakis put himself forward as a competent manager of the State-as-money-machine, leaving Bush to run unopposed in the realm of meaning.

It is hard to say why the Democratic Party and progressive forces generally have such difficulty understanding the ideas that I am outlining here, but my own sense is that the reason may be a partially rational streak of paranoia about what I will shortly call "the desire of the other" that is embedded in our liberal (postfeudal) political unconscious. The Right can frame its message in moral terms and appeal to images of community because it has no intention of actually bringing into being a society based upon mutual recognition or confirmation; such a society implies a kind of reciprocal openness and trust that would challenge the values of the competitive market and the hierarchies of power that the Right is fully committed to maintaining. The Left, however, because it defines itself as reaching out toward others in the name of equality and social justice and because this impulse implies a potential real dissolution of the distance between self and other that is quite threatening in light of our personal and cultural histories, tends to be more ambivalent about articulating the truly social dimension of its "wish" for social change. No one who has participated in more radical movements for social change can fail to see the way that they perpetually undercut their own alleged aims through the hysteria and quasi-intentional irrationality that tend to corrode their internal dynamics, and it may be the same "fear of success" that leads liberals to displace the heartfelt spirit that animates them into technocratic and narrow policy-based or economic thinking. Seen through this social-psychological prism, Bush and Dukakis can be understood as engaging in a kind of unconscious collusion—the former offering fantasies and the latter offering "programs"—which is designed to avoid confronting the real alienation and blockage of social desire that is our most serious problem as a people.

If we want to experience any real movement toward progressive social change in our lifetimes, we must develop an approach to politics that makes the generation of social connection and social meaning its central objective. But to bring about such a dramatic shift in political consciousness, we must come to understand our social resistance to such a shift, not just within political parties and their spokespeople but also within the society as a whole. If Michael Dukakis could not speak to the fundamental need for a connection that he himself shares, it was in part because he sensed that his own fear of opening up and speaking for this social desire would be rejected by his listeners. We as a people are in flight from the very spiritual needs that we most want our candidates—the spokespeople for our group and for defining who "we" are—to address. To understand the source of this flight, we must go more deeply into the dynamics underlying the "underconfirmation" and "blockage of social desire" to which I have been referring. We must see the way our collective alienation imprisons us in a collective isolation that does not—except in special circumstances—dare reveal itself.

The Blockage of Social Desire: The Circle of Collective Denial and the Problem of the Rotating Lack of Confidence in the Desire of the Other

Desire is a word whose meaning has been shaped in large part by the split-off nature of sexuality in our recent cultural history, the notion of sexuality that has been taken over by psychoanalytic theory and made into a more or less immutable fact about human nature. Within this cultural context and its associated conceptual framework, desire has become associated with "the id," with an instinctual force that pulses through us and that we must seek to control through the development of our consciousness during childhood and adult life. This model has had a number of destructive effects on our ability to understand the world, all of them with normative implications unconsciously intended to prevent this understanding from occurring. Among these destructive effects are the objectification or quasi mechanization of desire as a "force" that "aims" at an "object" and whose meaning is therefore not intelligible or accessible to the comprehension of human insight; the dissociation of desire from knowledge, analogous to the dissociation of passion from reason, leading to a belief in the possibility of a nonintuitive, dispassionate method of interpreting social phenomena (I would include here everything from positivist social science to structuralism and systems theory); the "individualization" of desire, because if desire is a "force" emanating from a series of organisms, if it is a drive that aims at an object, then it cannot be intersubjective or social in its very nature; the privatization of desire, because if desire is conceived to be an individual and unintelligible instinctive force inside us and outside our control, then it cannot be something public and shared whose meaning we can discuss and come to know together.

This characterization of desire is actually an effect of the process that I now want to talk about, which is the process by which we become alienated from the desire for mutual recognition and confirmation that I referred to earlier. As social beings, we do not originally enter the world divided up into a sexual, instinctive part and a mental, perceptual-rational part, but rather as a unified, sensual-expressive someone seeking a confirmation, by the other, that is at once sensual and conscious. This is perhaps easiest to see in the infant who seeks the sensual, intersubjective nurturing of mother's breast as well as the recognition that animates his or her search for eye contact. But if we are honest with ourselves, it is quite easy to see this also in the efforts we each make to give and to receive this sensual-expressive confirmation in our own lives. In fact, if we are honest with ourselves, this desire is constantly visible to us in the pain that covers the surface of the world and that reveals, self-evidently, the simple reciprocity that people want and are unable to achieve in their relations with one another.

The problem that confronts us is that from the time we are born, this desire for mutual confirmation is resisted and even opposed by those around us who have learned, owing to the fragility of their own cultural and personal histories, to deny this desire in themselves. The medium of this opposition I call "misrecognition" is a process by which the parent, instead of confirming the infant in his or her being, "throws" the infant and later the child into a series of roles that to a significant degree alienate the child, in his or her social identity, from the centered desire that is the social dimension of the child's soul. The child experiences the parent as denying his or her own desire for full recognition and confirmation and as conditioning the child's recognition and acceptance on becoming the uncentered, role-based "good child" that the parent seeks. Once this distance between the child's desire and his or her social self has been installed in the child's heart and mind, the child will then tend to reproduce this split in others with whom he or she comes in contact, including his or her own children. To the degree that we are all fundamentally animated by the desire for true confirmation, the child will continue to strive for this confirmation for the rest of his or her life—but to the degree that the child has internalized the sense that this desire must not be manifested because it will lead to the loss of what recognition and sense of self the child did receive, the child will repeatedly disown the movement of this desire and short-circuit its aim, returning to the safety of the earlier, validated forms of social connection.

This is not to say that the alienation of the child is the fault of bad parenting or even that the parent-child relationship is the key social location for understanding how alienation originates. It is only the first such location for each person, but the problem should be seen as located everywhere, to the degree that we are all being conditioned and conditioning each other to maintain this distance between our desire and our social selves—in the family, in the schools, in passing each other blankly as strangers on the street, and in the workplace. As I showed in "The Bank Teller," a corporate hierarchy is actually a perceptual-imaginary grid that a group of people collectively superimpose on their social relationships in order to regulate, through an ordering of disciplinary gazes accompanied by a conceptual schema (president, vice president, etc.), the flow of intersubjective availability and recognition. By remaining within the "de-centered" artificiality of one's "role" as secretary, supervisor, vice president, and so on, and by apprehending this role-performance as occurring within a top-down ordering through which the constraints of one's role-performance are enforced through what Michel Foucault called "disciplinary observation," the group conspires to block the revelation of everyone's real desire for a more supple and vital connection.

The same point can be made with respect to other forms of social mediation, like the media. The local TV newscaster when I was in law school would always start his newscast with something like "The Red Sox Win and a Fire in Dorchester—Back in a Moment," all spoken in a loud monotone with his eyes glazed over and his body clenched in the manner required for maintaining the kind of repression that I'm talking about. This newscaster was functioning to mediate the blockage of social desire among the viewers who were collectively passivized and atomized by his performance rather than being brought into connection by it, and he managed this controlling mediation by manifesting his social being through a de-centered role intended to (painfully) deny his desire for a more human and truer reciprocity.

These circular or "rotating" processes of denial in which each person passes the same doubt on to the next person (or often to millions of people at once, as in the case of the newscaster) also account for the phantom phenomena we usually refer to as "social structures." I call these structures "phantom phenomena" because they do not really exist—they have always served as shorthand formulations for talking about the odd fact that the social world always appears to be already constituted over and against us as existential individuals, even though we know that there really is no social world apart from the one we existentially create. To give these structures ontological intelligibility, we must be able to dissolve their objectlike character by reappropriating them as experientially understandable displacements of intentionally created externalizations of intersubjective, human meaning onto an "outside world."

The reason that the blockage of social desire makes these structures ontologically intelligible is that the role-based character of the social connection that results from it necessarily involves the reciprocal projection of the foundation of this connection onto an experiential "outside." The essential purpose and consequence of the deflection of true, mutual confirmation into a reciprocity of distancing roles is precisely to "de-center" the self-other relation, to inject a rejecting distance into this relation that deprives it of any "ground" or presence to itself. The "ungrounded" social self produced by this de-centration has the quality of being literally "anonymous" because the rooted desire of the self to confirm and be confirmed by the other has been withdrawn from the self's role-performance, leaving the manifested self floating in midair, so to speak, without the anchorage and immediacy of reciprocal self-presence. As a result, the underconfirmed social self, in a milieu of misrecognition and collective denial, must project a source of agency outside itself to ground its own identity, and then give this projected, external source of agency the quality of being "fixed" or "real," in the service of maintaining denial and containing the movement of desire. This is accomplished by the collective enactment of deference to an external source of meaning that is imbued with authority—the de-centered self looks "outside" for its "author" and defers to this author's authority in grounding its uncentered, role-based character so that the social desire that constitutes the force and movement of each person's true social existence can remain withdrawn and safe from the trauma of what we might call disrecognition. When the members of a de-centered group collectively attribute their respective, de-centered social identities to the same external source of agency or meaning, and then reify this external source of agency so that it appears "real" or objectlike, we get the appearance of a structure that seems to shape and define each of the subjects who defer to its constitutive power.

For a highly visible public manifestation of the ungrounded social self, consider the persona of Bush's running-mate, Dan Quayle. In Quayle, we could all see with striking clarity the withdrawal of authentic presence from the eyes in particular; in watching him we could not but see the surface of his eyeballs as ocular globes drained of the animation of desire and self-generated meaning. Mr. Quayle suffered from underconfirmation in the sense that I have been using the term, and precisely to the degree that he struggled to cover his authentic being with an anonymous outer self, he anxiously sought with equal intensity to defer to an external source of authority (revealed in his "following-behavior" in relation to George Bush) and to claim this as his substitute foundation. And although Dan Quayle is an exceptionally transparent, public example of the process of alienation that I have been describing, we are all like him to a degree greater than we would like to admit, because we suffer, in varying degrees, from the same history of underconfirmation. Our collective history is marked by a "rotating lack of confidence in the desire of the other," within which we each respond to the other's distance by installing this distance within ourselves and thereby become "one of the others" to each other, unconsciously complicit in creating the climate of underconfirmation that we imagine is created by others.

By the time we become parents, we have been buffeted about in these circles of denial for a very long time, and we cannot but pass a good part of the de-centration that results from it on to the new social beings we bring into the world. This is the reason why the problem of the blockage of social desire is a political problem rather than something to be treated only by individual psychotherapy—we can only begin to reverse the isolating effects of these circles of denial by gradually increasing the *public* confidence of a very large number of people that the desire for confirmation each of us feels within ourselves is also felt by everyone else around us.

When a critical mass of people do begin to recover their confidence that the desire for true mutual confirmation that they long for also exists in the other, in all others, we call the resulting release of energy a movement. The spiritual emptiness and seemingly eternal stasis of life imprisoned in the rotating lack of confidence in the desire of the other is often quite suddenly dissolved at such moments by the spiritual vitality of mutual presence, by a new rotating confidence in the desire of the other that emerges into and spreads across social space.

The job of a progressive political candidate is to inspire the emergence of this sense reciprocal confidence in those for whom he purports to speak—or, as we normally put it, to "represent." This is, so to speak, the ontological responsibility of the candidate, and it can be carried out only by the evocative articulation of a passionate moral vision that draws upon the historical possibilities in the present moment to enliven a concrete programmatic agenda and thus make it a vehicle for connection.

Michael Dukakis and the team around him did not understand this and so could not release the possibilities for the opening up of desire that accompanied the end of the Reagan era. Had he taken the risk of embracing Jesse Jackson and the legacy of the idealism of the civil rights movement and linked his own fundamental decency and his support for programs that expressed that decency to a vision of a new and caring community, he might have won. At least he would have planted the seeds for a progressive politics that would be capable of speaking to people's deepest spiritual needs and rekindling the now long-dormant movement of social desire that could carry these needs into public space.

As it was, however, the Dukakis campaign offered no hope of such a movement and so reinforced the apparent inevitability of our collective isolation. In these circumstances, as people wandered in collective isolation toward their voting booths, how could "a kinder and gentler America" not have defeated "a good job at good wages" in the realm of fantasy on Election Day?

CLINTON AND THE ID

The Moment of Hope

ONE OF THE MOST IMPORTANT ASPECTS of the 1992 presidential campaign was the failure of any conventional right-wing assault on Bill Clinton to affect his ratings in the polls or, ultimately, the election. The Republicans repeatedly invoked many of the same images that had worked for the last twelve years—such as patriotism, family values, and God—and sought to portray Clinton as someone who would undermine the sense of community conveyed in these images. This draft dodger, this "demonstrator on foreign soil," this womanizer, this husband of an "unfeminine" woman, this slick friend of the cultural elites (who don't care about our country or our families)—whatever they tried had no effect and even backfired, as if people were responding with "Come on, we don't care about this stuff."

Since the creation of these conservative images of community had played a major role in the rise and success of the New Right, it's fair to ask why they failed to move people this time. The conventional answer is that "all people cared about was the economy." But this answer can't be right. First, economic

realities never speak for themselves—their political importance is always deter-
mined by the set of meanings people give to them. When Reaganomics led to a
first big surge in unemployment and increased poverty in late 1981 and early
1982, economistic Democrats thought that the normal losses the presidential
party faces in off-year elections would be greatly intensified in 1982. What they
missed was that the energy and excitement generated by Reagan's "revolution"
had sufficiently gripped the minds of the public that they wouldn't allow "economic facts" to turn them against the Republicans. It is the social meaning that
people give to the economic facts that determine elections—and this has more
to do with the flow of psychic energy than with the lifeless statistics that were
available to Democratic candidates before Clinton.

Second—and more important—it is never true that people care only about
the economy. People care about connecting with others and come to life
through this kind of connection, and politics always is significantly about this
aspect of human desire, about its potential realization and repression. It is this
erotic aspect of politics that accounts for Clinton's victory, not because Clinton
is "attractive" in some superficial sense, but because he was able to be the carrier
of a hopeful "opening up to each other" that people were ready to affirm again.

People were not ready to affirm this impulse in 1980 when Ronald Reagan
was first elected because they were traumatized by the combination of the erotic
energy released by the sixties and the violent, dislocating craziness that had
accompanied it. The sudden feeling of being alive that swept the planet during
those amazing years overwhelmed the capacity of dominant institutions to perform their major function—to cool out the movement of desire in the service of
"alienation-management." We may not remember so well what it felt like to be
alive in that way now that we've endured so many years of concentrated cultural
assault aimed at convincing us that we weren't really there, that all that happened was the bad parts, the excesses, the ways in which we were immature, the
ways in which our ideals exceeded our level of individual and collective development. But for a while we did experience a rupture of the world's normal,
numbed-out surface and had a radically different glimpse of what social connection might be like beyond the paranoia and alienation that has held humanity in
its grip for much of human history. Unfortunately, as the id broke through the
ego's retaining walls, giving us a taste of pleasure, ecstasy, and excitement about
the possibilities of new forms of human relationships and new depths of human
experience, many people reacted with a combination of exhilaration and fear—
fear that they could not trust and contain the new possibilities, fear that they

were not enough to be what they would have to be to live with a new set of truths. As a result of that fear, people attacked, mistreated, and hurt each other—undermining their emerging belief in the possibility of a different world. Through the spread of a "rotating doubt" subtly passed from person to person, most of us came to feel that what we were experiencing really wasn't possible, that the experience itself was probably not real, and that fear led to an ebbing of energy and a decrease in the connection that had previously sustained us. The sixties didn't end—they gradually ebbed away as each of us confirmed the doubt in the other and then found ourselves alone, doubting ourselves, losing our confidence that anything had really happened. We became susceptible to a societal assault that would reduce the sixties to self-serving draft dodging and mindless drug and music infatuation.

Enter Ronald Reagan. Freud said, "The superego knows more of the wishes of the id than does the ego," by which he meant that conservative, repressive authority—a legacy of our personal and cultural past that we each carry around inside ourselves—is keenly aware of our desire to break on through to the other side and is ingeniously capable of preventing us from doing so. As the sixties began to fade because of the doubt that we ourselves felt about its promise, those grown-ups whose sense of cultural identity and traditional community were most threatened by the sixties formed an alliance with younger people who felt hurt and betrayed by the sixties and harnessed the still-loosed power of desire in the service of a new repression—the New Right. Led by Reagan, the New Right capitalized on our doubt, got control of "The Force" released by the sixties, and turned it against the sixties itself. Freud also made this point—that the superego, which has no energy itself, uses the energy of the id against the id to protect what he called civilization from all hell breaking loose (the standard paranoid fantasy of community).

The eighties succeeded in binding the energy of the sixties within a series of split repressive images—on the one hand, idealized images of community exemplified by the traditional family, church, and nation ("Morning in America"); on the other hand, the image of the "evil empire" against whom our collective rage was to be directed (along with other "others" like gays, liberals, and the like who—in the realm of the imaginary—were deemed to pose a threat to our idealized community). The disturbing, liberatory energy of the sixties, in other words, was literally converted into its opposite through the collective invention of Ronald Reagan as an idealized and also vengeful father figure projecting images of an authoritarian, false, and "safe" community. To give one reminder of the energetic power of this image of authoritarian community, recall the frenzied search for the Original Intent of the Founding Fathers led by Attorney General Ed Meese in the mid-eighties. As I show in my essay "Founding Father Knows Best" written at that time, this attribution of hallucinatory power to the "original" intent of the Fathers above all fathers was part of a symbolic effort to "cleanse" the Law of the permissive liberal impulses released by the sixties.

Understood this way, the Reagan revolution should be seen as what psychoanalysis calls a "reaction formation," a defense against, and a ruthless denial of, the erotic longings of human desire. Unlike the blandness of what we might call bureaucratic historical periods, the Reagan era was hot and powerful precisely because it converted the social-connection energy of the sixties into an antisixties wrath and a passionate commitment to the purity of the Nation, the Family, and other alienated images of connection, emerging from the McCarthyism and the kitchen culture of the fifties that the sixties sought to challenge. In this sense, Reagan was an erotic figure who bound people together through the invocation of an authoritarian, imaginary world fueled by the id-energy that the sixties had unleashed.

Yet precisely because the binding energy of the New Right was "false" in the sense that it was based on the repression of desire rather than the realization of desire, it was doomed to expire or dissipate. Offering nothing itself to the real human need for love, confirmation, and community, its energy was parasitic on the energy it sought to crush. And I think when Reagan left office in 1988, we all began to feel the erotic bind of the New Right weaken, even though George Bush was able to win by adapting Reagan's imagery (the Flag vs. Willie Horton) to his kinder and gentler persona. Beginning in 1988, we began to float as a country, unmoored from both the liberatory energy of the sixties and the antilibidinal power of Ronald Reagan, Jerry Falwell, Oliver North, and those Founding Fathers who slipped back into their actual place in the past. As the cultural id let go of the convulsive struggle between the sixties and the eighties, people began to lose interest in the supposed original intent of these long-dead men or the kind of patriotic bond offered by Oliver North.

It was in this "floating space" that the 1992 presidential campaign began, and it is quite possible that George Bush might have ridden the inert images of the New Right to power; the election might have been a bland extension of the status quo while the id within us—by which I mean the powerful desire for social connection and confirmation—simply waited for its next historical opportunity, like waiting to find a lover during a period of drift and solitude. But Bill Clinton emerged from whoever he had been (recall the puzzlingly boring speech introducing Michael Dukakis at the 1988 Democratic convention) to seize the opening created by the dissipation of the energy of the New Right. While the Right proceeded to exaggerate its increasingly lifeless images of its version of our social bond, Clinton stepped up to the plate to reclaim American society in the name of the long-dormant generation of the sixties.

To accomplish this, he had to both manifest a mature version of the erotic power of the sixties and dissolve the energy blockage that had been the political legacy of the failure of the sixties—the blockage created by the politics of "coercive deference" to special interest groups that had come to dominate the Democratic Party and the Left. The originally liberatory and potentially universal appeal of the labor movement, the civil rights movement, and the other transformative elements of the thirties and the sixties had settled—mainly as a result of the self-doubt I referred to earlier—into a collection of bitter and angry demands for more rights and benefits against an "outside authority" that was refusing to sufficiently recognize the victim status of these groups. This process, which had originally been reflected directly in countless organizations and meetings in the seventies, in which white "middle-class" idealists had been neutered and driven away by their politically correct, interest-group counterparts, had come to characterize the public politics of the Democratic Party and the Left in the eighties. We had these white grown-ups from our parents' generation—Jimmy Carter, Walter Mondale, Michael Dukakis—trying to "lead" a collection of groups to whom they were forced to defer and who therefore, quite understandably, held them in contempt. The crazy, denunciatory aspect of the sixties produced this form of impotent civility in the mass politics of the late seventies and eighties, a hopeless politics of blocked energy, resentment, and inauthenticity that could not possibly unite people with constructive passion.

Clinton had the courage and smarts to cut this Gordian knot by publicly and politely repudiating Sister Souljah and in other ways indicating that he would not ritually defer to the victimized anger of interest groups in order to get votes. In so doing, he became what none of his recent, deferential, predecessors could become—a source of power and energy that could enable whites, African Americans, union members, and yuppies to get turned on together about reclaiming the world from the pathological eros of the Right. By cutting through the politics of guilt-based, self-denying deference—and by combining this with the expressiveness, youth, and saxophone power of the now grown-up sixties generation—he enabled us to reenter public space and rediscover each other. Against this reemergent but less crazy force of the sixties, the old right-wing appeals to the id seemed like the phobic sputterings of a dying generation. At the Republican convention, Marilyn Quayle made an admirable attempt to win the battle for the sixties by asserting that "not all of us participated in the sexual revolution"—meaning: not all of us gave in to that exhilarating sense of connection that produced, and can only produce, betrayal, pain, and loss. But Clinton had already defeated this attempt to invalidate the sixties precisely by repudiating the destructive dynamics that had emerged from the contradictions of the sixties and providing a safe way back into politics for people who remembered what was good about that time and the ways in which we were right.

Now we will see if in our adult years we can begin to build the confidence in our transformative aspirations that we could not do twenty years ago. One of the most important symbolic aspects of Clinton's insistent focus on the economy during the campaign was that it demonstrated an attentiveness to improving people's real lives that contrasted with the Right's increasingly hollow fantasies of community. In this sense, focusing on the economy meant caring about people and creating real community, while "family values" meant denying the pain in people's real lives and exhorting people to keep believing in the expired images of the Reagan years. But for our generation's coming to power to be a true extension of the spirit of the sixties, Clinton and all of us supporting him must not let his economic rhetoric lose its communitarian quality and become a set of technocratic formulas and slogans. If that happens, we will lose the spiritual opportunity that this victory represents and set the stage for new id-based forces of reaction led, perhaps, by the passionate and compelling Jack Kemp.*

So let's have four years guided by saxophone power and the passion of a politics of meaning rather than the professional, moderately progressive reformism that can't engage people's life force and will set us up for failure. We need to join Clinton, embrace our generation's second chance, and pull him with us toward what still remains true and deep about the liberatory visions we once dared to hold.

---

* It turned out to be a relative unknown, Newt Gingrich.

THE RELATIONSHIP BETWEEN COMMUNITY AND TRUE DEMOCRACY

On the Need to Create a "Parallel Universe"
as the Lesson of the Republican Revival

IF THERE WAS A BRIGHT SIDE to the Republican landslide of November 1994, it is that it may have liberated those of us wanting to build a society based on community from having to identify ourselves with the impersonal conception of government associated with the Democratic Party. Newt Gingrich made his version of this point when he introduced the orphanage movie *Boys Town* for channel TNT with these words: "I can't imagine a better antidote to the modern welfare state than the sense of love, caring, and spirituality conveyed in this movie." If we put aside both our cynicism about whether orphanages like Boys Town really exist as well as our desire to affirm parent-child love in poor communities, wasn't Gingrich clearly right to have suggested that the mere redistribution of money to isolated poor mothers through a Democratic entitlement program has little to do with creating the kind of social transformation toward a radically more caring community that brought many of us into politics?

Like a kind of reverse Marxist, Gingrich was calling for the withering away of the State before rather than after the overthrow of capitalism. His positive message behind the call for less government was an affirmation of his version of what the communities of capitalist culture can and ought to be—loving, two-parent nuclear families, schools imbued with traditional values, prayerful and forgiving church groups, purposeful and loyal companies, the patriotic, unifying nation. However much we disagree with this vision, we can't oppose it with a liberal-Democratic (or Green, or Rainbow Coalition, or New Party) agenda that doesn't have an evocative communal vision of any kind. The opportunity in the present moment may be to build a new communal politics within civil society that can challenge the Republicans on their own terms ("underneath" the State) and be truer to our own transformative vision than we have been in many years.

First, let's clarify what exactly is wrong with the Democratic Party worldview and how our more or less forced allegiance to it has placed us in contradiction with our own communal aspirations.

The basis of the desire for community is the desire in each of us for a connection with one another that embodies the experience of mutual presence and confirmation. The effort to realize this desire impels us to resist and try to break through the isolation and alienation that envelops us, the artificiality of the roles we feel compelled to play, the cynicism and jokiness that pervades our everyday interactions, the temporizing and holding-back of "idle talk." The fear of reliving the trauma of a humiliating rejection, experienced first in childhood but reinforced by the denial of desire that seems to constantly surround us, tends to defeat our efforts, pushing us back into our isolating roles and routines. The whole society, the world, is in a state of denial of what we most want.

Changing this dynamic cannot occur through installing a new economic system or a new system of government because altering the externals cannot heal the paranoia. Just think of any political group you've ever been in. These groups often attract some wonderful people filled with hopefulness and a desire to make significant change. Yet all of us are filled with a level of paranoia and fear of humiliation based on our previous disappointments and the ways we have been let down by others in the past. No matter how hopeful people are about change, they approach these groups with suspicion, having already internalized the societal message that it is only in families and fragile friendship networks that we can find people to trust and that the people we are likely to encounter in these groups are going to put us down or otherwise humiliate us. This leads to a holding back on the part of most people in the group when a few of the more angry and wounded people begin to "act out" in ways that the group itself does not have the confidence to contain. The acting out takes many forms: dominating the discussion, putting others down, listening for the slightest politically incorrect or tactically mistaken suggestion and then jumping on the speaker for having made such a stupid remark, pushing for grandiose fantasies as "the necessary next step" that are guaranteed to lead everyone to feel nothing real is happening or, conversely, arguing that nothing is possible except repetition of political strategies that have gone nowhere in the past. Precisely because of the understandable tentativeness and insecurity that the majority of hopeful and decent people feel when they enter these settings, they quickly withdraw in the face of these negative dynamics and go back to the safer despair of private life. In different forms, these dynamics made possible the totalitarian manipulation of democratic forms in the Soviet Union, the apparent craziness of many Left groups in the sixties, and the continuing inability of smart and decent people to get a progressive movement off the ground in the 1990s.

The picture of society that has defined the politics of the Democratic Party since the New Deal has nothing to do with a communal vision or with creating the experience of community. To be sure, the social movements that gave rise to the reforms of the New Deal and the civil rights era did infuse these reforms with some communal meaning. The economic reforms of the 1930s were not merely dry, external changes in the economic system; they were enlivened communally by the solidarity of the labor movement and the "we're all in it together" feeling of struggling against the Depression. The expansion of legal rights that followed the civil rights movement involved more than technical extensions of the Fourteenth Amendment creating new rights to damages for discrimination based on race; these rights were originally infused with the lyrical upsurge of connection that spread from the churches and marches outward, giving these rights a transcendent communal meaning (the aspiration for true racial equality) that influenced their judicial interpretation for many years, transforming even a Republican district attorney like Earl Warren into the most progressive chief justice in American history.

But these communal influences were indirect and were actually in contradiction to the party's social paradigm. This paradigm was and is that our society is divided into (a) a liberal, noncommunal civil society in which everyone pursues his or her own interests and (b) a government that corrects social injustices through the redistribution of money from some individuals to other individuals and through the expansion of legal rights to assure no individual interferes, through discrimination, with the liberty of others to pursue their own interests ("equality of opportunity").

There are two important points to note about this picture: First, the image of civil society presupposes that as individuals we are inherently separate from each other except to the extent that we voluntarily form associations through, for example, contracts, marriage, partnerships, and corporations. There is no recognition of an inherent desire for social connection, for mutual recognition, or for a community of meaning and purpose because such a desire would define the individual as inherently social and in relation to others. Instead of such a social individual, we find the liberal individual whose only essential need is that of economic survival, whatever other desires he or she may choose to pursue in the exercise of liberty and the pursuit of happiness.

The second key point about this picture is that the State is pictured as "above" or apart from civil society, as literally not part of the flesh-and-blood reality of social life. It is democratic by virtue of elections characterized by individualistic voting, but it is not communal because in civil society there is no assumption that people are inherently connected in the absence of voluntary association. Thus the government can connect individuals to each other through, for example, taxing one individual in order to make a welfare payment to another. But the government cannot directly seek to bring people together in order to overcome their alienation and realize their communal bond.

The individualistic assumptions embedded in this worldview (and our unconscious psychological motives for adhering to them) go a long way toward explaining both the limitations of the social-change movements of this century and the eventual resurgence of the Republican Party in the century's last two decades. However important the specific economic and legal objectives of these movements were, the transformative aspect of the movements was precisely in their challenge to isolation and alienation, in the sudden thrill of connection and discovery of one another that gave them their movement character. This experience of community is what provided millions of people a glimpse that the world could be radically different from what it is and is what drew many of these people, including me, into politics.

But when these movements appealed to the government for legal and social change and increasingly adopted the Democratic Party as their expressive vehicle, they left the communal world of the movement (with its challenge to the alienation pervading civil society) and found themselves in the abstract world of the liberal democratic State. Because the creation of community could not be a political goal of the government within the abstract and unreal individualist "world" of this liberal State, because the paradigm itself required government to be perceived as a disconnected collection of "representatives" of collections of disconnected and separated individuals lumped together abstractly by state or congressional district, the transformative, communal aspirations of these movements necessarily became invisible. Wages and working conditions came to replace the vision of a cooperative and democratic workplace as the defining feature of the labor movement. Nondiscrimination in housing and employment within the liberal marketplace came to replace the civil rights movement's transformative vision of a society based on love across racial differences and mutual recognition. The women's movement lost some of its vision of a society based on cooperation rather than aggression and competition, on intuitive understanding and empathy rather than distanced male rationality, in favor of equal rights and nondiscrimination in the marketplace. And "helping the poor" through economic entitlements came to replace the vision of creating a world in which we share things equally because we want to, because we feel and want to manifest our common humanity.

Stripped of the desire for community that originally animated it, the liberal platform of the Democratic Party became increasingly absurd. A movement generates a feeling of connectedness that has appeal to those outside it because it promises a feeling of being with others that can lift all of us out of our painful feelings of meaningless and isolation. But if you take that promise away and replace it with a vision that leaves people in their painful isolation, reduces community to impersonal government programs that are based exclusively on the forced redistribution of money from one anonymous isolated person to another, deprives the donors of even feeling the caring of direct giving, and then tells the "taxpayer" that he or she doesn't need anything because he or she is not oppressed enough, people would have to be crazy to support you for too many decades. And let's face it: For those of us whose politics emerged from the experience of social movements, it was frustrating and even depressing to have to support a party that could never directly reflect back to us the most important desire that motivates us. How long should we be going on saying things to ourselves like, "Well, Clinton seems to have a sixties feel—even if he didn't say a single thing that is directly relevant to my universe."

So perhaps Newt Gingrich did us a favor by putting us out of our misery and freeing us up to come up with a new approach to politics that tells our real truth. His worldview is that if we can get the spiritually empty government with its "faceless bureaucrats" off our backs, we can find and nurture community within the institutions of American civil society as they already are, or were in some conservative golden age. For those of us who see these institutions as (not entirely, but significantly) alienated pseudocommunities concealing isolation, longing, and pain, contesting the Gingrich vision requires not a politics of more spiritually empty government (the liberal worldview), but a politics of building transformative community within civil society itself. It is a matter not merely of new economic programs or defending our rights, but of directly creating experiences of being together that feel better, more empowering, and more real than the alienated communities on which people are currently dependent for their social identities. It is a politics of civil society of this kind that will allow us to challenge the Republicans on their own terms, rather than continuing to saddle ourselves with the contradiction of relying on the anticommunal worldview of the state. And it is also such a politics that can revitalize the very meaning of government by respiritualizing it, by understanding government not as a political "entity" independent of and "above" civil society, but as the political expression of and carrier of our aspiration to community, our longing to connect.

What would this new kind of politics look like? The single most important first step is to shift our own attention in everyday life from frenzied activity aimed at "getting things done" to manifesting our presence to the other so as to "call" upon the desire for true connection that exists in the other's heart. This shift from an instrumental to a spiritual "strategy" has nothing to do with a Moonie-like conception of love—it is simply to take seriously that what people most want and need is to escape from the artificiality of the roles that imprison them and from the cynicism and evasion that they know will doom them eventually to a meaningless death. The power of a leader like Martin Luther King came not from his words alone but from how he manifested his presence through his words, and it was the developing reciprocity of this presence within the civil rights movement that gave the movement its communal life force. One doesn't have to be a gifted speaker to manifest a presence that begins to give confidence to the other—it is simply a matter of trying to embody, in the face of the massive denial around us, the truth to which we know others aspire and the possibility of realizing it.

No set of programs or policy proposals or organizing efforts can successfully challenge people's psychological allegiance to the existing system without this capacity to transmit confidence by example. But if we can succeed in gaining this sense of how to be present for each other, we can then pursue organizing strategies aimed not merely at passing new legislation or getting the Supreme Court to recognize some new right, but at spreading the experience. A labor organizer who has seen the transformative power of immigrant workers coming to stand up for themselves on a picket line can foster that experience of solidarity by creating discussion groups at the union where workers share their cultural history and backgrounds. Those who work in nontraditional or at least moderately progressive workplaces might move toward replacing work rules and employment contracts in favor of an ethos of mutual commitment, fellow-feeling, and voluntary cooperation. Groups of friends might seek to overcome the isolation of nuclear families—those often impacted havens in a heartless world—by finding ways to form committed villages in which they can help one another raise the next generation, share finances, and foster a sense of loving and playful—but permanent—comradeship that can't be fully achieved in our society's absurdly casual approach to friendship.

Thinking this way may at first seem "too small" and naively idealistic when confronted with the supposedly massive pressures of the capitalist economic system. But it's time to stop thinking of capitalism as an economic system, a kind of giant machine that determines our existence from the outside. Our society is not some kind of external machine organized for profit, but an alienated social reality, suffused with paranoia, that fosters domination in both the economic and the noneconomic spheres of life. Its Achilles' heel is that no matter how much economic prosperity it generates, it cannot address the spiritual impoverishment and the pain of isolation that haunts everyone's lives, even those in the ruling class whose interests the society supposedly serves, because it cannot satisfy our most fundamental desire for connection and meaning.

Changing the economic system from capitalism to socialism—even some new externally pictured model of democratic socialism—cannot solve this central problem because the healing required for the creating of community must be gradually brought into being through lived experiences that replace doubt with confidence, mistrust with trust, and cynicism with seriousness, hopefulness, and conviction.

It is the silent longing in everyone for such a transformation that makes a spiritual strategy within civil society plausible. But in order for such an effort to gain the confidence to spread, our private experiments must have a way of becoming publicly visible. So long as we remain isolated from each other in these efforts, we cannot gather the steam required for a new way of being to spread. As Michael Lerner has pointed out, in every single interaction we are conflicted between our desire to extend ourselves to the other and reach out for genuine recognition, and the temptation to pull back and hide behind the protective role-behaviors that were communicated to us as compulsory during the course of our alienated conditioning. So long as our transformative efforts are experienced as isolated and private, they will inevitably tend to fall apart from within because the vulnerability and the trust required to affirm at "meta" level the transformative aspect of the experience will be undermined by the legacy of doubt and mistrust that we ourselves have internalized. The sixties did not "vanish" because everybody sold out, but because the media would not reflect us back to ourselves as we really were, acting instead as a kind of cultural immune system that successfully encapsulated and caricatured our efforts so that we ourselves came to doubt our own transcendental discoveries and ultimately participated in spreading doubt rather than confidence among ourselves. So to be successful, a politics of civil society must build its own public sphere that will allow us not simply to learn from each other, but to build within ourselves as individuals and within our own face-to-face communities a conviction that the experience of unalienated connection to which we aspire can overcome the denial of that experience that constantly seems to surround us.

It may be that new publications that link spirituality and politics like *Tikkun, Yes!,* and *Sojourners,* the beginnings of a new spiritually conscious workplace activism that aspires to transform institutions into authentic communities, the recent formation (with the help of organizations like the Foundation for Ethics and Meaning) of groups within professions like law and medicine seeking to bring a deeper spiritual and communal awareness to the work of these professions, and the growing appeal of ecological and spiritual consciousness on university campuses are today helping to create this confidence-building mutual visibility, this new kind of public sphere "underneath the State" and within the civil society that is our real world. If so, I think we should understand our efforts as pointing toward a horizontal and narrative vision of social change in which our goal is neither some magical, instantaneous revolution nor vertical legal reforms that would try to fix the world with the Law's authoritative words, but rather the building of a parallel universe within our existing society that is simply truer to human needs than what Newt Gingrich and others like him have to offer. It is difficult to acknowledge this, but the closest model to the kind of spiritual organizing I'm talking about is the Christian Right, and we should learn from them.

How then should we think about the role of government in advancing our communal goals in the post–New Deal world? I think we should recognize from the long-term failure of the Democratic Party that the creation of an unalienated community is indispensable to the realization of democratic ideals. This means we must find ways of bringing into being an experiential reality that can overcome the split between an alienated, competitive, individualistic, paranoid society and an abstract democratic state. We should certainly defend New Deal reforms, entitlement programs, and the sixties-inspired expansion of legal rights on the basis of their communal and loving origins, but we should help to reconceive them so that they in fact advance the expression of community and love. Bill Clinton's National Service program is a hopeful example of how to do this because it directly creates social connection and human meaning—it brings young people into direct contact with other human beings in need and allows them to give of themselves, to create bonds of affection and solidarity. There are surely many, many other ways to do this if we can rid ourselves of the individualistic regulatory paradigm that has, for the time being, run us straight into the ground. But the deeper point I am making is that we should stop altogether thinking of the government as something separate from civil society that we can use in some manipulative fashion to change what is wrong with the world and think of it increasingly as an expressive medium of connectedness emerging from the parallel universe that we are trying on a daily basis, and through future generations, to bring into being.

It is the creation of such a parallel universe, existing alongside and challenging by example the alienation of the dominant culture, that will provide the social base for a communal government that can realize the ideal of democracy by connecting and thus constituting "the people" in a way that our current democracy of disconnected and mistrustful strangers never can.

CLINTON AND THE SUPEREGO

Hope's (Temporary) Expiration

LAST NIGHT AS I WAS GOING TO BED, I flipped on the TV to see if the Giants had somehow come back in the ninth to defeat the Rockies or had continued their midsummer swoon. To my surprise, on came Barry Melton of the sixties rock band Country Joe and the Fish, talking about how we in the sixties generation had been emerging millions-strong to create an alternative culture—a whole new way of looking at the world based on joy, love, and peace—that existed alongside the alienated mainstream culture that had produced the Vietnam War. His point was that we were not interested in political reform in the traditional sense, but in a consciousness-transformation, an emulsification of an alien and artificial world by a more real one.

I forgot about the Giants.

I had stumbled onto *Berkeley in the Sixties,* a documentary I had seen eight years ago. What struck me this time was how much even I had forgotten of the extraordinary liberatory energy of that time, the upsurge of connection and sudden insight that spread across the world like wildfire and caught me up in a way that decisively and positively shaped my whole existence.

How could I have lost touch with this? And why during the nineties rather than the more reactionary eighties?

The answer is: Bill Clinton. While Ronald Reagan and George Bush had represented the assault of my parents' generation against the liberatory energy of the sixties, they left the continuity of my generation's experience intact. But Bill Clinton "crossed over." He was one of us who decided to become one of them, albeit a liberal version of them. And because Reagan had succeeded (with a lot of help from us) in blunting our generation's movement energy, there has remained no force capable during the Clinton years of maintaining the visibility of our alternative spiritual reality in public space.

Once Clinton decided to fuse the embodied warmth and informal realness and longing for social justice that he got from being one of us with the globalization of capitalist values, he dissociated our generation's present from our past and left us, the real us who saw the promised land, invisible to each other and even to ourselves.

The irony is that Bill Clinton was elected in significant part because the We who elected him hoped he would carry forward the transformative idealism of the sixties in a more mature and compassionate form. Right after that first election in 1992, we at *Tikkun* devoted an issue to that hope under the heading "The Sixties Generation Returns." I wrote an optimistic piece for that issue entitled "Clinton and the Id," which tried to show how Ronald Reagan had, with the help of identity politics, contained the communal life force released by the sixties, and how Clinton might be able to combine eros and universalism in a way that could "get us moving" again.

I underestimated the power of the superego, the inherited voice of authority that, as Freud said, "knows more of the wishes of the id than does the ego," and that is so very skillful at co-opting those wishes of the id to defend the ego against the vulnerability required for its own liberation.

Misunderstanding the radical hopes and longings that first got him elected, Mr. Clinton has, no doubt unwittingly, used the idealism of the sixties to legitimize a self-centered, anticommunal, competitive marketplace that contradicts that idealism. Faced with a traumatic and confusing first year in office and lacking the confidence in any case to distinguish the integrity of his sixties-inspired soul from his childlike image-identifications with "presidents" from Jefferson to JFK, he chose deference to authority over the intimations of transcendence that had propelled him and us into public space during our younger years. So this week Hillary Clinton sent her plain wedding dress, bought off the rack at an Arkansas department store the day before her 1975 wedding, to be on show alongside the fancier gowns of Nancy Reagan, Pat Nixon, and Mamie Eisenhower at a Stanford University "First Lady" fashion exhibit, while Mr. Clinton led C-Span through a long tour of the Oval Office that was an idolatrous celebration of the "Founding Fathers" and their presidential children whose busts adorn the White House.

But: Let it be. Because of Mr. Clinton's crossover, the sixties are over. Because of that crossover, Mr. Clinton now "is" the sixties, the publicly visible embodiment of our generation. But the death of the sixties may at last be creating the possibility for a new social movement based on a new link between spirituality and politics that can enable the sixties ideal of a loving community to become less frightening and more sustainable.

PART THREE

THE SPIRITUAL DIMENSION OF PUBLIC POLICY

SINCE MICHAEL LERNER AND I BEGAN SPEAKING and writing about the politics of meaning, many people have responded with enthusiasm and excitement to the possibility of building a political movement that would challenge the alienation and isolation of our existing society and speak to people's longing to be part of a community of meaning and purpose. Particularly since our 1996 national conference in Washington, D.C., attended by almost two thousand people from across the country, and the publication of Michael's book *The Politics of Meaning* which followed soon afterward, local politics-of-meaning study groups have begun to form in more than ten cities, and task forces have emerged in the areas of law, education, psychology, and other professions—all hopeful about reimagining the meaning of social change in a way that speaks to the emotional, psychological, and spiritual dimensions of existence.

But while supporters of the politics of meaning resonate strongly to its critique of conventional economistic and rights-based politics and to the overarching vision of a politics that takes the spiritual dimension of existence seriously, they have had difficulty applying the perspective to concrete policy issues. In particular, local groups have been unsure how to distinguish a politics-of-meaning perspective on an issue such as health care, for example, from traditional liberal and progressive perspectives. Is it sufficient for a supporter of the politics of meaning to simply support health care for all? If so, what distinguishes the politics-of-meaning agenda on concrete policy issue like this one from the liberal and progressive agenda that is already supported by everyone from Marxists to the social-democratic Left to the liberal wing of the Democratic Party?

In this section, I try to bring out the distinctive character of a politics-of-meaning approach to concrete policy issues, using health care, opposition to standardized testing, affirmative action, and sex education in schools as my examples. The key distinction between a politics-of-meaning approach and a traditional liberal or progressive approach is making explicit the relationship between supporting progressive goals and the way that such support helps to realize the spiritual longing for mutual recognition and the creation of a loving and caring society. The essays on health care and affirmative action place the debates on these issues in their recent historical contexts, arguing that only a meaning-centered approach can explain why majorities at one time supported these social goals and that their recent defeats are explained by the *loss of transcendent meaning* in how proponents have publicly advocated for them. The essays on the SAT (including the exchange that follows it) and sex education contrast meaning-centered and meaning-less approaches to fostering intellectual development and loving sexuality in the context of education in schools.

The essay in part 1 on the creationism-evolution debate could have been included in this section, as could the foreign policy essays in part 5. The central point of all these essays is a simple one, yet one that is difficult to grasp because of the historical exclusion of subjective/spiritual discourse from the liberal conception of public policy and politics generally. The simple point is this: If we want people to support an ideal like universal health care, we must evoke the meaning of this ideal as an opportunity to be part of a society and a world in which we care for one another and for one another's families, not simply to be protected by monetary insurance against the illnesses that befall our individual bodies in isolation.

THE DESIRE FOR COMMUNITY
AND THE DEFEAT OF HEALTH CARE

Understanding (and Failing to Understand)
Government as a Carrier of Love

THE DEEPEST PROBLEM FACING OUR SOCIETY is that our common experience is colored by a fear of one another that precludes the development of community. This fear is the result of literally centuries of conditioning that has convinced us that if we seek to extend ourselves toward each other to achieve the affirmation that we desire, we will have to risk a vulnerability to the other's rejection that is too painful to bear. The experience of community requires a letting-go of our reserve and a becoming-present to each other that really entrusts us to the other's goodwill. But our experience of life has taught us that this goodwill is unlikely to be forthcoming. We suspect that if we approach others with this goodwill, we will be left "out there" without the protection of the reserve that has provided us with a sense of safety from each other thus far. Maintenance of the security of the self appears to require an internal hanging back from one another "within our heads" that contradicts the desire to become more fully present to each other in a community of mutual recognition and connection.

To the extent that our fear of one another holds sway over our desire to connect, the subjective experience that we each share as separate individuals is characterized by a withdrawnness into an inner "peering out" that we experience as our "self" and an outer self-presentation to the other that we constantly monitor from within to assure our presence to each other is under our control and retains the element of reserve. While this tendency toward paranoia and withdrawal of presence leaves us somewhat disembodied and outwardly anonymous (think of the blank gaze with which one passes strangers on the street, or the soulless artificiality of the typical television newscaster), this doesn't render us autistic or schizophrenic. To the extent that we are successful in stabilizing a pattern of reserved presence to each other, we tend to live a life of mild depression, with a poignant sense of longing for something missing.

But the desire to achieve a fuller, more direct connection to each other through a culture of a more fully embodied community is much too powerful for us to easily contain or conceal. In every social interaction, we pull for real recognition in spite of our simultaneous paranoid effort to ward off the very thing we most desire. Even a trip to the Department of Motor Vehicles involves an original interaction between each of us and the person behind the counter, a darting of the eyes at the possibility of contact or recognition that can't be totally deadened or robotified in advance by the bureaucratic script or our own familiar internal distancing.

The desire to break through our self-conscious monitoring and the distancing manipulations of our outer self—to "break on through to the other side"—is something we repeatedly extend toward each other and elicit from each other, even as we maneuver to avoid the connection because of our fear of rejection, humiliation, and loss. And it is the power of this desire and its possible outbreak beyond our inner constraints that makes history unpredictable and, for me, life hopeful.

From this point of view, the mild depression I just referred to conceals frustration and rage, and an anxiety at "loss of control" that haunts the stablest self-protective personality structure. But the power of desire also allows good things to happen constantly, especially if we find ways to encourage each other—through existential confidence-building measures—to trust our mutual impulse toward confirmation, acceptance, and even love.

You might get the impression from these words that I am advocating a psychological approach to the world that focuses on one-on-one interactions, like those in psychotherapy, as the route to healing our problems. And if I did mean this, you would be right to think such an approach could hardly be the basis for challenging the immense economic and social forces that seem so clearly to shape the larger social reality. But I am not advocating a psychological approach understood in this narrow way. Rather, I am saying that what we are used to calling "economic and social forces" must be reunderstood on the basis of a living, partly paranoid interhuman dynamic common to all of us, of which these "forces" are actually an extremely complex expression.

"Big" social phenomena such as class domination or xenophobic nationalism or even the Federal Reserve's regulation of interest rates, which we are accustomed to thinking about "from the outside" as external processes, are actually control systems that we participate in re-creating each day to ward off our desire for and fear of becoming present to each other. Getting at this reality requires a new way of thinking—thinking "from the inside" about what I call the "rotation" of social paranoia spread through a complex erotic modeling of authority and deference.

To see how this way of thinking alters our understanding of everyday matters of public policy, consider the issue of health care. When Bill Clinton was first elected in 1992, providing health care for all "from cradle to grave" was his foremost campaign commitment, and universal health care seemed to be an exciting prospect very much on the horizon. With this in mind, we must ask ourselves how that once central and popular platform plank of universal health care, supported by a majority of voters and symbolized by the plastic universal health-care card that President Clinton proudly held up for all to see during his first State of the Union address, was so rapidly repudiated by the country within a period of just a few months. Are we to assume that people simply had a rational change of mind, that instead of wanting to take care of each other's health as an act of universal human solidarity, Americans abruptly decided on the basis of rational argument that we should instead shift our national focus to disciplining a small number of irresponsible welfare recipients, perhaps even to the point of putting their children in state-sponsored orphanages (this was the actual policy agenda put forward by Newt Gingrich and other Republicans that rapidly replaced universal health care in public popularity during the months following Clinton's speech and leading up to the 1994 "Gingrich revolution")? Can such a rapid, widespread reversal of values really be explained by the power of the Republicans' arguments that a commitment to caring for every community member's health would be too expensive, too bureaucratic, too subject to abuse by the irresponsible among us?

The answer to this question is not that people figured out with their heads that universal health care is too expensive and too bureaucratic. It is rather that they lost faith in their hearts that the aspiration toward community that had fueled Bill Clinton's initial victory could actually occur.

In 1992, Bill Clinton was elected on the upsurge of a wave of desire and hope that he was able to elicit in vast numbers of us through his warmth and his capacity to care—qualities that he himself was able to embody in public space because of his participation in the affirmation of our desire for connection and mutual recognition that generated the "movement" aspect of the 1960s.

It was this capacity to affirm that we actually are connected, this direct experience of togetherness, that forged our generation's belief in the possibility of community, a conviction now passed on silently, in the form of an echo of our shared historical memory, to those born after us. The memory of our earlier experience and the conviction that it could and should be reaffirmed in our adult lives is what led so many of us to volunteer to help Clinton in 1992, why so many of us actually wanted to vote then, in contrast with our indifference at the time of the Gingrich counterrevolution of 1994, when so many of us did not vote or voted with heavy hearts and little enthusiasm.

During an outbreak of desire and hope, universal health care symbolizes a reciprocity of caring that we obviously all want and that we know on faith can be realized. When we are imbued with a spirit of hope, we simply know that we can and should find a way to care for one another if we get sick, and suggestions that we can't afford it because we simply must keep building more nuclear weapons seem absurd. In a spirit of hope, those who will staff a health care system do not appear in our minds as "faceless bureaucrats" but as people like us who are participating in saving the lives of ourselves, our parents, and our children. And at the moment of Clinton's election in 1992, people actually wanted to pay more taxes to create such a community of caring, because participating in building a community is much more meaningful and satisfying than saving a few tax dollars that would only allow us to buy a bigger TV to help us numb ourselves into oblivion in the quiet desperation of our isolation.

But the opening of the heart required to hope for an emergent community also leaves us vulnerable to the pain of nonaffirmation. Every gesture toward mutual affirmation that we extend toward another person exposes us to the risk of rejection, the risk that the other will avert his or her eyes and hide behind a role, like the newscaster. And in one area of policy after another, the Clintons lacked the confidence to affirm the desire for connection that got them elected.

When a fresh expression of hope is not reciprocated—when we take the risk of hoping again when we have been hurt before and then we are hurt again—the energy of hope is converted by a kind of ontological alchemy into the anger or even rage that we have spent a lifetime feeling toward a world that will not recognize us. At that moment, people voted for Newt Gingrich to express their anger and despair because he already occupied that place in their social experience as the person who best articulated the danger of hope. That danger is the basis of his convictions, so in the rotation of confidence and doubt that shapes the political arena, when we turn away from our shattered confidence, a cynical voice like his is always there waiting in the wings to speak for that anger.

To understand how this shift from confidence in our shared longing to connect with and care for each other to shared doubt about the possibility of that connection can sweep intuitively, like a kind of spiritual virus, through the consciousness of millions of people, think of the social fabric as a *rapidly moving common experience,* rather than as an externally pictured entity called "society" made up of a collection of discrete individuals with different views. In this account, how I experience what's happening around me and what my possibilities are is dramatically affected by my intuition of what everyone else is experiencing. What I am willing to affirm as real is dramatically affected by what I sense everyone else is willing to affirm as real. And so it is for everyone else also. In our lifetimes we have witnessed moments when people could intuit that others would affirm their mutual connection in public, and other moments when fear predominated over hope. In the 1960s we experienced a rapidly moving outbreak of desire for community (not without its craziness!) that spread worldwide from Berkeley to Des Moines to Prague to Paris to Beijing to Guadalajara in a virtual instant of historical time. That same ricochet or rotation spread among us in a negative fashion when Clinton elicited our hope that others would hope, and then seemed to abandon us, thereby transforming Newt Gingrich from an almost comical and marginal naysayer into a legitimate and powerful national spokesperson for our despair.

When we think of universal health care in a spirit of mistrust and fear, the whole thing seems like a terrible idea, the height of liberal folly. What was conceived as a community of caring for one another from cradle to grave suddenly appears as a monstrous gulag of betrayal. The very same program undergoes a transformation of image akin to the conversion of Dr. Jekyll into Mr. Hyde. At such a moment, universal health care seems to mean that everyone will be forced to participate in and pay for an army of faceless bureaucrats, indifferent to our fate or the fate of our loved ones, who will mechanically follow rules that will deny us life-saving medical care while paying off the claims of fraudulent doctors providing unneeded services to those who don't even pay taxes.

The Clintons actually fostered this conversion of image when they began to compromise with those who seem least likely to really believe in community—the insurance companies, the conservative medical establishment, and the Republican opponents of health care itself. The final straw was Bill Clinton's abandonment of his supposedly unshakable commitment to the universality of coverage itself. Can we expect people to believe in a community in which 90-odd percent of us will be covered and the rest of us will be left to die in the streets? Never mind whether this is realistically what would have occurred under the final Clinton plan—the point is that we can't take the risk of moving toward all being in it together and committing ourselves to caring about each other and at the same time be entertaining thoughts like, "Well, some people won't be covered but at least it won't be me." This leads one to suspect (usually, quite correctly) that everyone else is having the same thought, that self-interest and lack of caring have crept back into the core of the system, and that any resulting government program will therefore probably be a bureaucratic nightmare.

But it would be wrong to blame the national change of feeling about health care on the Clintons' handling of the health care issue alone. That same lack of confidence in the upsurge of the desire for community that elected them, their chronic refusal or inability to be present to us in public space in a way that was needed for us to continue to be present to each other, pervaded everything they did.

You can compromise from a position of hope, standing firm for the common hope you're upholding while trying to win over those who retain the capacity to hope but still doubt you. From this standpoint, I thought it was right to struggle to include doctors in a substantial way in the health care discussion, because most doctors spend their lives trying to heal the sick even though they have also been selfishly conditioned to guard their elite social position and economic interests. Even insurance agents could have been engaged at the level of their idealistic, real satisfaction at protecting people from catastrophic loss, as opposed to deferring to their economic power and supposed efficiency as profit-seekers. But you cannot compromise with hope itself, as if you, too, don't really believe in the desire for community that animates it.

Although hope has the truest human desire behind it, it cannot survive with halfhearted support in the climate of mistrust and doubt that remains such a big part of our social inheritance. Yet Clinton radiated this lack of hope in his compromises.

So what we witnessed and were a part of during the first two years of the Clinton presidency was an outburst of hope for community converting, through nonaffirmation, into an outburst of anger and paranoia. It is this that explains the shift in metaphors in the national debate from universal health care to the preoccupation with weeding out welfare cheats and irresponsible dependents ripping off our tax dollars. It is the dominant sense of whether we can trust each other to affirm each other's need for affirmation that determines who votes and who doesn't and what metaphors of social reality are fore-grounded in the nation's political consciousness. When California governor Pete Wilson suddenly conjured up the metaphor of the freeloading illegal immigrant during his come-from-behind reelection campaign in 1994 (a virtu-ally nonexistent issue at the time), he unconsciously used his own paranoia to provide the perfect fetish-object for a wounded national mood.

If the Clintons could not sustain whatever confidence they had in the power and presence of the idealism that elected them—if they could not see or hear our pull for recognition through the cynicism, rejection, and doubt that they were subjected to in the media and elsewhere—it is in part because we our-selves lacked the existential infrastructure capable of manifesting it. FDR understood the need for this reciprocity between group and spokesperson when he told a labor leader advocating a progressive reform, "That's a good idea. Now go out there and make me do it." The Clintons' incapacity to stand up for their highest ideals against the cynical barrage to which they were subjected mirrored the same doubt within the sixties generation as a whole. Seen in this light, their retreat speaks to the need for a politics aimed at strengthening our confidence in each other within the interspace where this reciprocity must occur, the interspace that Martin Buber so beautifully called "the between."

In the area of health care, such a politics means recasting the policy debate in spiritual terms, affirming in the rhetoric we use and the legislative program we advocate that health care is about realizing our shared desire to actually care for each other and each other's families, to fill the space between us with empa-thy and compassion, rather than being simply about insuring each other's dis-connected bodies through impersonal public *or* private benefit schemes.

ABOLISH THE SAT

Standardized Tests and Meaningless Thought

WHY ISN'T THERE MORE PUBLIC CHALLENGE to the legitimacy of standardized tests, whether it's the SAT, the comparable tests for professional schools, the civil service exams with their incredibly important social and economic consequences, or the IQ tests themselves, which continue to be given to children as a legitimate measure of their "intelligence"? As far as I can tell, the answer is that the vast majority of people actually believe that these tests are measures of intelligence, ability, aptitude, and merit, while being secretly humiliated by their own test scores. We have created a society where we are addicted to feeling dumb, inadequate, and like failures, no matter how inaccurate and even childish the "measures" that create and reinforce this impression.

The SAT does not measure how smart you are or your aptitude or your merit. It measures your capacity to think like a machine—by which I mean to think without employing the faculty of human understanding (or more accurately, while suppressing the faculty of human understanding)—under highly abusive competitive and authoritarian social conditions.

The abusive conditions consist of herding together in one room young people who since early childhood have been conditioned like rats to believe that love and approval depend on the quick and correct public answering of magical questions, and then subjecting them under extreme time pressure to what they are told is the one Big Test that will determine the degree of cultural validation they will get for the rest of their lives.

The machinelike thinking demanded by the test is more difficult to see because we have spent centuries developing this capacity and mythologizing it as "natural," as simply "what thinking is" with those who are skilled at it being thought of as the best thinkers, the most intelligent, the most able to discover truth and advance the human race. In fact, the dominance of this way of thinking has increased our alienation from ourselves, from one another, and from the natural world. That this is not obvious to us in the face of the state of present-day human relations and our continuing, possibly fatal destruction of the environment is a measure of how much repression and forgetting the valorization of this way of thinking has entailed.

The key to the machinelike thinking tested by the SAT is the detachment of the thought process from the intuitive understanding that gives ethical direction to life itself. An infant "understands" that he needs his mother's recognition and sensual nurturance or else he would not and could not seek it. This understanding is a kind of knowledge that emerges from his embodied existential engagement with his life-world; his desire for mother teaches him intuitively that love is good and impels him in this good direction and away from the badness and pain of love's absence. As he learns to think, initially through internalizing meaningful sense-images of mother and connecting them to current perceptions of his mother's presence as a way of "finding" her, his motivation for doing so is guided entirely by the goal that he already intuitively understands. His thought process is anchored in and directed by an intuitive moral understanding, call it love-knowledge, that is prior to it. Or to put this slightly differently, thought and understanding are linked by a relation of meaning.

The SAT is structured to test meaningless thought. Students are not expected to understand anything about the world, about their own lives or the lives of their parents, or about the aspirations of human beings as a whole and the difficulties we face in realizing those aspirations. On the contrary, the multiple-choice format of the test requires that students disconnect themselves from any such understanding and adopt a hypothetical rather than an engaged relationship to reality. Meaningful thought requires that there be a relationship between thinking (representing or imagining the world) and a heartfelt end that motivates the activity of thinking itself. The SAT requires that students detach themselves from any compelling engagement with the world whatsoever and manipulate the conventions of "language games" from the position of a "linguistic calculator" who cares nothing about the questions or the answers. The only "intelligence" or "scholastic aptitude" measured by the random collection of analogies, so-called reading comprehension passages, and aphorisms that make up these tests is the ability to very rapidly recognize abstract formal properties of a language that one already speaks under circumstances in which the language is treated as an object severed from its meaningful origins (thus it can only be "right" to conclude that cold is to hot as life is to death as Nazis are to Jews if one relates to temperature, existence, genocide as if they were interchangeable). This type of recognition of formal and interchangeable properties is exactly what computers do in relation to their own language when they perform "grammar checks" or, to take one of their newer talents, when they tell you that "you are writing on a tenth-grade level."

Those who do well on such tests will for the most part be members of the dominant culture because they have both the greatest preexisting immersion in the language of the culture and the greatest capacity to accommodate themselves to the alienated consciousness that the test makers require. Our culture calls upon us to separate mind from body, thought from feeling, and analysis from the intuitive empathic understanding of human longing that is indispensable for comprehending the ethical call of being. These separations are embedded in and reinforced not only by the tests but by the very same detachment from meaning that characterizes much of journalism, legal reasoning, scientific research, corporate decision making, and many other aspects of our culture. As a kind of trial by fire that we all must go through in late adolescence, the SAT plays an important part in cementing this pervasive cultural distortion. Apart from its cultural bias, it is also brutalizing to the soul of everyone who is subjected to it because it requires that we alienate ourselves from everything that matters to us in order to be recognized by the prevailing criteria of merit as deserving, worthy, intelligent members of our community.

❖   ❖   ❖

Exchange on the SAT

To the Editor:

Peter Gabel's "Abolish the SAT" is overwrought and betrays a lack of understanding of the nature of these exams, their significance, and their purpose. They do not measure one's capacity to "think like a machine," for, indeed, machines don't think, nor can they parse sentences or solve more than the simplest verbal problems. The SATs measure, albeit imperfectly, a student's basic vocabulary, ability to read simple passages and extract their meaning, mastery of the basic principles of logical reasoning, and familiarity with concepts of mathematics and elementary mathematical problem solving. Like any test given over and over, there are certain types of questions that are repeated and hence that can be prepared for, but this also tests a not unimportant ability to memorize facts and techniques. There is a lot in this world that requires technique, and we should expect that our students have developed some of it. The SATs have two parts: verbal and mathematical. Kids who like to read books, magazines, and newspapers, and think about what they read, generally do reasonably well on this part—without any "prep" course. Similarly, average students who don't cut class and do their math homework can do respectably on the mathematical part.

For gosh sakes, the SATs are taken only by students interested in going to college, and to measure to what extent they have the basic skills for reading and computation that are needed to learn. You can't benefit from the works of the greatest humanistic philosopher if you can't read adequately. You can't become a loving public defender if you can't read critically. You can't be an effective doctor unless you have learned a minimal amount of mathematics and mathematical thinking. The SATs provide cutthroat competition only for the small handful of students vying for spots in the elite colleges. Nearly every college and university these days has a highly qualified faculty, and most students who want to go to college can gain admission somewhere. Gabel's description of test takers as conditioned "like rats to believe that love and approval depend on the quick and correct public answering of magical questions" fits only the tiniest percentage of students I have encountered in thirty years of teaching. Furthermore, students who have certain learning disabilities or have extreme difficulty with time pressure can take the SATs untimed. In his zeal to demonize the SATs, Gabel gets himself so worked up he resorts to a really cheap shot: "thus it can only be 'right' to conclude that cold is to hot as life is to death as Nazis are to Jews . . . " This is his straw SAT question. He certainly knows how to play to the galleries.

I do not believe that the SATs alone provide an adequate criterion for college admission. Contrary to what Gabel may think, neither do colleges themselves. For most colleges, SAT scores and high-school academic record provide some sort of minimal cutoff. Below a certain level, students just aren't ready for college work. However, in addition, every college asks for a personal essay. Most years the topics are chosen so as to provide the student with an opportunity to show his or her personality and values. Colleges also value nonacademic activities, especially those demonstrating community service. Gabel's blather about "language games" and "linguistic calculator" is in fact humbug. Students can prep for the SATs, but, by the same token, anyone can learn the calculus of some style, whether it be conservative dogma, liberalism, eduspeak, psychobabble, or the "Politics of Experience." Gabel would like to see some sort of "Good Person" index to rate college applicants. Are they respectful of the humanity of their brethren and the "aspirations of human beings as a whole"? I imagine the *Princeton Review* or Stanley Kaplan could prep them on how to answer this as well. I'd just like to know if they can read and calculate.

MARK BRIDGER
ASSOCIATE PROFESSOR, MATHEMATICS
NORTHEASTERN UNIVERSITY
BOSTON, MASSACHUSETTS

To the Editor:

Peter Gabel seems to believe, with the Beatles, that "All you need is love." Does he really believe that all the technically demanding work of our society can be performed by anybody at all? Apparently he does, since he will tolerate no selection criteria because every such criterion is, by its very nature, elitist.

SAT math scores are the single best predictors of academic success in technical fields. Selection made on the basis of these tests permits instruction to be delivered at a higher level to those who make the cut. I presume that Peter Gabel regards this as bad also, and that he would have instruction dumbed down to enable everyone to get through.

If I need brain surgery, I want my surgeon to be selected for his mastery of surgical technique. I don't want a sympathetic bumbler who couldn't master the sciences that are the basis of the surgeon's craft. I also insist that my electrician, CPA, and every other technical professional to whom I entrust my well-being be qualified by selection and examination that excludes a significant fraction of the applicants.

Imposing Peter Gabel's noncriteria for educational opportunity on society will endanger us all. Communitarian thoughts are not enough. Whom do we hug to keep that airplane we are on from falling out of the sky?

Were Gabel's ideas applied in society generally, the few who survive would be shivering around a smoky fire at the mouth of a cave and have no time for hugging at all. Civilization depends upon advanced technology; advanced technology depends upon special expertise; and conveying that special expertise depends upon selection of qualified students.

Barry Bunow, Ph.D.
Rockville, Maryland

Peter Gabel responds:

We live in a society in which journalists cannot experience the meaning of their own stories ("The Red Sox Win and A Fire in Dorchester! Back in a Moment!"); in which corporate managers cannot experience the meaning of their own decisions (employing criteria of efficiency that destroy plant and animal life to make, say, copier paper); in which engineers and scientists are trained to calculate, irrespective of the meaning of their own calculations (laying railroad tracks to convey human beings to concentration camps); in which lawyers manipulate rules without experiencing the meaning of their own legal reasoning (the insanity of present-day Los Angeles, with its smog and its sprawl and its traffic jams, is the result of the neutral application of property and contract rules that treat land like a thing); in which the world may end without any of us realizing our responsibility for it because we never experienced the meaning of what we were doing.

My essay "Abolish the SAT" was based on the fact that the SAT equates merit with this very capacity to detach thought from meaning. A reading-comprehension passage on "Fig Trees in the Amazon" is presumed to be as good a measure of one's capacity to read as a passage from Buber's *I and Thou*—the only question is, "What is a good title for this paragraph?" Analogies treat the most banal aspects of reality as if they were "like" the most profound—thus cold is to hot as life to death because they are both "opposites." Questions about the measurement of the physical world (so-called "math questions") are exactly like "Fig Trees in the Amazon": whether you can figure out when a train leaving Chicago at a certain speed will pass a train leaving New York at a different speed is presumed to be no different from whether you can employ the same or similar knowledge to save or improve human life or the environment. The only question is, can you apply the formula—to anything.

Of course I am not saying that all you need is love to perform a surgical operation or that pilots shouldn't be tested before they fly planes. I'm saying that we should stop equating one's merit to go to college with how well one can very rapidly answer standardized test questions that reward the very worst alienations of our society—the separation of mind from body, thought from feeling, and analytic skills from the capacity for empathy and ethical understanding, which give moral direction to human existence. The point isn't that we should have some new kind of test, but that we should stop measuring each other with dehumanizing exams and realign education toward the fostering of wisdom, goodness, compassion, and healing a world that is lost to itself.

When I published these ideas in the *Chronicle of Higher Education,* dozens of people contacted me to thank me for making them feel less stupid, less inadequate, less "lacking in merit." One mother, whose son was taking his SAT for the second time the next day and had been frantically preparing by taking one of the many courses that have become a spin-off industry spawned by the exam, felt compelled to tell me almost apologetically about the community service her son performed in high school and what a good, caring, intelligent boy he was. It was only his initial SAT score that first made him doubt himself and think perhaps he was destined for a lower track. My reply to her was the same as the response I would make to the professor of mathematics who so sarcastically dismisses my article: The worse you do on these tests, the smarter you may be in the eyes of God.

THE MEANING OF AFFIRMATIVE ACTION

*Making It as Individuals
in the Competitive Marketplace,
or Climbing Together to the Mountaintop?*

This essay was written just as the Republican backlash against affirmative action was beginning, some two years before the passage of California's Proposition 209 outlawing affirmative action in that state. Perceived as controversial at the time because of its criticism of what I call the "liberal" defense of affirmative action, the essay nonetheless accurately explains, I believe, why the backlash has subsequently been so successful. I campaigned strongly and publicly in my capacity as a college president against Proposition 209, and believe the "No on 209" campaign would have won if the politics-of-meaning perspective advocated in this essay had been adopted.

UNLESS THERE IS AN UNFORESEEN UPSURGE of emotionally compelling support for affirmative action by a cross-racial coalition in the near future, its demise appears likely to be the next nail in the New Deal coffin. Should we understand this as being the result of a new wave of mean-spiritedness or even racism that is sweeping the white population, of which the first indication was the anti-immigrant Proposition 187 in California?

No.

No more accurate was former secretary of labor Robert Reich's economic explanation that non-college-educated white males have been facing declining real incomes, or the more conventional Left economic analysis that ruling elites have been shoring up their own power by pitting white and minority sectors of the working class against each other.

The reason for the success of the assault on affirmative action is that the idea of affirmative action has largely lost its idealistic meaning, emanating from a vision of true racial equality, of inclusion of all people in a loving and nonexploitative human community that emerged from the spirit of the civil rights movement. That idealistic meaning was part of a larger challenge to the alienation that pervades American society, to the selfishness and individualism that is fostered by the competitive marketplace and that makes the creation of loving human relationships and cooperative human community so difficult.

This idealistic meaning of affirmative action has been replaced by its virtual opposite, a meaning that actually defends the legitimacy of the competitive marketplace and the alienation that it engenders while claiming that African Americans and other minorities should be given preference over "more qualified" whites for jobs and for admission to college and professional schools. The justification for this special treatment is that past discrimination resulting from the history of slavery and legalized segregation has created an unequal playing field that favors whites and denies minorities "equality of opportunity" in their effort to make it in the marketplace—therefore, minorities should be given a leg up in spite of their relative "lack of merit" until the effects of the past discrimination are eradicated.

When Martin Luther King, Jr., proclaimed that he had been to the mountaintop and was never coming down, he wasn't talking about making it in the competitive marketplace. He was talking about transforming our cruel and alienated world so that people would recognize, respect, and love one another across the richness of their racial differences. Within this idealistic vision, affirmative action was an expressive call to act together affirmatively to eradicate the antihuman humiliation of racism. And affirmative action does still retain an echo of this deep ethical meaning that spread through American culture as a result of the transcendent energy and spiritual presence of the civil rights movement itself. Few of us can see clips of that famous "mountaintop" speech by Dr. King and not be deeply, momentarily stirred by the memory of our own connection to the sense of ethical purpose and community to which he was able to give voice.

As I argued in "The Relationship between Community and True Democracy," it was precisely the failure of progressive forces to make this idealistic vision of a transformed human community the centerpiece of its political and legal claims that in significant part led to the erosion of the transformative appeal of this century's social movements, including the civil rights movement. In place of the vision of a higher ethical community evoked by the images of the mountaintop and the promised land, civil rights activists and lawyers found themselves arguing only for "equal rights," for the elimination of discrimination within the alienated world of competitive capitalism. In part, this narrow view of racial justice was forced upon them by the individualist assumptions of American law, by the absence from the Constitution and from the history of American political and legal culture of any substantive ethical/communal vision of what our collective life ought to be like. In part, our political imagination was constrained by the legacy of Marxism and the New Deal to think of racial justice primarily in terms of economic redistribution and liberal rights, rather than in terms of the creation of a spiritually transformed civil society.

The consequence of this despiritualization of the meaning of affirmative action has been to make it rational for whites and even many African Americans and other minorities to oppose it. Affirmative action today implicitly affirms the idea that the goal of life is to make as much money and get as much status as possible in a market of scarce opportunities, and that people generally succeed in this competitive struggle according to their own merit, measured by more or less objective criteria. This is the background framework of social meaning against which people are expected to measure their success in life, their ultimate sense of self-worth. The theory then assumes that objectively less-qualified minorities should be allowed to deprive their white competitors of deserved success, recognition, and money because of past discrimination of which their current white competitors are not guilty.

Except in the narrowest legalistic sense, I think it is impossible to defend this impoverished market-based meaning of affirmative action.

First, it is an approach to law and social policy that legitimizes the very competitive and individualistic social reality that has to be changed if people are to begin to lead meaningful, socially connected, and humane lives. However they express it, most people know this at a gut level. Why would they be motivated to fight for a program that, in its despiritualized form, is basically an affirmation of the status quo?

Second, most white people do not feel "privileged" in this society—they feel isolated, disconnected from any sense of social validation, and like failures, according to market criteria of success and worth. Why should they give up the modicum of potential recognition and success that affirmative action tells them they have won fair and square in order to help someone else "less qualified" whom they have not personally injured? Most white people are secretly enraged that nobody seems to care about them, and they blame themselves for not having made it on their own. You can't tell them they have a moral responsibility to sacrifice their hopes of escaping their humiliation for the sake of helping others because of sins they believe were committed long before they were born.

Third, just as market-based affirmative action implicitly legitimizes the competitive marketplace, it also legitimizes meritocracy (by making an "exception" for minorities). As it operates in the United States, meritocracy is an evil because it denies people unconditional acceptance for who they are—each of us is made to feel we must achieve something to "merit" recognition, worthiness, and love. Instead of eliciting people's talents and capacities in a climate of trust and support for their intrinsic value as fellow human beings, we have created a system in which people chronically feel they are about to be "found out" as lacking. They spend their lives frantically trying to measure up to some external criteria of merit, while often dreaming of failure.

Not only that, the actual criteria used to measure, say, one's merit to attend college or law school are frankly absurd, and they breed injustice and racial hatred. They are absurd because standardized tests that require anxious young people to read and answer questions about, say, "Fig Trees in the Amazon"—under pointless and sadistic time pressure—have nothing to do with the true social or ethical reasons why we should want the younger generation to pursue an education or a profession (for example, they value shallow cleverness and meaningless manipulation of concepts over engaged empathy and the desire to create a good world).

Such criteria breed injustice because they purport to be objective measures of "merit" when they were in fact developed by white ruling elites, following the collapse of the supposed "natural" superiority of the aristocracy, to measure the capacity of test takers to perform the arguably shallow, detached, and manipulative tasks that they, the test makers, value. As someone who has been a law professor for more than twenty years, I feel confident in saying that the Law School Admissions Test and then the Bar Examination measure value-laden skills of this type that neither "objectively" measure one's merit to be an attorney nor measure in the slightest degree the ethical and empathic capacities or the sense of justice that one ought to demonstrate to become a lawyer. These tests breed injustice because they tell whites they objectively merit things that they do not objectively merit, and they breed racial hatred because minorities know this to be true, but they cannot influence the negative judgments imposed upon them.

Why should we support a market-based theory of affirmative action that legitimizes meritocratic judgments that are evil in themselves and that breed injustice and racial hatred?

Fourth, market-based affirmative action is often humiliating to African Americans and other minorities because it treats them as unqualified and defective, as if they do not "really" deserve their admission to college or professional school or their job. This is one reason polls find that almost 50 percent of minorities are opposed to affirmative action. It is unjust for them to be made to feel this way because it is not true that they are "less qualified" except on the basis of (usually) superficial nonobjective criteria that are utterly stacked against them. In the case of legal education, this injustice is made worse by the fact that law schools for the most part value the same shallow, detached, verbal manipulations that the tests measure (compassion and a sense of justice are largely irrelevant to success in law school, although they are essential to a morally significant legal practice).

This structural humiliation inevitably leads African Americans and other minorities to act out their rage at being disrespected and humiliated, often in the form of politically correct, victimized denunciations of whites that frighten most decent white people, who, after all, believe they have done nothing wrong. Contrary to the charges often leveled against them, most of these whites are not racists, and, in addition, they have been told by the society (through policies like affirmative action) that they "deserve" whatever they've managed to achieve. When they are attacked, guilt-tripped, and threatened with losing even the patina of self-worth that they might have gained from becoming a professional, they are even less able to hear the echo of idealistic meaning that affirmative action once had and further lose hope that they can be part of an effort to bring about the kind of community that would embody true mutual recognition and racial justice. Although these whites would prefer to be part of just such an effort to build a society based on transcendent meaning and high ethical purpose, they settle for a retreat into private life and for the crumbs of professional recognition. And they move toward a conservative politics that validates both their anger and their retreat from hope, because the alternative seems so unsafe and crazy.

Although I strongly oppose any attempt to abolish affirmative action and have fought for it as an activist and later as a college president all my adult life, I don't see any real promise of salvation in supporting a market-based approach to it that seems so clearly ridden with contradictions and assumptions that we are opposed to. I think we must recognize that such a market-based approach may well increase rather than heal societal racism. But what is the alternative?

Think again of the original impulse behind affirmative action, the impulse to go beyond the mere removal of barriers ("overcoming discrimination so we can all be free to compete in the marketplace") and instead to take affirmative steps to achieve true racial justice and equality. The key point about this idealistic meaning is that far from appearing to exclude whites, it served to connect whites to a higher sense of purpose, something that would give our lives meaning in part by freeing us from the so-called privilege that is actually an empty prison. That idealistic meaning of affirmative action also connected us to African Americans and other minorities rather than separating us from them.

Redeeming that impulse today means developing a cross-racial strategy that, instead of pitting whites and African Americans against each other (threatening one group or the other with invalidation and social exclusion), unites them in a challenge to the phony meritocratic criteria that historically have divided them.

As an example, consider the following possible ballot initiative:

> Public employees in the State of California shall be hired not on the basis of race, gender, or other external characteristic, nor on the basis of standardized tests, but on the basis of a history of service to their community and State as revealed by exemplary work with church groups, schools, the elderly, and other populations in need. In order to increasingly link public employment with an ideal of service emerging from all of California's communities, hiring policy should to the extent possible seek participation from every neighborhood within each locality and from each Assembly District within the State. The capacity to foster the development of racial harmony, as demonstrated by an applicant's history of service, may be one factor considered in determining qualification for public employment as defined in this initiative.

The point about this proposed initiative is that it begins to foreground the idea that empathy and caring for others are the qualities that we value in public officials and public employees, from politicians, to police officers, to housing authority staff, to street cleaners. It begins to redefine worthiness in a way that assumes one must go through a process of moral development to be selected to work for one's community, rather than passing a shallow multiple-choice test. It makes inclusion of all communities, rather than the selection of one over another, a moral value for its own sake (as opposed to a manipulative strategy for remedying past exclusion). And it explicitly includes race in a way that speaks to people's belief in and longing for cross-racial mutual recognition rather than placing races in opposition to each other, as market-based affirmative action does.

You could, no doubt, find a million things wrong with this initiative: What about necessary qualifications for skilled positions? What about ways it might be manipulated? What about the civil service, and so on? But if we could start by thinking about what's right about it, about what kind of society it points toward and what human needs it speaks to, and about what contradictions in our current market-based thinking it begins to overcome, I'm sure we could fix it. And it would pass.

TRY A LITTLE TENDERNESS

On Sex Education in Schools

This essay was written in response to an article published in Tikkun *by Amitai Etzioni, professor at George Washington University and the leading theorist of and spokesperson for the Communitarianism movement, on the subject of sex education in schools. In his article Etzioni argued against a strictly physiological/biological approach to teaching sex education, criticizing that liberal approach for its amorality, for its failure to address the inherently moral relationship between sex and human intimacy. Etzioni's article was unabashedly "moralistic," emphasizing the importance of transmitting to high-school students moral content he regards as central to the creation of moral communities: among them, abstinence, faithfulness, and the moral bond between sexual pleasure and love. My reply is meant to link the moral dimension of sex education with fostering the natural unfolding of the inherent goodness of human sexuality.*

COMMUNITARIANISM AND THE POLITICS OF MEANING are both open to conservative as well as progressive interpretations, and it is hard to imagine a piece that better reflects the ambiguity than Amitai Etzioni's piece on sex education. On the one hand, I agree with Etzioni's effort to bring a moral perspective to the way young people are taught about sex, to the extent that what he means by this is that our schools should affirm that sexuality is the beautiful embodiment of the longing for human connection and mutual recognition. Understanding sexuality as an erotic energy flow of reciprocity that goes beyond intercourse, that is in some way present in all touching and even in the rhythm of the sound of the spoken word and in the aura of another's presence—this is a far better way to present the moral meaning of sexuality than are the biological metaphors of "healthy human functioning" or mere empirical statements about the facts of reproduction. By presenting the meaning of sexuality in its true interpersonal context, schools would be able to foreground the critiques of exploitation, objectification, and shallow sexual experiences Etzioni speaks to in a way that is not possible when the matter is relegated to a biology or hygiene class.

So far so good. But when Etzioni begins to describe sexuality as "raw impulses" to be "channel[ed] into socially constructive and morally sound avenues," or later as a "primordial urge" that must be "subject to self-control," he begins to slide toward repressive descriptions that actually cause the very social distortions in sexual relations that he is rightly concerned about. Sexuality does not begin as a raw urge in need of control—on the contrary, an infant sensually nursing at his or her mother's breast is a beautiful example of exactly the broadened understanding of sexuality that Etzioni is advocating. It is the social alienation and lack of community that corrodes our entire social dynamic—or to put it in more concrete terms, it is the fact that we have to spend so much of our time relating to each other like numbed-out robots trapped inside our heads and cut off from our sensual in-touchness with one another and with the natural world—that leads sex to become the distorted raw urge that Etzioni is worried about. And it is this legacy of everyday repression that must be gradually and lovingly healed so that one day sexual morality and sexual liberation are not perceived as being at odds with each other, but as two ways of describing transcendent and meaning-giving sensual human connection. A moral approach to sex education ought to be aimed at helping the next generation understand and feel the difference between alienated and unalienated sexuality, not at telling them to control their so-called "raw impulses" until they can be expressed in a socially responsible form.

I'm not necessarily rejecting any of Etzioni's practical points, even the idea of telling kids not to sleep together until they're old enough or encouraging them to go to Shabbat services or the basketball game instead of making out in the park. I, too, am against the liberal paradigm of do-anything-you-want-as-long-as-you-wear-a-condom. But if we are really going to take responsibility for the moral development of the next generation in the area of sexuality, we have to realize there is a limit to how much we are going to accomplish by telling them good moral precepts or anything else. We have to try to be more wholesome sensual beings and create more wholesome sensual environments, including the environment of the school and the classroom, in order to really begin to alleviate the sensual pain that our individualistic, despiritualized society produces. Schools, for example, are often anticommunal, pain-inducing, sensually dead places preoccupied with competitive testing like the SATs, macho sports, and authoritarian, indifference-fostering routines. "Education for intimacy," in the words of Etzioni's title, can't occur without fostering experiences of intimacy to ground the verbal discussions of it, no matter how true the teacher's words alone may be.

In the context of sex education, this means schools must try to do a very difficult thing—create an environment of tenderness and sensual openness that is not intrusive or offensive to families and that remains appropriate to the classroom. It is this environment that should serve as the experiential background for the kind of moral discussion Etzioni wants to encourage, in order to prevent students from experiencing such discussions as authoritarian and irrelevant to their developing sexual feelings. Among the ideas that occur to me that might help to create this kind of environment are providing students with (a) the chance to watch and talk about movies that bring out, in a poignant and nonprurient way, how attraction, sexuality, and love emerge in adolescence (*David and Lisa* is an example from my own teenage years); (b) playful participation in forms of dance and movement that allow the expression of sensual affection without it being charged or frightening or potentially explosive; and (c) more sensory contact with the natural world, including the world of the birds and the bees that Etzioni is perhaps too dismissive of.

But the best people to help imagine this kind of curriculum are high-school teachers, parents, and students who are dealing with these issues directly and who share our goal at *Tikkun* of healing the world rather than trying to control what is wrong with it. The point is not to avoid telling students the difference between right and wrong but to reconcile this need with the need to tenderly elicit in them the open-hearted longings of their early erotic experience.

PART FOUR

THE LAW NOT AS RULES BUT AS A MEANING-CREATING PUBLIC CULTURE

WHILE THE PREVIOUS SECTION HAS ARGUED for enlivening the normally flat and despiritualized discourse of the "policy wonk" by making this discourse a carrier of the desire for mutual recognition and social connection rather than a denier of that desire, this section provides an example of a politics-of-meaning approach to transforming an entire profession in this same direction. Developed over many centuries as the cultural centerpiece of the individualist worldview that finally defeated its predecessors in the liberal revolutions of two hundred years ago, the legal system that we have inherited has become both a creator and a legitimator of the social alienation that envelops us. Instead of resolving conflicts in a manner designed to create community by fostering empathy, compassion, and healing, the current adversary system fosters mistrust, antagonism, and mutual deprecation. It sacrifices the longing for community on the altar of protecting the rights of the isolated individual. And this current system is constantly being reproduced through the collective work of an enormous army of elite professionals—

lawyers, judges, and law professors—who have been trained to believe unquestioningly in the system's ethical validity.

Without minimizing the importance of the Bill of Rights and other elements in our current legal culture that protect individual liberty from group oppression, I think it is nonetheless a testament to the power of the fetishism and awe that accompanies our conditioning to "believe" in the Rule of Law as it exists today, with the semisacred aura attributed to original texts like the Constitution, that we have been unable as a culture to progress beyond legal and political ideas that were thought up two hundred years ago. As I show in the essay "Founding Father Knows Best," our society appears transfixed by the ideas of a group of mainly twenty- and thirty-year-olds who lived a very long time ago and have been transformed into icons—Founding Fathers who serve as rulers of the cultural superego to whose thoughts we owe a near ontological deference. As a society we appear to have conditioned ourselves to believe that we are not to have any fundamental new ideas that would be a next step, that would continue *in our time* the spiritual and political development of society to which that earlier generation made an important contribution *in their time.*

A politics-of-meaning approach to law sees the taking of this next step as a necessity. Our legal culture must be transformed in a direction that fosters empathy, compassion, and mutual understanding and sees the longing for connection to each other, and the healing of the alienation that divides us, to be as important to the cultural aspirations of law, and as important to the achievement of social justice, as is the protection of individual rights.

The analysis of the limitations of the existing legal order and the vision of legal transformation presented in this section offer a way of thinking that is relevant to the transformation of other professions as well. All our professions—journalism, medicine, education, even social work—suffer from the legacy of liberal individualism that disables those who practice these professions from seeing their work as a way of fostering the emergence of the I-Thou relationship at a social level. For readers who are members of politics-of-meaning task forces on transforming their profession, I hope the essays in part 4 help you in your thinking and strategy.

FOUNDING FATHER KNOWS BEST

The Search by the Framed for the Intent of the Framers

During the mid-1980s, a number of mainstream judges and legal scholars became preoccupied, under the influence of the Reagan revolution and the conservative backlash against the social movements of the 1960s, with searching for the "original intent" of the Founding Fathers as the correct method of interpreting the Constitution. Progressive constitutional law professor Mark Tushnet wrote a critique of this "jurisprudence of original intention," deconstructing the conservatives' efforts by showing that the meaning of the founders' "original intent" was inherently indeterminate and subject to multiple interpretations. What follows is my response to Tushnet, which emphasizes the importance of comprehending the underlying alienated social-psychological meaning of the new conservative jurisprudence (an approach still very much alive today) rather than simply demonstrating its impossibility through a deconstructive, analytical critique. As such, the following essay reveals the difference between a politics-of-meaning progressive critique and a progressive critique animated by the ungrounded analytics of deconstruction.

MARK TUSHNET'S CRITIQUE OF ED MEESE'S "jurisprudence of original intention" is an example of the kind of work being done by a number of scholars in the critical legal studies movement, an influential left-wing force in contemporary American legal scholarship. Most liberals (including not only Judge Brennan but also well-known legal theorists like Ronald Dworkin and Owen Fiss) think that Meese's call for a return to the intent of the framers in interpreting the Constitution is "wrong." They believe that the correct method of constitutional interpretation requires that the meaning of the constitution's language be drawn from a contemporary understanding of the nation's political morality as that understanding has developed over two hundred years, and that such a method tends (correctly in their view) to favor the enlightened expansion of altruistic and egalitarian ideals expressed in liberal case results. Meese, they argue, is just trying to disguise his desire for more conservative outcomes on such issues as abortion, affirmative action, and school prayer, by advocating an interpretive theory that is at best outmoded and at worst hokey and disingenuous.

Tushnet's point is that the liberals' position is just as wrong as Meese's because there is no such thing as a correct method of interpretation that can properly determine the outcomes of cases. He shows that the intent of the framers' view can be used to legitimize not only conservative results, but liberal results as well, and that the liberal notion of principled adjudication informed by an enlightened, modern ideal of justice—although it has been used to justify liberal outcomes—could, with a little conceptual finesse, be invoked in the service of conservative ends. The thrust of Tushnet's argument, in other words, is that it is futile to seek salvation from having to make difficult ethical or political judgments by calling upon some higher interpretive scheme that could "correctly" tell us what to do because such schemes are inherently indeterminate and are themselves open to multiple interpretations. The critique of Meese is, therefore, not that his position is wrong but that it is incoherent, internally contradictory, and essentially meaningless, just as its liberal counterpart.

Other critical legal scholars have developed critiques similar to Tushnet's in virtually every important area of American law, arguing, for example, that there is no such thing as a distinctively "legal" way of deciding when workers have the right to strike under the National Labor Relations Act, or whether industries that dump toxic wastes into rivers and lakes are creating a "nuisance" giving rise to actions for money damages under tort law. Since the law itself is always indeterminate in its application with a stock range of arguments on all sides, Critical Legal Studies writers assert that the resolution of these issues always requires frank political choices, that a legal argument is simply an opinion about right and wrong dressed up in an elite, technical discourse. The radical aim of this work is not simply to show that all legal decisions are actually political decisions, but to undermine the legitimacy of "legal reasoning" itself as a powerful symbol of cultural authority, a symbol that tends—along with other such fetishized symbols as flags, black robes, and the elevated judicial "bench"—to reinforce people's passivity before imposing cultural institutions like the Supreme Court, which is imagined to be the repository of a wisdom inaccessible to the average person and the oracle of American political truth. In alliance with the deconstructionist work of Jacques Derrida and the related work of Michel Foucault on the multiple ways that "official" forms of knowledge tend to crush people's self-confidence and sense of self-activity, this strand of critical legal scholarship means to expose "the law" as basically a lot of posturing baloney, and to empower people to think and feel for themselves. If we are to decide important social questions by reference to a constitution, then only a democracy of interpretations emerging from genuine political debate can give the document and its words an authentically democratic content.

If we return to the question of the *meaning* of Meese's efforts, however, we can see that there is a limitation to the form of criticism that Tushnet puts forward, and, in fact, to the entire "deconstructionist" enterprise. This limitation is that a critique demonstrating the indeterminacy and essential irrelevance of interpretive method in relation to judicial results cannot account for the meaning of the debate over method itself. Tushnet says that Meese's haranguing about the intent of the framers seems "particularly pointless" since Meese knows the results his judicial allies will reach no matter what theory they use; but to Meese there seems to be something very important at stake, something that goes beyond naked results and focuses on the worldview to which he wants those conservative results to be linked. It would not be enough, in Meese's eyes, for the Supreme Court to simply overrule its prior liberal rulings on, say, abortion (which it could easily do without a jurisprudential revolution); he wants an antiabortion ruling to be based on a belief in a particular vision of how we are "constituted" or united or brought together through the Constitution and through our relationship to the Founding Fathers who framed it. Why?

The answer to this question seems to me to require a critical method that goes beyond the detached, analytical skepticism of deconstruction, to one that seeks to grasp and unveil the social meaning of Meese's worldview itself as an aspect of the New Right's effort to fashion a lasting ideological hegemony. Seen in this light, the question of whether the "jurisprudence of original intention" is somehow rationally required for judges to reach conservative results is really quite irrelevant. The desire for a shift in judicial philosophy must, rather, be understood as an attempt to reshape prevailing cultural images about how "we" are constituted as a political-legal group, a reshaping that conservatives like Meese feel is needed if they are to retain their momentum during the current phase of their ascendancy, and consolidate their hold on popular consciousness. For however strong the New Right's cultural dominance may seem today, we should not forget that the vitality of its evocative appeal has yet to channel itself (at least at the level of "mass," or national culture) into legitimated institutional forms that might enable this dominance to reproduce itself without reliance on Ronald Reagan himself or on an endless series of contrived emotional highs. To achieve this degree of anchorage in mass consciousness, the Right must generate and sell a new mythic, historical narrative about the origins and nature of "our society" that can then serve as what might be called the psycho-political foundation for a passively accepted, conservative legal order. This kind of transformation in the "national belief system" is a part of what is needed to convert the passion of the Reagan revolution into a set of habitually obeyed conventional norms.

The "jurisprudence of original intention" is intended to accomplish this transformation by seizing upon certain emotionally charged fragments of New Right ideology and integrating them into the conventional imaginary account of the source of our connection to one another as political beings. The imaginary account is roughly what everyone is taught in eighth-grade civics class— that there was a group of "Founding Fathers," that they came together in certain sanctified buildings, that they created this great document, and that "We, the People" were born as a result. I describe this account as imaginary not because the historical events on which the account is based did not occur— obviously, they did. The account is imaginary because it is communicated in a way that transforms these actual historical events into a symbolic fantasy that has a mass-psychological significance independent of the events themselves. The people who wrote the Constitution are presented as exceptionally wise and virtuous; the document they produced is treated with great awe and reverence; and the feeling conveyed is one of belonging and oneness, as if by virtue of their words we were rescued from alienation and homelessness and brought into connection and harmony. The content of this fantasy, in other words, is that "We Americans" are magically bound together in a great democratic group, and that we owe this bond to the will of idealized father figures who transfigured us by the frame they provided for our existence. And the mass-psychological significance of this fantasy is that it generates in our conscious-ness an image of social connection that compensates for the feeling of disconnection and loss that suffuses our actual experience of each other in everyday life—at work, on the street, and even in our most intimate relation-ships—while allowing us also to deny that this lack of connection exists.

It is at this symbolic level that Meese's call for a return to the intent of the Founding Fathers must be understood, but understanding it requires some sense of how the fantasy functions psychodynamically in relation to the sense of alienation and loss that underlies and gives rise to it. Here we need to draw a contrast between a real sense of "we" and the false sense of "we" that acts as a substitute for it. A real sense of "we" emerges from the realization of a desire, immanent within each of us as social beings, for mutual recognition and con-firmation; it is a feeling-bond that is grounded in the actual connection of those who generate it, and as a result, it has no need of a ground or source out-side itself in order to exist. The false sense of "we" is quite the opposite: it emerges in social contexts where the feeling-bond among people is for various reasons blocked, and it can only come into existence as a relation of withdrawn selves to a fantasized common image of connection whose fantasy-based nature is collectively denied. Since the actual relation underlying the false sense of "we" is one of mutual isolation and withdrawal, and since those who create it are therefore incapable of affirming its pseudoreality on the basis of an underly-ing experience of mutual reciprocity, the false sense of "we" must always be sup-ported by the projection of an "outside authority" invested with the power to constitute it. It is here that we find the function of the Founding Fathers in the fantasy of our own "constitution": since we know by virtue of our own alien-ation that we are unconstituted and feel incapable of generating a real "we" based on true reciprocity, we give ourselves over to the fantasy of being "united as a people" and invent the Founding Fathers to provide the authorship for this unity that we cannot provide ourselves. We then invest these imaginary figures with a "belief" that makes them seem as if they really exist, so that we can deny that our sense of national connection is a fantasy and sustain our own belief that we are a genuinely constituted, real group. Since the continuation of our false sense of "we-ness" depends upon the continuation of our belief in their authority, this belief becomes "reified," or collectively insisted upon as being true on pain of excommunication from the false group. Any sign of disbelief in the authority of the projected source upon whom the group's false sense of "we-ness" depends threatens to revive the underlying experience of loss, isolation, and pain that the group's common image of connection is created to deny.

Meese is putting his ideas forward during the rise of a movement whose aim is to restore people's loyalty to the false sense of "we-ness" embedded in the patriotic imagery of Americanism, a loyalty eroded by the social dynamics of the previous twenty years. This erosion has in part been due to the success of the movements of the sixties, which were able to generate a powerful "movement" of actual, embodied community, multiple hints of real social connection spinning more or less out of control on a worldwide level. And it was eroded even further by the failure of these movements, leaving people feeling that the Vietnam War, for example, had been a "defeat for America" rather than a victory for a movement of humanity that no longer existed. The rise of the New Right was in part made possible, in other words, by the fact that the countercultural energy of these movements, which went far toward stimulating people's hopes for, and actual experience of, social transformation in the direction of creating deep and genuine connection between people, was defeated—and defeated in a way that led people to feel, however unconsciously, that they had been seduced and betrayed. Whatever the confluence of preexisting cultural conditions that make them possible, social movements are founded fundamentally on an outbreak of desire that resonates throughout the social body and that cannot but revive, precisely because of its vitality, the memories of loss and disappointment associated with this desire that stems from our earliest childhood experiences. This is why people like Meese so fiercely resist the development of these movements, and it is also why such movements tend to defeat themselves by losing confidence in themselves from within. While the collapse of the movements of the sixties did not lead directly to the consciousness of the eighties in some simple, casual sense, the heightened vulnerability produced by these movements played an important role in people drawing themselves back from the risks associated with the revelation of desire—a drawing back that in some cases is manifested in a commitment to a kind of hopelessness or spiritual deadness, and in other cases, especially in those who struggled to resist the utopian aspirations of the sixties, is manifested in a desire for revenge against these aspirations and ultimately against the desire for deep connection itself.

Taken as a whole, this historical experience has generated a social reaction in the direction of reclaiming the paranoiac and defensive social armor that is meant to keep us from feeling even the possibility of another revival of our wounds. At the surface level, this reaction has taken the form of a middle-class populist revolt against liberal entitlement programs, but at the deep psychological level, the revolt is against the "permissiveness" that allowed too much vital and spontaneous social connection to be released in social relations, generating a renewed need to reconstitute the old authorities that could provide the vehicle for reconstituting a "false we" requiring obedience to proper boundaries.

Understood against this background, Meese's call for a return to the intent of the framers should be seen as an attempt to reconstitute these old authorities by revitalizing their mythological appeal. He does this first by blaming our current sense of collective isolation, of not feeling part of something anymore, on the actions of judges like William Brennan who have substituted their own interpretation of the Constitution for that of the Founding Fathers. This symbolically transposes the real historical experience I described in the last paragraph into an imaginary narrative in which "we" are imagined to exist by virtue of how authority figures interpret the Constitution and in which "our" present nonexistence or sense of disconnection is imagined to have been caused by the failures of these authority figures. Such a transposition or imaginary renarration has the effect of acknowledging people's real experience of desire and loss while denying the real source of this experience, placing the blame instead on the keepers of the false we. At the same time, it acknowledges that we have tried to generate a real movement toward each other on the basis of our own ontological power and capacity for love, but it "transfers" this generative movement to the actions of those bad judges who have given in to their impulse to "substitute their own interpretation" for that of the Founding Fathers, thus transforming our own desire and actual effort to create a real we into a transgression by the priests we select from among ourselves to maintain the boundaries of the false we, against the higher authority of the "outside source" whose will creates the false we. The imaginary schema that Meese is offering has mass-psychological appeal, in other words, because it allows people to recognize their own historical experience of, and continuing need for, true social connection, but in a symbolic form that disguises this need, characterizes it as giving rise to the very impulses that must be suppressed if we are to maintain our "national unity," and channels the energy generated by this need toward the re-creation of an imaginary pseudocommunity based on a revitalized shared belief in authority. The political message is that passivity and dependency on the authority of the framers are required for continued membership in the false group, and that false group is the only group there is.

At the same time that it transposes our real history into a symbolic history that acts as a defense against our awareness of real historical meaning, Meese's jurisprudence revitalizes the erotic appeal of the image of the Founding Fathers by infusing our imaginary relationship to them with a new sadomasochistic fervor. I use the word "sadomasochistic" here in the same sense that I have used the word "desire" throughout this essay, to refer to an organization and movement of social energy that is not strictly sexual in the Freudian sense but is nonetheless erotic in that it designates the "pull" that impels us toward each other as social beings. Meese's imagery is sadomasochistic because it seeks to redirect our desire away from the immediacy of real relations (in which we might form a real we by developing our own "interpretation" of our constitution) and toward the safe arena of controlled, internalized images of connection based upon our carrying out the framers' will in its most essential and undiluted form. The symbolic message is that we must sweep away the impurities that we have allowed to accumulate in our law, impurities that have resulted from a succession of judges who have allowed our constitutional connection to dissipate in a thousand directions, and we must return to the original state of obedience to the Founding Fathers that gave us our original unity. But the real message is that we must (a) stop seeking vital recognition and confirmation in real life by withdrawing from each other; (b) fuse our withdrawn desire with the rage that results from the disallowal of its expression; (c) channel this eroticized aggression into an image of a punitive authority sadistically controlling a masochistically obedient and dependent group of subjects; (d) act this sadomasochistic identification out through a rigid compliance with the dictates of social hierarchies. Within Meese's symbolism, we are to displace our potency onto the Founding Fathers and direct our eroticized aggression against the liberal judges who are symbolic carriers of our own authentic impulses for connection, impulses that, if followed, lead to betrayal and loss. In the real world we are to command ourselves and each other to conform to an artificial social facade characterized on the one hand by passivity and role-compliance, and on the other by repeated elicitations of "evil" impulses that are repeatedly subjected to control and punishment.

It is in this last respect that the call for a return to the intent of the framers is related most closely to the rest of the New Right's program—to the call for a return to a docile vision of the family of which *Father Knows Best* is perhaps the model, a vision of religion founded upon obedience to God, a righteous and nationalistic militarism that stamps out evil empires wherever they appear, and a domestic policy that seeks to disassociate the State from "programs for the weak" while associating the State with the effort to cleanse the social body of such exciting impurities as drugs and oral intercourse. Whatever valid elements there may be in some of these positions, they are all directed in their symbolic dimension to the intensification of sadomasochistic control over our fundamental desire for spontaneous and genuine social connection. The distinctive meaning of Meese's jurisprudence is to be found in its attempt to place this perverse passion for control at the heart of our social and political bond, to make it part of "the law" in a way that would extend its cultural power beyond the appeal of any particular issue and, as I suggested earlier, beyond the appeal of Reagan himself. For if a generation of college students, for example, can be induced to revere the intent of the Founding Fathers at the expense of their own human needs, they will be less likely to challenge the many more secular forms of authority whose legitimacy is linked to this intent by law and onto whom their reverence is therefore likely to be transferred.

The symbolic reading of the "jurisprudence of original intention" that I am proposing here is representative of a competing critical method within Critical Legal Studies (CLS) to the deconstructive method exemplified by Mark Tushnet. It seeks to understand—by recourse to a kind of sociopsychoanalytic theory of alienation—how cultural phenomena acquire and "hold" social meaning at nonrational levels, and I believe it therefore complements the deconstructionism that goes in quite the opposite direction in seeking to undercut the pseudorational surface meaning attributed to oppressive ideologies by those who advocate them. Tushnet shows that the call for a return to the intent of the framers is irrational, since what evidence there is of such an intent is so vague as to be inherently inconclusive in resolving any important legal question, and since to the extent that the evidence is clear it reveals contradictory intentions that would be likely to support opposing results. My claim is that this "call," however irrational in appearance, is nonetheless expressive of an intelligible nonrational meaning that must be comprehended if it is to be effectively opposed. Both strains of CLS work seem to me important in providing the forces of humanity with the kind of articulable insight that must be partly constitutive of any confident movement that seeks to challenge the level of estrangement that we face today.

THE POLITICS-OF-MEANING PLATFORM
PLANK ON LAW

This platform plank on law, drafted with the help of lawyers Thane Rosenbaum and Nanette Schorr, was presented at the National Conference on the Politics of Meaning, which was held in Washington, D.C., in April 1996.

THE LEGAL SYSTEM IS ARGUABLY the most important public arena in our society; it defines how we are expected to relate to one another within civil society and how the government is expected to treat us as citizens. It also shapes our understanding of the meaning of injustice and justice, and therefore profoundly influences our society's ethical consciousness, our perception of right and wrong in human relations. While other aspects of our culture—in particular, religion—also speak to these issues in important ways, it is law and the legal system that provide the society's "bottom line" on matters of ethics and social justice, even in defining the permissible scope of religious practice and influence, and the public relevance of other nonlegal sources of ethical values.

The ethical understanding reflected in our present legal system is heavily tilted toward validating individualism, selfishness, and materialism, and shows little concern for fostering a sense of community or a spirit of caring for the well-being of others or for the natural environment. The basic individualistic orientation is reflected in the following core elements of the legal system:

❖ The basic rules of substantive law embodied in, for example, the laws of contracts, torts, corporations, and property assume that people are essentially unconnected monads who wish to pursue their own self-interest in the competitive marketplace, and whose main social concern is limited to protecting their persons and property against unwanted interference by others. Even the Constitution, often thought to be among the world's greatest legal documents in securing social justice, provides no recognition of the human longing for community, for social connection, for mutual caring and recognition. Instead, the protections of the Bill of Rights are restricted to protecting the isolated individual or family against government incursion, oppression, and discrimination, protections that are very important, but that in no way provide a basis for challenging the selfishness and the materialism that are otherwise largely legitimized by the rest of American law.

❖ Dispute resolution takes place within the framework of an adversary system that defines differences as antagonistic clashes of conflicting interest, fosters hostility and mutual depreciation, and normally exclude any community interest in the resolution of disputes beyond the self-interested goals of the litigants themselves. The adversary process is characterized by the assumption that all participants should treat each other with skepticism and mistrust, and that justice is best served by the use of rules that are limited to the proof of empirically verifiable facts. As such, the underlying social meaning of disputes is presumed to be "subjective" and irrelevant; healing underlying social causes of an injury is not considered to be an aspect of legal justice; and empathy, compassion, and forgiveness are neither fostered by nor relevant to the legal process.

❖ In their training, and in the disciplinary and ethical rules that govern the legal profession, lawyers are encouraged and even to some extent required to ignore ethical considerations beyond the narrow self-interest of the client. Legal education is almost exclusively directed toward the technical manipulation of specialized professional rules; the best students are seen as the ones who can demonstrate their capacity to shape precedent to argue for any side; no part of a law student's education is directed toward instilling in the student an obligation to promote the creation of a more humane or more caring society. The ethical rules of the profession reinforce the view of the lawyer as a hired gun with no transcendent ethical consciousness: the "duty of zealous representation," for example, virtually requires the lawyer to not allow his or her own ethical concerns to interfere with the zealous legal pursuit of the client's ends, irrespective of the impact of these ends on others, on the community as a whole, or on the environment.

❖ The intense individualism, empiricism, and mistrust of any transcendent ethical or community values that characterize all these aspects of the present legal system are understandable if we recall that this system emerged in reaction to the abuses of communal and religious norms that characterized feudal society and feudal law. Protecting the liberty of the individual against the coercion of others and of the State was the highest priority of those who first imagined our liberal legal order during the Enlightenment, and those who made it a reality following the American and European revolutions of the eighteenth century. At that time, the creation of our present legal system was a great accomplishment. But today that same system has become both a symptom and a cause of the ethical indifference, the cynicism, and the lack of community and caring that pervades our wider society.

In the area of law, our challenge is to preserve the core value of individual liberty that earlier generations fought for, while transforming our legal culture to foster the healing of our disintegrated communal fabric. To that end, we propose the following initial changes in the American legal system:

1. We call upon all those affiliated with the legal profession—including lawyers, judges, law professors, legal scholars, and law students—to declare that the healing of distortions in human interaction and the fostering of mutual recognition and respect shall be acknowledged as a central aspect of the meaning of justice, and a core objective of law and legal processes. This "declaration" might be accompanied by the holding of public conferences in which the role of legal culture in promoting social healing is discussed, by the writing of scholarly articles that help to advance public understanding of how specific legal reforms can further

the creation of meaningful social connection, and by experimentation by individual members of the profession, bar associations, law firms, law schools, and legal service offices in developing innovative legal interventions consistent with a healing-centered objective.

2. The American Law Institute and other influential associations of judges and practitioners, as well as members of state legislatures in states where the state legislature plays an important role in defining the rules of court and rules of evidence, should seek to modify the current operation of the adversary system so as to foster a greater sense of empathy and compassion in the parties to a lawsuit toward each other, and in the minds of the jury and the public generally, regarding the social causes of legal disputes. One key element in accomplishing this goal must involve modifying the existing evidentiary rules regarding relevance away from the narrow empiricism of the current "fact-finding" process and toward the telling of meaningful stories or narratives that place disputes in their meaningful social and personal context, and therefore reveal more of the full human meaning of each party's actions. Other possible methods for furthering the dissemination of empathy and compassion within legal proceedings might include the encouragement of contextualizing opening and closing statements by judges, attorneys, and litigants; encouraging judges to make "findings of social meaning" instead of just the traditional findings of fact; encouraging judges to use expressive rather than narrowly objective language when writing legal opinions, with the goal of revealing how empathy plays a part in both the understanding of a legal problem and the construction of a just response.

3. The American Bar Association and other affiliated state and local bar associations should modify the existing ethical rules governing the legal profession to provide that in addition to having an acknowledged duty to the client and the court, a lawyer must also assume an ethical responsibility for the welfare of the broader community. In order to better accomplish this objective, the principle of a lawyer's "duty of zealous representation" should be reoriented so that it no longer is limited to advancing the individual self-interests of clients, but also contemplates an ethical obligation to work toward promoting substantive and social justice, as well as the larger goals of a good society. Within this new framework, the existing attorney-client relationship, and its attendant

confidentiality rules, can still be preserved, but the nature of that relationship, and the "calling" of the profession, should also seek to address
the broader problems of social justice that the client's individual problem might have raised.

4. The American legal system should adopt and recognize, as a new princi-
    ple of tort law, a duty to care for others in distress. This duty would be
    broader than the historical duty to rescue, but would be limited by a
    reasonableness condition subject to common law interpretation. The
    purpose of this duty would be to create a new ethos of responsibility for
    those who are in personal and economic crisis—the homeless, the
    infirm, the elderly, family members.

5. The criminal justice system should adopt a second stage of all criminal
    trials. Where there is a conviction, after the sentencing of the defendant,
    all those who participated in the trial—the judge, the jury, the attor-
    neys, the public, the defendant—should convene for a second stage of
    the trial, at which there will be a discussion of the deep social meaning
    and pain in the community that the trial uncovered. The purpose for
    the second stage would be to seek opportunities to explore healing,
    repair, acknowledgment of responsibility, as well as understanding and
    compassion for the defendant, the victims of the crime, and the larger
    community. In addition, criminal law should increasingly seek to adopt
    the principles of "restorative justice" in response to community violence
    of all kinds. As reflected in the work of the South African Commission
    on Truth and Reconciliation, these principles seek to shift the law's cur-
    rent focus from an emphasis on individual guilt and punishment to an
    emphasis on acceptance of responsibility by the wrongdoer, apology to
    the victim for suffering inflicted along with other appropriate restitu-
    tion, and, where possible, forgiveness of the wrongdoer and reintegra-
    tion of the wrongdoer into the community.

6. With respect to civil remedies, the focus on money damages should be
    changed so that liability can be redressed by directly healing the wrongs
    committed by the defendant. Such an approach would focus on face-
    to-face reconciliations and would also recognize the value of contrition
    and the acknowledgment of pain caused by the defendant—all in the
    hopes of seeking the possibilities for forgiveness. Moreover, those who

have been found liable for civil damages could be required to undergo some process of public education that would speak to the nature of the personal and social injury for which they were responsible. In addition, the law should promote remedies that result in changing workplace dynamics or other social contexts that caused the injury.

7. The current system of legal education breeds an unhealthy culture of anger, resentment, and rage. Law school education should adopt the following reforms: law schools should try to create opportunities for sharing and caring in the law school community; there should be less focus on individual grades and more focus on group activity and problem solving; students should be taught how to counsel clients in a way that develops an appreciation of the moral and psychic dimensions of a client's suffering and pain; there should be more clinical opportunities, so that students can see the value of working within the community with people who have real problems; law school instruction should move away from traditional methods of teaching that intimidate students and mystify "legal reasoning" and move toward methods that encourage students to work together, share information, and not be made to feel isolated and alone; law schools should place more emphasis on teaching students the role and value of being a counselor, as well as an advocate; students should be taught that ethical principles are not merely code words for how one goes about avoiding legal consequences, but in fact are real moral imperatives that make all of us in society better off.

In addition, consistent with the ideal of teaching the law as an ethical calling rather than a rule-manipulating trade, students should be asked to reflect deeply in their classes about the meaning of justice itself and the relationship of justice to fostering mutual recognition and the building of authentic community through the healing of moral wounds.

TRANSFORMATIVE POSSIBILITIES
FOR PROGRESSIVE LAWYERS

Toward a Politics-of-Meaning Conception of Public-Interest Law

The Impoverished Political Meaning of Existing Legal Culture

THE NEED FOR PROGRESSIVE PEOPLE to develop a new approach to politics does not apply only or even primarily to national elections. Presidential elections are an important element in the development of such a politics because they define—with special force because of the finality of the collective act of voting—what "we" regard to be the legitimate scope of national debate over ideas and social vision. On the one hand, it is often said quite rightly that presidential elections are too abstract and removed from the concreteness of people's everyday existence to be expected to have much of an impact on the reality of people's lives. On the other, it is much easier to get people to believe in the possibility of social change or in the possible realization of a new social vision if the people as a whole express themselves as taking such ideas seriously. There is a reciprocal relationship between the ways of being and the kinds of ideas legitimated in national elections, and more local and concrete forms of social-political involvement (including everything from actual participation in specific political activities to the things that we talk to our friends about and the degree of passion with which we feel able to talk about these things); each arena—national and local—helps to define the other's horizon, and each works to enable or limit the content and spirit of what can be expressed in the other. To give a simple example from a situation I was involved in, it is much easier for a health care advocate in Madison, Wisconsin, to say to a local legislative sub-committee that our ethical obligation to care for one another, as we face death or infirmity together, requires Wisconsin to provide statewide health care to all its citizens, if the same compassionate vision is being expressed by a recognized national leader. If there is little or no indication that there is a larger "we" giving legitimacy to this kind of "soft" ethical discourse, the subcommittee is likely to respond cynically or with boredom to what they will think of as touchy-feely, unrealistic arguments, and rely heavily on the "hard" data in the staff's cost-benefit analysis to make their decision.

The legal arena plays a particularly important role in shaping people's sense of the legitimate and the possible, because it is the democratically validated, public context for mediating the relationship between every specific local case or conflict and the agreed-upon universal vision that gives these values meaning. Lawyers, judges, law students, law professors, media commentators on the law and the legal process, high school civics teachers, and legal secretaries are but some of the people who shape this culture, not to mention the long-dead architects who designed the hierarchical-majestic courtrooms in the local Hall of Justice or the producers, directors, and actors of TV law shows like *The People's Court, Law and Order,* and *American Justice.* Taken together, this congeries of persons, images, and publically transmitted ideas about law convey the culture of law, expressed through such phenomena as the evocative qualities and sub-stantive content of legal doctrine and reasoning, the symbolic meaning of the architecture of legal settings and the uniforms lawyers wear, and the way lawyers manifest themselves through their physical presence.

Here I will focus on only two aspects of existing legal culture—what I will call the "disembodiment" of lawyers and judges, and the technical-rational character of legal reasoning. Although each of these aspects of our legal culture at one time may have manifested a certain resistance to the religious moralism of preliberal society, they have now become part of the spiritual and moral emptiness of liberal political life.

To understand what I mean by the "disembodiment" of judges and lawyers, think of the physical bearing of a soccer goalie in the midst of a game. She bends her knees and moves with quickness and suppleness from side to side, anticipating the next shot on goal, the feint that she must sense to avoid losing her balance, the fully extended leap to one side or the other that might suddenly be required. In her play this goalie is present in her body, and her mind and body are relatively unified in the sense that she lives her project as a goaltender through the coordinated "praxis" of her movements. In light of the weight and the poise of her presence, it would be difficult to casually push her backward.

Contrast the physical presence of a judge. He sits on an elevated platform, his body almost entirely concealed by a black robe. His movements are usually minimal and narrowly functional, involving mainly the head and the hands. We could say that *his being is in his head* and withdrawn from his body, so that we experience his presence mainly through a disembodied and slightly elevated style of speaking or writing, as if the law were above and outside us and he were bringing it to us with his mind. This separation of mind and body corresponds to a separation of thought and feeling revealed in both the content and the manner of his self-expression. In light of this absence of bodily presence, if he were standing, it would be very easy to push him off balance with a slight push.

The same disembodiment is characteristic of lawyers also. I have taught contracts for twenty-five years and never fail to notice the change that comes over law students during October and November of the first year, when they first begin to learn how to "make arguments." The tentativeness, the intuitive orientation, and the feeling for justice that characterize the first weeks gradually give way to a glassy-eyed stare and a rigidification of musculature as a student learns to say in a monotone, "Well, it seems to me that you could argue there was no consideration at all here since the paper was entirely worthless." Full-blown lawyers tend to become quite addicted to this kind of glassy-eyed, disembodied power-discourse in spite of the strain required to keep it up, because the esteem and recognition attributed to it within the circle of collective denial makes it seem to be worth the repression required to keep it up.

My claim is that the effect of this separation of mind and body and thought and feeling is to reinforce the isolation of both the judge and the lawyer, as well as those who experience them, by blocking the empathic channel required to link the person to the community of meaning that a good legal culture should constantly be in the process of constituting. The disembodied lawyer or judge withdraws his being from his public self in order to manifest a detached neutrality that mirrors and confirms the felt detachment of the client or citizen from the political community that the lawyer or judge is supposed to represent.

To the degree that this way of being pervades legal culture as a whole, it serves to replicate the alienating structure-producing process I described in "Dukakis's Defeat and the Emphasis on Postmovement Politics," because the law is made to appear as an authoritative system of thought outside and above everyone, and something to be "obeyed" as a condition of group membership, rather than as a contingent and developing expression of social and political meaning that we actively create and interpret.

Complementing this disembodied way of being is legal reasoning itself, which for the most part aspires to be a kind of disembodied thought. The training that lawyers undergo draws them toward becoming primarily technical analysts who learn how to "make arguments" as if their thought process were simply a function of the law as an external and authoritative discourse. If I am right that the desire for mutual confirmation is as fundamental an element of our existence as any biological need and is central to understanding the meaning of any cultural phenomenon, then legal reasoning should not aspire to the kind of analytical rationality that places the reasoner at a distance from the world and that relies upon the "logical application of the law to the facts" to resolve human problems. It should aspire to an empathic comprehension that requires the thinker to immerse his or her soul in the so-called "facts" and to interpret their meaning in accordance with the moral and social end to which he or she believes the law should be directed. Yet the existing methods of legal education and law practice actually tend to invalidate and suppress this kind of comprehensive understanding, valorizing instead an unempathic and objectified way of looking at "fact" situations and "analytical rigor" in applying rules as well as in doing policy analysis. If the legal world were concerned about empathic rigor, the entire nature of law practice and legal education would have to be changed.

The reason for this misemphasis is not that people haven't thought the whole thing through properly, but that the processes that generate the collective denial of social desire also generate forms of social thinking that reinforce and justify this denial. The predominance of technical-rational over ethical-emotional thought within legal culture succeeds in draining legal reasoning of the qualitative dimension of human situations. By attributing a privileged authority to legal thought as the carrier of our political values and by excluding this qualitative dimension from it, we privatize and define as nonpolitical what is probably the most important distinctively social aspect of our existence—the desire for social confirmation and meaning—even though the absence of this confirmation and meaning can be overcome only through a politics that produces public social change. This split in the law is paralleled by a split in the lawyer, who has a "personal" life in which she seeks qualitative satisfactions and is guided by comprehensive or intuitive knowledge and a professional life in which she converts herself into a kind of observer-analyst, funneling her client's goals into the essentially anti-intuitive conceptual knowledge of legal argumentation. As I will discuss in a moment, this division has had very bad consequences for both social-change movements and public-interest lawyers themselves, but it has bad consequences for all of us to the degree that it requires collusion with the social dynamics that inhibit the realization of our own deepest social need. For the insulation of legal reasoning and of the lawyer's self from the qualitative pull of social desire just fragmentizes or serializes this desire, pooling it up within each of us as individuals, instead of allowing it to have a public voice seeking qualitative public remedies.

A second aspect of the way that existing legal discourse reinforces what I have been calling collective denial is through the reification of legal categories. I have described the way that the internalized mistrust of the other's desire gives rise to de-centered or unconfirmed subjects who collectively project (through a kind of conspiracy of rotating doubt) an externalized source of social authority or agency, which is then experienced, defensively, as fixed or "real." This dynamic is embodied in existing legal discourse, in the sense that people believe the law to be a something outside and above us that acts upon us when "it" is "applied" to our situations, and also in the sense that the categories of legal discourse form a perceptual grid that is experienced by most people as "the way things are."

To most nonlawyers as well as lawyers, the categories of "landlord" and "tenant" or "management" and "labor" or "employer" and "employee" are experienced not as contingent descriptive concepts subject to change, but as more or less fixed and immutable characteristics of the people enveloped by them. The *rights* of the landlord or tenant may be subject to change, but the categories of landlord and tenant themselves tend to be experienced as simply "part of the law of property that governs us." As I will argue in a moment, this might not have to be the case if legal interpretation were animated by a disalienating vision, because the vitality of such a vision might have the effect of allowing us to remember the contingency of these categories as we use them. But so long as these categories are flattened out and hardened through the objectification that envelops phenomena when seen with a detached, analytical eye, they help to give a thinglike appearance to the very forms of blocked connection—to the "housing hierarchy," for example—that ought eventually to be opened up.

It is, of course, not the case that the existing legal culture is based upon no moral vision at all. The disembodiment of lawyers and the conceptual rationalism of legal reasoning are expressions of the aspect of liberal political theory that wants to use neutrality to secure the boundary between the individual and the group (to put it conceptually) or between self and others (to put it experientially). The ostensible goal of this view is to prevent totalitarianism whether feudal, fascist, or communist, and to protect individual freedom. Without denying the importance of this idea to the development of human culture, it has always been based on a mistaken notion of social existence because its individualist ontology has failed to grasp the a priori reality of intersubjectivity and the absolute need of each person for the empowering confirmation of the other. Seen from this intersubjective perspective, the political morality of liberalism can tend to strengthen reactionary movements as much as to prevent them, because it fails to recognize the nature of the social inclusion and meaning that people have no choice but to seek out. If liberal legal and political culture fails to speak to and validate this intersubjective need as a central constituent of political meaning, that culture will tend to create pathological forms of community (fundamentalism, for example) that do speak to this need in a distorted and dangerous way.

Transformative Possibilities for Progressive Lawyers

Whether they are Democratic Party liberals or political radicals who continue to believe in the possibility of a fundamentally different and more caring world, lawyers who want to work for social change must transform the way that they think about law practice in much the same way that the Democratic Party must transform its approach to politics. The failure to have engaged in this rethinking has played an important role in the spiritual enervation of the entire generation of public-interest lawyers who were produced by the sixties. The splitting of desire and reason within existing legal culture has had its worst effects on these lawyers because they have for the most part accepted its inevitability, defining their legal work as the endless "making of arguments" within the confines and assumptions of existing legal discourse and roles, while relegating the expression of their true political selves to meetings or demonstrations or participation in volunteer organizations in their private lives. Many of these lawyers are now in their forties or fifties and are burned out—because of this schizophrenia and because their often-exhausting work within their official legal personae has produced so much less than they had originally hoped for. It seems to me that as a group they feel both demoralized and confused about what went wrong.

Although "what went wrong" is a very complex story that certainly should not be blamed on these often courageous and self-sacrificing attorneys, it is nonetheless true that the public-interest law movement of the late sixties and early seventies tended to undermine itself through its own very limited self-definition. From the beginnings of this movement until the present day, it has been difficult to tell most public-interest lawyers from their corporate counter-parts; they look, act, and speak alike, using the same legal language and sharing the same underlying assumptions about what law is, the difference being that the public-interest lawyers represent relatively oppressed people and try to help them get their rights and entitlements, while the corporate lawyers represent relatively rich people and do more or less the same thing (if a tax shelter is an entitlement). In public-interest law schools like New College where I work, we use "skills-training" classes and an apprenticeship program to teach our students the same things that corporate firms teach their young associates in their first years of practice—essentially a collection of specialized technical skills coupled with role training in how to act like a lawyer.

This approach to practice has allowed the lawyers' political and moral aspirations to be assimilated to a set of cultural meanings that contradicts these aspirations. Whether they were drawn into politics by the civil rights movement or the antiwar movement or more recently by the environmental or feminist movements, most of these lawyers originally conceived of social change in something like the qualitative terms that I have been using—they would not have used the theoretical vocabulary of desire, mutual confirmation, denial, and so on, but they would certainly have said they wanted to help create a more humane world where people related to one another and to the natural world with more respect, affection, and even sacredness. Yet the course that they chose, to the degree that it meant giving over their being to the existing legal culture, served to help reproduce in their own political arena the very social dynamics they wanted to change. However they expressed themselves and acted in their personal lives, in their public roles they felt they had to translate their socially transformative aspirations into a disembodied way of being and a technical-rational way of thinking, talking, and writing that suppressed precisely these aspirations.

In addition, the narrow outcome-oriented focus of the typical public interest practice, coupled with a theory of social-change strategies that was limited to reform litigation versus service cases, meant that they were accepting a priori the moral and political assumptions of liberal legalism as the framework for articulating the meaning of their own and their clients' goals. It is difficult to expect to generate movement toward the realization of greater social connection and mutual respect when the moral and political assumptions of your own legal discourse conceive of people as discrete, competitive individuals who want to relate to each other at arm's length and who lack any common emotional-ethical desire except the desire to be free from governmental tyranny. Although most lawyers have not fully realized the nature of this ideological contradiction (in part because they were trained as legal technicians who simply use liberal-legal doctrine rather than reflecting on its meaning), many of them have been demoralized and confused by it and now really have no clear notion of how their work can have a social impact.

The alternative to this older public-interest law model is for progressive lawyers to build a legal culture that rejects the strategy of trying to win cases on the other's terms and that asserts in all its manifestations the political legitimacy of its own moral and social vision. I use the term "culture" here to make it clear that I am referring to more than the substantive content of legal arguments. Actually the idea that the law "is" nothing more than a conceptual-interpretive schema to which lawyers are more or less appended is itself part of the problem to be overcome, because it derives from the disembodied character of the existing legal culture that I described earlier. If the aim of social-change lawyers is to give a new political legitimacy to people's psychological and ethical need to be part of a meaning-giving community, then they must actively try to reconstruct the political culture within which they work and which they partially constitute, so as to overcome the existing separations between mind and body, thought and feeling, and analysis and comprehension as these separations manifest themselves in the public space of legal settings. This is to say that in the way they organize their offices, the qualities of being they manifest with their clients, and in the way they relate to judges, jurors, and other legal workers, they should seek to recover the relatively spontaneous and supple embodiment of the soccer goalie (obviously in a form appropriate to being a lawyer). The aim here is to reunify legal practice with the world by grounding it in being and to pull the law back from its imaginary location "above" and "outside" the concrete settings where it is actually created and acquires its social meaning.

I don't mean by this that lawyers must wear blue jeans to the office or continually get deeply involved in personal conversations with their clients, but rather that they should systematically challenge, with a keen awareness of the customary constraints that limit the scope of their freedom, the modes of role-based, disembodied interaction that reproduce on an everyday level the divisions between private and public, and desire and reason, that I have been addressing. A new kind of "skills training" is required for this because the legal arena is suffused with so much authoritarian symbolism (think of the portraits alone that are found in the average courtroom) that one must develop a highly disciplined sense of how to retain the expressive forms of the existing legal culture enough to be recognized as a legitimate member of the legal community and yet infuse these forms with a new, morally autonomous cultural meaning. I doubt that one can do this effectively, for example, without understanding the psychoanalytic idea of "transference" as it applies to both the fearfulness and the idealization that tend to characterize the way clients see lawyers, the way lawyers see judges, the way judges see the Founding Fathers, and so on. The idea is not to strike out against the existing system of roles in a self-marginalizing and self-defeating way, but to manifest in a disciplined way—in the totality of the manifestation of one's being as it appears in the preverbal but intuitively accessible expression of meaning revealed through the lawyer and her surroundings—her affirmation of the social desire that others have formed a "system" to deny.

The same kind of transformative possibility and constraint exists in the area of legal doctrine and reasoning. The analogue to the disconnected laundry list of redistributive entitlement programs so common in Democratic Party platforms is the endless demand on the Left for more rights for oppressed groups. The problem with defining political aims in terms of entitlements or rights is not the appeal for entitlements or rights themselves (I usually support these liberal efforts), but the failure to frame these appeals within an expressive or evocative moral vision that could give them a potentially universal, desire-realizing social meaning. At best, the pursuit of more rights within the presupposed liberal framework of conventional legal reasoning simply extends the post–New Deal, liberal welfare state—that is, the ideological meaning of a conventional Fourteenth Amendment argument justifying the expansion of political rights serves to justify rather than transform an individualistic, competitive model of social and political life. At worst, this translation of transformative political aims into existing legal consciousness serves to actually destroy the transformative hope contained in a legal claim—as when an affirmative action argument based on past governmental discrimination that has impeded "equality of opportunity" to compete on the Law School Admissions Test affirms both the legitimacy of competitive exams as ciphers of social value and the legitimacy of the narrow and antiempathic analytical rationality tested on these exams as the kind of "skill" needed for mastering legal reasoning (while also tending to intensify societal racial conflict between relatively powerless whites and minority groups, since the ethical message embodied in the interpretive schema tends to reconfirm that the whites really merit success on the competitive ladder and are being punished for sins they themselves had nothing to do with).

The way to surpass this contradiction that has plagued progressive lawyers for at least my adult lifetime is to start telling the truth about the vision of social life that we are trying to make real, and to treat the American people as a whole as if they also can and should believe in it. I have already stated the philosophical/ontological basis for the possibility of this occurring—the desire for mutual confirmation and the felt need of everyone to overcome the blockage of this social desire means that people will want to respond to (and in some cases, to defensively resist the pull of) evocative moral appeals that convey a sense of transcendent social purpose. Claims of right, when they are formulated with clients in law offices and whether they are made in court or through the media, should be justified legally in a way that is continuous with the qualitative political meaning that inspires them. As for the possible objection that this kind of thinking is "idealist" in the sense of not being grounded in the real socioeconomic and cultural conditions that shape people's responses to such appeals (a view shared by both Marxists and conservative economic rationalists), let me say simply that any claim must be contextualized so that it expresses some particular tendency, already alive and moving within the culture, that carries a disalienating, potentially transformative meaning that can legitimately support the political expression of this meaning in public legal discourse. If the Constitution is an "evolving document," then its meaning should always be subject to a contested debate over who "we" are as social beings and how we are or should be "constituted" as a political community.

Here is one contemporary example of what I mean. The doctrine of comparable worth has emerged from the spread of mutual confirmation that gave rise to the women's movement, but the social meaning of both the movement and the doctrine at the moment is in doubt. In its early phases, the women's movement sought to fundamentally challenge the qualities of social interaction that have been valued in male-dominated society and are reflected in everything from the market economy to positivist epistemologies in the social sciences. Today, this transformative dimension of the women's movement is being contested by a more conservative notion, which defines success and failure primarily in terms of the number of women who occupy positions formerly held only by men and by the amount of money women earn relative to men. Certainly these two meanings of feminism are potentially compatible in the sense that the struggle for sexual equality within the existing society does not imply an abandonment of the more transformative goal—but I believe that the two visions are often in tension and that the latter threatens to co-opt the former or to neutralize it enough so that it no longer carries the sharp critique of prevailing forms of social alienation that it once did.

The choice of how to articulate a comparable-worth claim reflects this tension. The principal way that comparable-worth claims are currently formulated is to claim a right to equal pay for jobs traditionally occupied by women that are comparable, in terms of educational and skill requirements and other measurable factors, to higher-paid jobs held primarily by men. The remedy sought is money damages. In one sense, this formulation does express the transformative dimension of feminism because it seeks to value—in the manner currently recognized as the measure of value—the compassion and intuitive wisdom that have long characterized many forms of so-called "women's work." But on the whole, those who have made these claims have tended to accept the division of desire and reason that feminism originally sought to oppose, emphasizing instead a quantitative meaning of equality defined by such factors as number of years of training and amount of monetary compensation that are assimilable to the prevailing liberal models of both market-based social relations and rights-based redistributive political intervention. Like labor-law jurisprudence in the decades following the rise of the labor movement, which to some degree redefined that movement's goals so as to emphasize higher wages and safer working conditions while de-emphasizing the qualitative and more transformative goal of workplace democracy, this approach to feminist jurisprudence may in the long run contribute to the dissolution of the transformative vision of human reciprocity that is at the heart of the women's movement's power to create social change. The law always has this potential power of dissolution because legal interpretation constantly reflects back to those inside and outside a social movement what society as a whole considers to be the legitimate aims of the movement; the law therefore offers its own promise of social recognition and inclusion, however alienated, that may subtly erode the movement's own self-understanding and original conception of its aims.

My claim is that it would be better, for the women's movement and for society, for feminist lawyers developing their legal theory to have as their goal a redefinition of human worth that challenges the market-based definition more directly than a pay equity theory does, and to seek a remedy that calls for some plausible modification in the organization of a workplace aimed at realizing a more nurturant and socially confirming conception of the nature of socially valuable labor. I cannot say at the moment exactly how such a claim would be formulated using the existing legal materials (there is certainly support in American legal history for a qualitative ideal of equality), but the great virtue of this approach is that it would allow the legal claim to be expressed in a way continuous with the moral passion and sense of social purpose that originally animated the women's movement itself. Not only would this fusion of desire and reason within an openly political discourse challenge the apparent inevitability of people's sense of underconfirmation by challenging the prevailing system of measuring social worth that produces that sense; such a fusion would also challenge the technical-rational character of existing legal reasoning and the reification of legal categories by calling for an interpretation of social equality that relies upon the "softness" of heartfelt thought and the kind of empathic comprehension of social qualities that dissolves the detachment of the anti-intuitive and hyperanalytical "legal mind." The moral power of such a claim, in other words, would not only be in its assertion of the possibility of a transformed workplace sensitive to the realization of a common social desire that women are speaking for, but in its assertion that political and legal reasoning must reform itself so as to be able to recognize this kind of desire if it means to really express the will of the people in the truth of their social being.

It may be that this way of framing a comparable-worth claim is not currently feasible because of the constraints within the social context or the available legal materials are too great. But even if the precise right asserted is more narrowly framed and the remedy sought is more conventional, the meaning of what is being asked for can be stated so as to express the deeper political goal, perhaps emphasizing primarily the intrinsic worth of the qualities immanent in the work to be valued rather than equivalence in educational qualifications. There is virtually no case to be litigated or bill to be lobbied for that does not offer progressive lawyers some opportunity to infuse their practical objective with a larger meaning that exerts a pull on the desire and longing of those who hear them, including their own supporters who face the same conflict between confidence and doubt that everyone else does.

THE MORAL OBLIGATION OF CRIMINAL DEFENSE LAWYERS IN THE WAKE OF THE O.J. SIMPSON TRIAL

A Debate with Alan Dershowitz

OUR EXISTING LEGAL SYSTEM—WITH ITS EMPHASIS on protecting the individual against oppression by the government—emerged as a heroic response of the human spirit to centuries of class and religious domination that were justified by feudal law. The adversary system, with its emphasis on the confrontation of opposing positions as the route to discovering truth, the guarantee of freedom of contract with its emphasis on liberating the individual from any preexisting status constraints on freedom of action, the emergence of evidentiary rules that rejected the word of twenty bishops in favor of empirically verifiable facts, and the protections of the Bill of Rights, which sought to protect the innocent individual citizen against all forms of officially sanctioned group power—all of these liberal inventions represented an important advance for humanity when understood in the context of the injustices of the feudal aristocracy, the Divine Right of Kings, or the Salem witch trials. And they gave rise to the (partly justified) romantic view of the criminal defense lawyer described by Yale Kamisar and perhaps to some extent identified with by Alan Dershowitz.

But that was over two hundred years ago, and the advances of that earlier time must be reexamined in light of the problems of our present era, problems that the liberal legal system has itself helped to produce. Today we live in a world of radically isolated individuals creating a public culture without ethical or communal meaning. Our problem is not liberating ourselves as individuals from State oppression, but rather finding a way to heal the cultural alienation that has disabled us from creating a loving and caring society. In this present context, we need to envision a new kind of legal culture that preserves individual liberty against group-sanctioned injustice but that also understands the legal arena as a moral environment within which to build greater empathy, trust, and solidarity. We must stop seeing the legal system as an amoral, hyper-individualistic environment in which protecting civil liberties becomes a justification for criminal defense lawyers doing anything they can to get their clients off even when they know or strongly suspect or even believe that their clients are lying or have been guilty of acts of cruelty or brutality.

It is difficult for me to imagine that anyone could wholeheartedly endorse a defense of the existing system after enduring the drawn-out painful spectacle of the O.J. Simpson trial. Here we have an extraordinary situation in which the general public has substantial direct evidence that the defendant has brutally murdered his ex-wife, the mother of his own two children, and her friend, a random victim who could have been any one of us. The immense human suffering engendered by this terrible crime obviously calls upon us to recognize the death experience of the victims and the horror and trauma of the families as well as to expect whoever is responsible for it to be compelled to acknowledge that responsibility. Yet we were forced daily to watch a team of criminal defense lawyers act as though they had no responsibility for assuring that this recognition of suffering and acknowledgment of responsibility would occur, and indeed that they were the ones pursuing justice by, to use Mr. Kamisar's words, "challeng[ing] the conduct of the government officials involved in the case every step of the way" irrespective of the probability that Mr. Simpson had actually committed the murders. At least as morally offensive to the conscience of the country were the "legal experts" who covered the trial on television. Steeped in the same legal tradition as the defense team, they speculated excitedly hour by hour on what "move" Johnnie Cochran et al. would make next, about whether Marcia Clark and Christopher Darden were up to the challenge and what "moves" they would make in return, suppressing people's experience of the pain at the murders and their longing for justice beneath an obscene fascination with the lawyers as celebrities, and gossip about who was more skilled at the legal-manipulative chess game.

It is not surprising that applications to law school have dropped since the Simpson trial. People know instinctively that it is wrong and unjust to use every tactic to challenge the prosecution's case when you know your client is guilty of brutal and violent acts. The moral situation is not changed significantly when you strongly suspect or even believe that your client is guilty of such conduct. Why should people want to join a profession that exalts cleverness and adversarial challenge as its highest virtue and calls it the pursuit of justice, and that shows little or no concern for the seriousness and openness to suffering that the actual pursuit of justice calls for in any human situation where injustice exists?

The reason that Mr. Dershowitz and his colleagues were able to convince themselves that what they were doing was not only permissible but right is the belief that the presumption of innocence, combined with the right to counsel, justifies and even requires the criminal defense lawyer to do whatever is legally allowable to secure his or her client's acquittal. I submit that this position is valid only when the defense lawyer actually believes the client is innocent and has been unjustly accused (or in some situations in which the lawyer believes the law itself is unjust or its application will lead to an unjust result). In cases in which the client is charged with committing acts of brutality or cruelty, neither the presumption of innocence nor the right to counsel justifies an effort to obtain a verdict of not guilty if the lawyer does not believe his or her client is in fact innocent.

The basis for the current ethical rules that allow and even require the criminal defense lawyer to zealously pursue the acquittal of all his or her clients so long as he or she does not know them to be guilty as a matter of fact is found in the hyperindividualism of the pure civil liberties model. To reiterate, the principal concern of the architects of our existing legal system was the protection of the individual against all forms of group tyranny or coercion. In the area of potential incarceration or even execution during a historical period that had witnessed the abuses of the Star Chamber, this version of the presumption of innocence was thought to require the absolute protection of the individual, whether in fact guilty or innocent, unless the prosecution could prove its case by empirically verifiable evidence beyond a reasonable doubt. The guilty client was not expected to take responsibility for his or her own conduct and was even protected from having to do so by the Fifth Amendment, which guarantees a defendant's right not to have to testify against himself or herself. The guilty client's lawyer was also insulated from responsibility for knowledge of the client's probable guilt because the lawyer's sole legitimate and even socially exalted role, within the civil liberties framework, was to defend the legal "presumption" of each individual's innocence, irrespective of that individual's actual responsibility for suffering inflicted on other human beings, until and unless the State proves its case.

As Mr. Kamisar says in words that I personally consider to be morally shocking, "It is not the defense lawyer's job to pass judgment on his or her client." It is this same consciousness, when applied in the "noncriminal" context, that allows lawyers representing large corporations to use every legal means to destroy the rainforest—it is "not their job" to pass judgment on their clients' ends.

Enough already! The vast majority of Americans find this amoral conception of the lawyer repugnant and are pained by the injustice—the lack of real caring about consequences—that this conception of law routinely sanctions. And because liberals and the Left regard the pure civil liberties position as some immutable idea that cannot even be questioned for fear that the group (liberals) or the System (the Left) will reduce them to slavery, more and more people quietly come to identify with a right-wing that shows itself to care about the suffering of victims and expresses its rage at the protection of the violent and cruel people for whom liberal lawyers disavow any responsibility. To put it simply, the pure civil liberties position drives people to the Right and turns what would have been an appropriate concern for recognition of suffering and the need for responsibility into a potentially fascist rage.

The solution to this that the politics-of-meaning law task force will soon propose in its call to the American Bar Association for what we term "legal renewal" is a new conception of the lawyer and of legal culture itself. We believe that lawyers must reject their current public identity as technical rule-manipulators indifferent to their clients' ends and free of moral responsibility for their clients' conduct, whether that conduct is labeled criminal or civil in nature. Instead, we will put forward a conception of the legal profession as a "calling," a spiritual and activist pursuit aimed at healing the social alienation and ingrained distortions in human interaction that disable us from repairing our communal fabric. Among the changes we will argue for will be abolition of the adversary system as it exists today, revamping of the evidentiary rules to include the incorporation of meaning into the public resolution of conflict rather than just rules and facts, and the rejection of the belief that money is the primary proper remedy for civil wrongs in favor of recognizing the importance of apology and forgiveness.

With respect to ethical rules governing the legal profession, we will call for the affirmation of a lawyer's duty to take every step to reconcile the client's goals and needs with the well-being of the wider community and the creation of a more humane and just society. In the case of the criminal defense lawyer, this will mean no longer permitting attorneys to ethically participate in justifying false denials by their clients of responsibility for violent and cruel acts. If we are to bring about a *tikkun olam*—if we are to heal, repair, and transform the world—the only possible path is to expect our practitioners of justice to make the truth visible and to respond to it as a community in a compassionate and caring manner reflecting our individual and collective responsibility for it.

Alan Dershowitz, Professor of Law, Harvard University, Responds

Dear Editor:

There are few more dangerous ideologues than those who believe that truth can be arrived at without process. You would have thought that Peter Gabel might have learned that lesson from both communism and Nazism, which adopted procedures closely akin to the one he proposes. Those who tried witches and conducted inquisitions also believed that they were serving "the well-being of the wider community and the creation of a more humane and just society." Gabel's road may be paved with good intentions, but it will surely lead to hell.

Gabel says, "In cases in which the client is charged with committing acts of brutality or cruelty, neither the presumption of innocence nor the right to counsel justifies an effort to obtain a verdict of not guilty if the lawyer does not believe his or her client is in fact innocent." Indeed he goes further and says that "The moral situation is not changed significantly when you strongly suspect or even believe that your client is guilty of such conduct." This approach virtually abolishes the role of defense counsel and turns every "defense" lawyer into a prosecutor and judge whose job it is to "suspect" his or her client and treat the client as guilty based on mere suspicion. It is a role with which I am quite familiar, since I encountered it when I represented Soviet dissidents in the 1970s and 1980s. To illustrate the naive nature of this simple-minded approach, I challenge Professor Gabel to respond to the following questions:

1. Assume a system in which the exclusionary rule—either under the Fourth or Fifth Amendment—continues to exist. Assume that you have been appointed to represent a woman facing the death penalty for killing her abusive husband. Assume that the police broke into the defendant's home without a warrant and discovered evidence suggesting that the murder was planned. Would Gabel preclude the woman's appointed lawyer from invoking the Fourth or Fifth Amendment so as to exclude this evidence? Would Gabel also deny the lawyer the right to object to hearsay testimony in cases where the lawyer suspected that his or her client may be guilty?

2. Assume the same case. Would the appointed lawyer be obliged to tell his client in advance that whatever the client told him would not be kept confidential and that if the client told him anything incriminating the lawyer would no longer vigorously defend the client. Would that not simply result in clients never telling their lawyers anything of an incriminating nature?

3. Would lawyers who adopt the Gabel approach, as distinguished from the Kamisar/Dershowitz civil liberties approach, have to identify themselves as Gabel lawyers, rather than as defense lawyers? If so, can you imagine any reason why a defendant who might suspect that this lawyer might believe him guilty, would ever go to a Gabel lawyer?

4. Does Gabel concede that under the current constitutional and ethical rules, a defense lawyer who suspects or believes that his client may be guilty and who refrains from invoking all ethically available legal and constitutional defenses—such as the exclusionary rule—would be violating both the Sixth Amendment and the ethical requirements of the legal profession? (If he does not, he should read *DeLuca* v. *Lord,* 77 F3d 578.)

5. If Gabel does concede this, does it not follow that accusing a defense lawyer who complies with his obligation to current law of having "his hands still dripping from the blood of the victims whose assassins he protected"* reeks of blatant

---

* The words of Michael Lerner from the *Tikkun* editorial that initiated this debate.

McCarthyism and fails to understand the constitutional obligation of defense counsel under current law?

Arriving at truth in a system committed to civil liberties is a complex phenomenon. Gabel's simple-minded solutions will move us back to the Dark Ages where truth could be found by the rack and the Star Chamber.

Peter Gabel Responds

My dear Mr. Dershowitz:

Before I respond to your "challenge," may I reach out to you across the mental and spiritual constraints imposed on us by our legal training to ask that you hear the main point that I was making in my initial response to you and to Yale Kamisar?

America is in the midst of a spiritual crisis that is being spoken to only by the religious Right, the Promise Keepers, and various marginal new age movements that cannot really counter the moral suffering engendered by the selfishness, individualism, and materialism of the competitive marketplace. In spite of an outpouring of a kind of inflated-balloon pseudo-optimism generated by the Internet and other new technologies, people feel isolated from one another, trapped in meaningless routines, peering out at a world of artificial role-performances (think of your local newscaster) and social and cultural violence. We are also probably—not possibly, but probably—eroding the world's ecosystems and extinguishing natural species at an increasing rate so that it is not clear that our own species will survive for many more generations. Yet the collective psychic pain associated with our sense of isolation and disconnection from each other and from any collective sense of meaning and purpose is so great that we cannot even respond decisively to this moral and spiritual crisis. With the help of Prozac or Valium or alcohol (or crack cocaine for that matter), people survive day by day in a state of collective denial, which is maintained in significant part by everyone communicating to the other that everything is basically fine. As a result, each person in his or her peering-out isolation imagines that the floating pain of everyday life is a result of his or her own personal failure and to avoid humiliation covers this up by joining the spinning circle of collective denial and putting on a good face, the face of the artificial role-performance. If you think I'm exaggerating the matter, then I challenge you, Alan Dershowitz, to turn on your television, turn off the sound, and watch fifteen minutes of professional wrestling; then turn on the sound and watch fifteen minutes of *Melrose Place* or listen to the grotesque violence and cynicism of *Crossfire* or *The McLaughlin Group* or watch the "lighthearted" collective put-downs of family life and friendships contained in the endless series of vapid sitcoms that have now dominated evening cultural life for several decades.

If I am exaggerating, I'm exaggerating for effect. Of course we care for our loved ones, and life continues to have its positive aspects, even its joys. But what I'm saying is essentially true.

This "system" of spiritual immiseration is maintained by routinized organizations of experience that we call cultural institutions—the family, schools, corporations, professions, the entertainment and sports industries, and so on. These institutions all have positive aspects that form our very cultural and personal identities—they are conduits of social connection, but in spite of their positive aspects they are overloaded by negative coefficients of adversity. They tie us together and at the same time profoundly alienate us from each other. They bottle up our longing for mutual affirmation and authentic social connection at the same time that they provide us with the socially legitimate channels for experiencing what affirmation and connection there is.

In order to overcome the spiritual crisis that I have briefly described, we must transform our cultural institutions—we must infuse them with spirit, with the spirit of community expressive of our longing for empathy, trust, connection, solidarity, recognition, and meaning. And we must reshape the channeling process that organizes our social experience within these institutions so as to gain traction for, and foster the development of, this spiritual foundation. It won't do any good to seize State power or replace capitalism with socialism or pass campaign finance reform or engage in any other external manipulation of the cultural landscape—because what is needed is a healing of an internal distortion in the interspace of human relations, in the "between," as Martin Buber put it, where we connect through reciprocal recognition with the life force, with the force for Good in the universe itself.

Among the most important of the cultural institutions that we must transform is what we call the legal system, although it is not really a "system" but a culture masquerading as a system in order to make it appear as a fixed thing that can't be changed. As the single most important public arena for addressing the distortions and breakdowns in human relations that reveal themselves in our everyday life, the legal system plays a very important role in establishing our society's ethical culture. As I emphasized in the first part of this debate, the current legal system is obsessed with protecting the isolated individual from State power and from other isolated individuals or institutions. Two hundred years ago, it was a stunning achievement to invent and instill a set of cultural understandings like those contained in the Bill of Rights that confirmed the sanctity of individual existence—of conscience, of family and home life, of the autonomy and presumed innocence of the individual mind—against the many forms of group coercion that had desecrated and abused the individual for thousands of years up to that time. But in our time, this very achievement has become an important source of our spiritual crisis. In the name of protecting the individual, we have created a legal culture that fosters mistrust and mutual hostility and that blocks our ability to heal the cultural distortions that imprison our longing to reach each other, to understand and recognize each other, and to help each other up (not out, but up). And within this legal culture, we have created lawyers who have been taught to win at any cost (the duty of "zealous representation"), to manipulate rules to serve their clients' ends while being indifferent to the moral consequences of those ends (the Bar Exam requires you to "argue both sides" as if legal reasoning were an amoral skill), and perhaps most important, to see themselves as professional appendages to a "system" that is external to them and absolves them of moral responsibility for the practical and spiritual consequences of their own actions. If you collude with your client's lying in a murder case or if you win a clever procedural motion that allows your client to continue to pollute lakes and streams, it is the "legal system" and not you who bears responsibility for the consequences. You are just following orders, which in this case corresponds to the current ethics of the profession.

My differences with you, Mr. Dershowitz, are reflected in the first phrase of the set of questions you pose to me. You say, "Assume a system in which the exclusionary rule . . . continues to exist," referring to the current practice of excluding evidence illegally seized by the police. But I do not perceive the legal arena as a fixed external "system" to which I am a technical appendage, but as a spiritual and moral culture that I help to create and shape. If I were to try to respond to you within your framework, you'd have me in a box—how could I not apply the exclusionary rule if that is my predetermined role as defense counsel within "the system"? With all respect, it is this kind of "rigorous" Socratic questioning by their professors that leads each new generation of law students to become amoral technicians rather than spiritual and moral agents. They make the law review by giving correct answers to leading questions.

From my point of view, the question you pose leads in quite a different direction. In seeing the law as a very important moral and spiritual culture rather than a system, I think it becomes the responsibility of all of us engaged in it either to affirm the hyperindividualism and social alienation that the current culture produces and reproduces or to challenge those values by our own cultural interventions. If you believe as I do that it is a moral imperative to foster a process of empathic healing in resolving conflict in order to save the planet and realize the longing for mutual recognition immanent in the human soul, then the "role of the lawyer" is to contest the prevailing culture while working within it. This is why I described the politics-of-meaning view of the lawyer as "a 'calling', a spiritual and activist pursuit aimed at healing the social alienation and ingrained distortions in human interaction that disable us from repairing our communal fabric."

It is on this basis that I argued that criminal defense lawyers should no longer routinely participate—citing the presumption of innocence and the State's obligation to prove its case—in justifying false denials of responsibility by clients who commit violent and cruel acts. If they are going to publicly represent such clients as practitioners of justice, they should manifest a compassionate moral presence and exercise compassionate moral judgment in every phase of the representation—from the way they relate to their client and the victim and victim's family, to the conduct of the trial, to the probable consequences of a conviction or an acquittal for the client's life and the lives of others.

Consider your hypothetical case. First, let me make it clear that I support the attorney-client privilege because it is right that every person have a loyal confidant, familiar with the complexity of legal culture, who can advocate for him or her with moral integrity. But the nature of this confidential relationship should correspond more to the priest-penitent relationship than the currently prevailing attorney-client relationship. When one confesses to a priest, the priest does not respond by either threatening to turn you in or promising to try to get you off. He or she offers a moral and spiritual engagement that seeks to help you heal yourself through absolution and makes himself or herself available to assist in that process.

The use of the prevailing attorney-client relationship by criminal defense lawyers is often morally obscene. Since the ethical rules governing lawyers constrain the type of defense lawyers can put on when they know their client will perjure himself or herself, all criminal defense lawyers are taught from the first year of law school on to subtly or openly discourage their clients from acknowledging their own guilt. They are taught to want to learn only enough to mount the best defense in light of the State's evidence or to negotiate the best plea bargain. Since as many as 90 percent of a defense lawyer's clients are guilty, this means that the practice of justice is often directly correlated to collusion with lying. This inevitably fosters a moral cynicism that may already deeply affect the client's being and, from my experience, also gradually has a spiritually deadening effect on the lawyer.

Therefore, the first thing I would want to know if I were representing a battered woman charged with killing her husband is not whether incriminating evidence seized by the police could be kept out of evidence by use of the exclusionary rule, but whether she actually committed the killing. Certainly, if I believed she did kill her husband, I would only be reinforcing the amoral individualism of the existing legal culture if my first act were to seek to exclude the evidence that formed the basis of my belief. Instead, I would seek to have a profound encounter with my client that revealed to both of us the tragedy and violence of their relationship and, if she did kill her husband, the awesome nature of that act even if it was a response to her own suffering at his hands. True justice in these circumstances calls for a public telling of this story and a public acknowledgment and a public taking of responsibility by the defendant for what she did. Then I would seek to defend her on the grounds that her act was justified, or understandable if not entirely justified, depending on a moral consensus that she and I sought to arrive at together.

The exclusionary rule has nothing to do with restorative justice of this kind that is based on the truth of what occurred. Although this rule is sometimes justified by the idea that the State should not be able to convict someone with evidence that is "tainted" because of how it was obtained, the rule is primarily intended to discourage police from raiding the homes of innocent people without a warrant by prohibiting the use of even incriminating evidence seized in this manner. In the good society toward which we are aiming, in which only conduct that ought to be criminalized were criminalized and in which police were no longer the inheritors of a paramilitary and patriarchal history, the exclusionary rule would make little sense because it seeks to correct one injustice—improper police conduct—by arguably facilitating another—restricting access to the truth of an entirely different event. In your hypothetical case, its use would serve to deny the client the opportunity to be vindicated for what she actually did by pretending that she did not do it.

However, we do not yet live in the good society toward which we are aiming, and this brings me to an essential point about the nature of the spiritual struggle within existing legal culture that I am arguing for. The point is raised very powerfully by the presence of the death penalty in your hypothetical case. It is also raised by the reality of the influence of class and race on crime, by the inhumanity of the present prison system, by the irrational criminalization and sentencing practices associated with drugs, and many other structural injustices that distort the cultural reality of the criminal law.

That point is that the effort to transform legal practice into a spiritual and activist calling, to see it as an important means of healing the misrecognition of one another underlying so much social conflict, is a morally and politically complex one. At the political level, it requires building a movement of lawyers who reject the spiritual insensitivity of current legal processes like the adversary system itself and who make their presence felt in organizations like the state bar associations, the American Bar Association, and the American Association of Law Schools. At the moral level, it requires making difficult decisions all the time that take account of the realities of the existing system—a process that could well lead a lawyer and a client facing the death penalty, like the battered woman in your case, to use the exclusionary rule to keep out evidence of a killing the client did in fact commit. By the same token, if the parties were reversed and the evidence led the lawyer to believe that the batterer had probably killed his wife—which may have been true in the O.J. Simpson case—the moral context may call upon the lawyer to urge his client to acknowledge his act and the suffering it has caused, while seeking some mitigation of the sentence based on compassion for the cultural brutality the defendant himself has suffered (I thought the Simpson case cried out for some discussion of the story of a black man raised in the projects of San Francisco who made it in white society by adopting what the writer Franz Fanon called a white mask, and the effect of this history, if any, on his experience of rejection by his wife). In still a third complex circumstance, if the lawyer has genuine doubt about his client's responsibility for the murder, but knows he was a batterer, I think he should condition his willingness to represent the client on the murder charge on the client's willingness to face the causes of his battering behavior and perhaps apologize to his victims who are still alive. Any lawyer who simply uses the exclusionary rule to gain an acquittal of a known batterer of women who may have brutally murdered his wife—without assuming serious moral responsibility for ameliorating the suffering of the client's past and future victims—is in my opinion behaving unethically because he is denying responsibility for the effects of his own acts as a lawyer. And in the larger sense, his cultural intervention will have contributed to the notion that we are all disconnected individuals without responsibility for each other's fate—the very means by which the existing legal culture contributes to the spiritual crisis of the larger society. To answer your fourth question, it is precisely the problem with the existing legal profession that such conduct is considered ethical and even compulsory. Fortunately, no lawyer is compelled to take a case with important moral consequences if he or she knows existing cultural constraints will force him or her to behave in an immoral manner.

And yet I must also acknowledge the moral complexity of your own position in light of your worthy claim that you never turn down a capital case. If the lawyer does not believe that pressing his client to acknowledge responsibility and seek mitigation in sentencing based on his social and cultural history will succeed, the lawyer may have to support a plea of not guilty and use all available defenses to save his client's life. My point is that even in this circumstance, the lawyer must to the best of his ability assume responsibility for the moral consequences of the acquittal. Confront the client with his battering. Expect reciprocity for your defense of him. Consider what is likely to happen to others if he is freed and try to influence what happens, perhaps by consulting with the client's friends and family (to the extent consistent with the attorney-client privilege). Insist that he seek spiritual and psychological counseling and honestly face his terrible sin.

But however morally complex and sometimes contradictory the lawyer's position is, the point is that the legal profession must transform its very conception of what it means to "represent" someone before a court of justice, which is to say before God (whether you believe in God or not), if the profession is to contribute to healing the world rather than continuing to contribute to harming it. Justice is a spiritual and moral healing of a distortion in human relationships: it can occur only if "representation" means seeking to manifest the client's presence as a spiritual and moral being engaged in meaningful and morally consequential relationships with others, rather than as the isolated and abstract rights-bearing individual that is the hallmark of existing legal culture. This kind of representation requires lawyers themselves to be present to their clients as moral beings rather than as technical "experts in the law" and to develop the capacity for moral empathy required to link each particular case, each "representation," to the creation of a less alienated and more spiritually connected world.

I am certainly not saying that responsibility for this transformation falls uniquely upon criminal defense lawyers, and I fully recognize that there are many who are struggling to embody this kind of caring, ethically committed presence in the often Kafkaesque settings of the lower-level criminal courts throughout the country. I most certainly do not think that these courageous lawyers should abandon traditional rights-based strategies and sacrifice their clients to punitive sentencing schemes and the prison system. For many of these lawyers who have devoted their lives to the cause of the oppressed, I have nothing but admiration.

But if progressive defense lawyers want the criminal justice system to change, they need to join those of us who are in revolt against the moral and spiritual bankruptcy of the entire legal culture that envelops us. That culture is partly constituted by the narrow, individualistic rights-based model that these lawyers are struggling to use for good purposes but that nonetheless both mirrors and helps to create the spiritual fragmentation—the awesome global disconnect—of the entire society. It is this very environment that generates the zeal for retribution and the public thirst for blood criminal lawyers must struggle with every day, and changing that environment requires that we build a movement that rejects the cynical paranoia that characterizes our adversary process and affirms the possibility of a legal culture founded on empathy, compassion, and the capacity to actually see each other in our common humanity. This may take a long time, and its success will depend upon the ability of movements like the Politics of Meaning to introduce a whole new paradigm of spiritual politics into the larger culture. But there are already small steps that suggest the effort is far from impossible—the transformative mediation movement; the efforts of visionary prosecutors like Ronnie Earle, district attorney of Austin, Texas, who has helped create community justice courts that provide the opportunity for nonviolent offenders to be reintegrated into their communities prior to arraignment through a redemptive process of apology and forgiveness; and the beginning efforts of our own politics-of-meaning law task force to introduce these ideas into bar associations and legal education. Against us, we have what is; in favor, we have what everyone is longing for, however invisible this longing sometimes appears to be.

PART FIVE

SHORT ESSAYS ON THE NATURE OF MOVEMENTS, THE MEDIA, AND FOREIGN RELATIONS

T HIS LAST SECTION OF DESCRIPTIVE ESSAYS CONSISTS of a series of short takes that are intentionally miscellaneous in character. Their miscellany is meant to show that a politics-of-meaning perspective can be helpful in illuminating any aspect of American society, precisely because the politics of meaning speaks to a fundamental human desire, a social longing present in every aspect of our society.

The first two essays are about the nature of social movements, meaning the nature of all social movements that are liberatory, and the nature of the resistance—the legacy of centuries of alienation—that inhibits their emergence as well as tending to undermine their lasting success. Taken together, they offer a simple and short summary of some of my central ideas that have been presented in heavier philosophical form at various points elsewhere in the book.

The next two essays are snapshots of the core of "media consciousness," that cynical and frightened voice that emerges as the "media-tor" of what I have been calling "the circle of collective denial." My aim here is to show how two prototypical manifestations of media consciousness—the television commercial and journalistic coverage of an important political event—serve to cement the false "realness" of the alienated world by "mediating" this alienation across the culture and reinforcing it as a cultural norm. "The Meaning of a Maalox Commercial" shows how actors, technicians, directors, and the executives who employ them unconsciously collude, in the making of an ordinary antacid commercial, to disconnect us from our desire for authentic social connection by representing the "whole world" in a way that denies that this desire even exists. The essay that follows on the media's coverage of the 1988 Democratic Party convention reveals the fearful core at the heart of journalistic cynicism and the self-protective detachment through which the journalist forms a perverse "savvy alliance" with the viewer, an alliance intended unconsciously to prevent spiritual authenticity from gaining a foothold in public space.

The final two essays in this section point toward what a politics-of-meaning approach to foreign policy should look like. "Left Meets East," an account of a trip I took with a group of progressive lawyers to Eastern Europe shortly after the revolutions, reveals the necessity of interacting across national and cultural boundaries in ways that thaw out nationalist and ideological stereotypes. "Looking at the Gulf War before It Began," a speech that I gave at a teach-in before the Gulf War, illustrates a healing-based approach to foreign policy that is a prerequisite to successfully dissolving our paranoiac attachments to these stereotypes and the sense of pseudocommunity they offer us. The breakfast diplomacy among Norwegians, Israelis, and Palestinians that made possible the Oslo Peace Accords in 1995 are a perfect illustration of how the politics-of-meaning foreign policy I described in the Gulf War speech can succeed in creating an experience of mutual recognition that contrasts sharply with traditional diplomacy, with its formal and distant delegations with attachments to hardened nationalistic allegiances negotiating repeatedly over the shape of negotiating tables. Here again, the distinctive point about a politics-of-meaning approach is to imagine new kinds of intervention capable of thawing out the delusional attachment to nationalistic pseudocommunities, both positive (the "good us") and negative (the "bad them"), that impede the capacity for empathy that is indispensable to achievement of the authentic mutual recognition that these delusional attachments are precisely a defense against.

The recent war in Kosovo has again demonstrated the necessity for such a new kind of foreign policy, one that recognizes the necessity of using force in some intractable situations to stop immediate genocidal brutality, but that also emphasizes public manifestations of empathy and compassion that alone can undermine the terror of the other that pathological nationalism is based upon. Ultimately, the United Nations itself must aspire to a new spiritual understanding of its mission and tactics, a mission informed less by the goal of rationalistic international cooperation among self-interested nation-states and more by the effort to foster a transnational reaching out across all national boundaries and identities that can heal the alienated origins of pathological nationalism itself. To this end it has been Doctors Without Borders and other nongovernmental groups working outside the nation-state, interest-based paradigm that have begun to show us the way.

WHAT MOVES IN A MOVEMENT?

EVERY MORNING, EVERY ONE OF US WAKES UP with the desire to overcome our isolation and connect with others in a meaningful, life-giving, passionate way. We long for the sense of confirmation and validation that can come only from participation in real community. As we peer out at the day in front of us, however, we feel compelled to suppress this desire, to actually forget about it as best we can, because we have become resigned to the fact that no one else seems to want what each of us wants.

Having grown accustomed to a life deadened by bureaucratic work and family routines, to passing people on the street whose blank gazes seem to indicate an inner absence, we each internalize the sense that in order to feel part of what little community there is in the world we must deny our deepest needs and adjust to things as they are. And so we don our various social masks and become "one of the others," in part by keeping others at the same distance we believe they are keeping us. In this way, social reality takes the form of a "circle of collective denial" through which each of us becomes both agent and victim of an infinitely rotating system of social alienation. Trapped in this alienation, people in the West are often unable to imagine themselves acting to change things, no matter how deeply they may desire a different kind of world.

Whatever the cultural context in which they arise, social movements are in significant part attempts to overcome this circle of denial, to replace alienation and distance with connection and solidarity. The very idea of "movement" suggests this, since no one physically moves anywhere. What "moves" is social desire itself, as it partially breaks free of the denial that has enveloped it. People "take to the streets" with a new feeling of mutual empowerment and possibility, instead of consigning each other to the sidewalk where they (we) feel weighted down by a world that seems to be going on outside us—an illusion that results from our collective feeling of powerlessness and passivity.

But it is very difficult for a social movement to "arise," for reasons that go beyond the mere power of everyday roles and routines per se. To understand why there is no true social movement in the United States today, we must understand both the elaborate social mechanisms we have set up to prevent us from fully recognizing and confirming each other, and the psychological scars—dating from our earliest childhood—that undermine our ability and even our motivation to do so.

Human beings have many sophisticated methods of containing social desire in order to maintain the status quo. One of these is to shape the world into hierarchies. We are shaped by hierarchical pictures of the world to the extent that we believe that our self-worth depends on the approval of a "higher authority" and to the extent that we come to feel that our sense of social well-being and inclusion is satisfied by deference to that authority. The prevalence of hierarchies in our workplaces, schools, and families leads us to develop a virtually erotic attachment to all cultural images of authority beginning in childhood.

A second such social mechanism is the media. One result of the isolation engendered by the circle of collective denial is an overwhelming longing to be seen for who we really are—and, concomitantly, an immense rage at rarely, if ever, being able to achieve this recognition. Television, videos, the Internet, and even multiple editions of afternoon papers like the *New York Post* help people to tolerate these emotions by satisfying their volatile repressed feelings in an imaginary way. In watching TV, we can remain withdrawn (as "watchers") and at the same time experience some emotional relief through fantasy by identifying with the images of both social connection and violence that pervade the soaps, real-life crime shows, and even the news. The mass media thus becomes an aspect of social reality that we have created in order not to feel the threatening need to act on our desire for change.

It is remarkable to see the lengths to which we have gone to ward off the contact with reality that might come from true connection with one another. Everything from the majestic symbolisms of The Law and "organized religion" to the micro-messages transmitted by billboards and cereal boxes ("*TOTAL* brings you these words from the Founding Fathers") works to protect us from the contact we both desire and fear.

If these dynamics were simply imposed upon us from the outside—if it was all something that "they" were doing to "us"—we could rightly expect to find many more ways in which people would be consciously engaged in resisting the isolating effects of these dynamics. But the truth is that we all bear psychological scars—from our very first encounters with other people—that interfere with our motivation to emerge from the dreamy pain of our isolating routines.

Families are rarely pockets of social movement, and parents—themselves conditioned within the circle of collective denial—are rarely capable of fully reciprocating the desire for empowering confirmation that emanates from the soul of every newborn child. So they inevitably transmit to us a sense of self that has a small hole in it, a hole that exerts a drag upon our capacity for building a more meaningful social world.

Before we speak our first words, we come to sense that in order to remain "with" these others who are the first to hold us and shape us by their sight, we must accept the boundaries of what is possible. This notion of the "possible" is communicated to us through the sense of loss and compromise that others have come to feel. And as we grow up, we become partly addicted to the poignancy and depression that accompanies this memory of loss, because these painful emotions allow us continually to relive our initial bond with our parents in the face of a world that seems to offer us little possibility of a deeper and more fulfilling form of community. The paradox is that these early attachments tend to reinforce the circle of collective denial and thus make it difficult for such a community to come into being.

Unless new social movements find a way of addressing the psychological and social dynamics that inhibit us from developing a confidence in each other more powerful than our dependency on the status quo, any political activity is likely to fail, even if in the process it is successful in bringing about important economic or political reforms. That is why we need to stop thinking of social change simply in terms of fighting for more economic benefits or more legal rights, and focus instead on developing new forms of activism that can overcome the doubt in our own hearts.

Sustaining What Moves in a Movement

The Politics of Meaning as Embodied Connection

We are all animated by a desire for social connection. A desire for mutual recognition. A desire to be confirmed by one another and validated by one another in our being. It's an embodiment that we seek of feeling whole where we feel partial and small, of feeling strong, validated, and seen by others in a life-giving and empowering way.

In the world that we live in, that desire for social confirmation or social connectedness is systematically denied. Instead, our experience is dominated by an experience of alienation. By virtue of not being fundamentally recognized in our full humanity, we find ourselves split into outer and inner selves. The outer self is shaped by the artificiality of the role performances that we all feel compelled to engage in, and that we feel surround us and isolate us. Within we feel a smallness, as though we were an inner core peering out against this apparently infinitely expanded alienated facade.

This phenomenon of alienation is the central *social* basis for our struggle to transform the world. Of course, hunger, shelter, and the need for fundamental material safety are central elements in that struggle. But to the extent that previous movements have been successful in mobilizing people around economic issues, they have done so in part because they have also spoken to people's need for solidarity; for workplace democracy; for personal power that comes through being experienced as equal by others, and the experience of being validated by others in one's political activity. That's what a movement actually is because, of course, it doesn't actually move anywhere—except down the street, if you're demonstrating.

A movement is a movement of being, in which the passive, fragile part of us that is normally underrecognized, unconfirmed, turns into a powerful force because it begins to feel the possibility of real recognition, and very suddenly—if you think of the few years that the sixties actually were—very conservative environments can be transformed. We assent to the notion that the world can be radically changed, and we discover within ourselves and within one another capacities for love, happiness, playfulness, fun, and a radical spirit enlivening everything in ways that seem virtually unimaginable at the times of our life when we are dispirited and withdrawn, when the alienated facade seems to extend everywhere and we ebb away from each other, peering out from isolated plateaus at a world that seems immune to change. At those times, we feel ourselves "going through the motions," which is the very opposite of social movement.

The politics of meaning seeks to speak to that desire for social connectedness and confirmation by creating a culture of meaning and purpose through which each of us can have the experience of being recognized and confirmed. But this means whatever we create must actually *embody* the connection rather than simply talk about it in utopian terms. It is not enough to say that the politics of meaning is about "values" because values suggest too much that we are talking about verbal formulas—like saying we are against individualism and for caring for others, for example. We do support this shift in values, but a politics of meaning must also be linked to an embodiment of the experience of confirmation that I'm speaking of, or the words are cut off from the underlying reality in being.

The struggle, in other words, is to develop an alternative to the alienated processes that I was describing, so that where people experienced emptiness and distance they can now experience fullness and presence to one another.

When people believe that in order to feel recognized or confirmed by others they must adopt an outer self that's kind of a half-second behind, like the newscaster on television, then what occurs is a splitting between the artificial outer self and the underconfirmed or invalidated inner self. Because they lack anchorage in connection to others, many people develop a dependency on external authority and seek the recognition of someone higher who has "more" in order to feel worthwhile themselves. The lack that is experienced inside is compensated for in an unsuccessful way by an attempt to inflate one's image in the presence of an external authority.

Sometimes this self-inflation is called narcissistic self-grandiosity. But its roots are in our desperate attempt to compensate for the pain of nonrecognition and to compensate for the emotional falsity of daily life. The only way to counter these dynamics is to build a movement like ours, among Jews and non-Jews who are trying to move forward behind the evocation of the politics of meaning, and connect that up to our previous experiences of validation and insight.

In order to develop this kind of movement, we need an experience of social connection. We need to discover ways of being together that break the artificiality of the distinctions in our own lives between the isolated family unit where intimacy can become too much a mere refuge from work based on functional behavior that feels largely like meaningless routines, and larger friendship circles and communities. The only way to challenge this dichotomy is to be part of groups that slowly, over time, develop our capacity to mutually confirm each other in wider and wider circles. The rituals of Judaism are one way—a religious way—of trying to widen this experience of connection. Including close friends in lifetime financial planning is another way—a secular way—of spreading confirmation beyond isolated family units; it can reduce reliance on individualistic pensions and widen the community of those to whom we feel indispensable.

I am the president of a college in San Francisco. I regularly get mail advocating "Total Quality Management," or TQM, and it often uses the kind of language that I sometimes hear coming from communitarians and from the Clinton administration. But it uses this language in the service of more efficient management, not in the service of deepening human connection. If you watched C-Span when Vice President Gore met with employees in the federal government to talk about improving how the bureaucracy works, there was a strongly hierarchical and deferential quality to that supposedly caring group process meeting that was taking place. Rather than conveying an experience of mutual solidarity and validation, the meeting conveyed an artificial informality and friendliness that can simply be a means of masking the alienation of capitalist culture with a façade of community.

Quality circles are another example of the development within the workplace of new forms of worker cooperation that challenge the old assembly-line, atomized, hyperindividualistic model in favor of people performing tasks together. There are possibilities in quality circles for building a true politics of meaning and for figuring out how to make that a basis for workplace organizing and expanding the power of unions to include more issues than the bread-and-butter issues that unions have typically focused on. But there are also possibilities for greater manipulation of workers without giving them greater power, opportunity to actualize their deepest capacities, or occasion for real connection and mutual recognition with others. So the language of a politics of meaning could be co-opted to a new, psychologically oriented mode of control at the workplace, leading to the institutionalization of new forms of hierarchy—a more humane version of the alienated and empty capitalist process that I criticized earlier.

Consider Bill Clinton's labor policy and its promise of retraining workers to work at computer terminals. The Clinton plan doesn't address the loss of meaning that workers have had to face through the disintegration of crafts that were characteristic of much traditional blue-collar work. Retraining is done without regard to the kind of work that will be offered—as long as people can fit into the job market. The argument for getting people off welfare, the challenge to the traditional liberalism of welfare and the emphasis on people's responsibilities to the community, while having a positive element of truth, may also become a new form of caring that actually is oppressive and seeks to integrate people within the alienated system rather than seeking to transform that system. So a politics-of-meaning approach must critique this manipulation of language and always focus on the nature of the experience being offered to people, and to what extent it provides possibilities for real human connection. At the moment, gang membership offers a greater sense of embodied connection and social meaning and purpose than does President Clinton's call for us to roll up our sleeves and retrain ourselves to operate high-tech machines so that we can, as he so often says, "compete and win in the world market."

The task of a politics of meaning is to build forms of social connectedness that would enhance empowerment, mutual confirmation, and recognition, thus helping rid us of the split between the false outer self and the weak, impoverished, underconfirmed or underrecognized inner self—so that people can become present to each other as equals. That's a radical politics of meaning. It has, in my opinion, strong correspondences with the radical aspect of socialist movements of the last two hundred years.

To emphasize this goal doesn't require that we reject Clinton's qualities of openness, the sense of genuine caring that I believe characterizes aspects of his administration. But it does mean keeping our eye on the ball and figuring out how we, not they, are going to develop communities of meaning and purpose that are actual embodiments of the connection we seek rather than being mere verbal advocates for that connection. As a verbal phrase, "the politics of meaning" is a mere abstraction that can be manipulated to mean almost anything, even its opposite—as Shakespeare put it in words that history has repeatedly proven true, "The devil can cite Scripture for his purpose." Only actual embodiments can transmit felt confidence, teach by example, and spread from group to group in a way that can sustain our movement's initial inspiration.

MEDIA CONSCIOUSNESS (I)

The Meaning of a Maalox™ Commercial

AS HOSPITAL TECHNICIANS PUSHING CARTS full of medicine quickly move past each other with a clear sense of purpose and commitment on the busy first floor of a high-tech American hospital, a well-dressed young woman sweeps into view of the moving camera from screen right. The techs acknowledge her superior presence with deferential nods and smiles as they make way for the woman, whose clipboard, badge, and smart-looking suit identify her as in some way in charge—perhaps an administrator or a professional expert hired by the hospital to make sure that things are working at peak efficiency. As she sweeps through a door marked "Pharmacy" with her heels clicking on the metallic floor, moving past other technicians rapidly filling vials and important prescriptions, she turns to us and tells us what we now already know: "In hospital pharmacies, they work fast. They dispense medicines that work fast." And then she tells us what we don't yet know: "For heartburn, that means one-minute Maalox."

As the woman opens the glass door of a refrigerated case to remove one of what appear to be hundreds of bottles of Maalox, we cut to the familiar graphic of two side-by-side stomachs, each upset, half-filled with stirred-up liquid. As we watch a white fluid flow down the esophagi and into the stomachs, the woman's firm voice reminds us (for we already know this) that Maalox quickly and completely calms the stomach on the right while the competing substance is hardly noticed by the stomach on the left. As the fifteen-second clip comes to an end, we see her emerge with continuing confidence out of the pharmacy door, past the efficient technicians moving to and fro with their carts, and right up to the camera, where she looks us right in the eye. "Hospital pharmacies count on the speed of one-minute Maalox," she says with the authority of one who has made it in today's world by knowing all about hospital pharmacies, and she concludes, "Shouldn't you?"

In one sense this commercial is designed to get us to buy Maalox. But that is not its meaning. Its meaning is something like this: Contrary to the preverbal desire you feel at every moment that you want to break through the pain of your isolation, break through the somehow artificial and unreal surface of reality and connect with others in a vital, passionate, spontaneous, joyful way, you must learn that the world really does correspond to this artificial, role-playing surface, and it is your desire to break through that is unreal, your private problem that you need to somehow get over. So stop hoping, viewer, because your hope threatens the rest of us with a horrible rejection by eliciting our hope, our desire for exactly what you desire.

And who is this "us" that is threatened? It is the entire society talking to itself through the "media."

It is true that the media bosses and the Maalox management and their advertising agency are the ones who actually make this particular commercial—their special interest in this commercial is that they want to keep making more money so they can postpone, as long as possible (hopefully until they're dead), having to rely on the goodwill and love of others to take care of their material needs (for food, shelter, protection from bodily illness). This is the true, fearful social meaning behind the profit motive—it's got nothing to do with the so-called economic system, which is only the collective form that this fear takes. But behind this special interest that motivates those who finance and project the commercial through our television sets, we have the deeper reality of society talking to itself. We could say that the fear of the makers of the commercial "capitalizes" on the fear of all of us, helping us to protect ourselves against the pulsion of that preverbal, kinesthetic desire for love and authentic recognition that is our only salvation. Thus, "capitalism."

The Maalox commercial works on us by removing the presence of desire from the depiction of something purporting to be a real experience. This purported "real experience"—a highly competent professional woman overseeing dedicated medical technicians in a busy hospital pharmacy—in turn refers outward to the whole world. What we see is not just the depiction of a discrete or isolated event, but an event we as viewers experience as an instance of the totality, a few frames of a whole movie. That biped with hair and cloth covering is self-announcing as a "successful woman professional" and thus carries with her the entire professional world of which such women are a part and in which they are at last making their presence felt. The dedicated technicians had childhoods, have families, and buy groceries, as do all the doctors they implicitly work for and all the patients they implicitly serve. The commercial would not make an ounce of sense but for the fact that we instantly already know how this scene fits into the whole world. And therefore, by removing the presence of desire from its depiction of what purports to be a real experience, the commercial is also able to convey, in a mere fifteen seconds, that this desire does not really exist in the entire "real world" within which the depicted hospital pharmacy experience is occurring.

Commercials, in other words, transmit the artificiality of everyday life as though it were indeed as real as our alienating conditioning forces us to pretend that it is. In a true interaction with the woman professional who emerges from the pharmacy with her Maalox bottle and looks us straight in the eyes and says, "Shouldn't you?", our experience would be quite different. If we could leap from being "viewers" trapped in detachment watching this canned pseudo-event, if we could leap through the television screen and actually encounter the woman as she comes out of the pharmacy, we would have a very different experience from that portrayed in the commercial. The experience would be pervaded by contingency, meaning that the woman's attempt to play her highly competent professional-expert role would be somewhat awkward, somewhat undermined by her spontaneous desire to connect with you or me in a relation of true presence to each other, and we would feel her somewhat self-important and hyperconfident professionalism as an artificial attempt to deny us access to the presence she really is. The encounter would be ambiguous and would have an ambiguous outcome—she might stumble in the performance of that self-protective role; she'd probably have to avert her eyes to avoid the direct gaze that could reveal the artificiality of her allegiance to the images of her corporate hospital culture. If we could leap through the screen, we would be there as real others pulling for real recognition and contact, rather than being detached observers on the other side of a screen that protects her from our gaze, a screen that seals her off from our ontological presence and the pull of desire that always constitutes that presence.

The fascinating thing is that the transmission of the commercial's meaning—its attempt to convince us that we are in fact detached observers of an artificial role-spectacle rotating outside us that we are powerless to affect—is accomplished by the intense concerted effort of actors, technicians, directors, prop managers, film editors, the entire production crew. Many takes may be required to eliminate all vestiges of the human being behind the actor's persona. The cameramen and women will work with great intensity with the director, and later the director will do the same with the film editor, to present the bustle of the hospital, or the woman's delivery of her professional advice, as a flawlessly constructed and thus impenetrable artificial reality. Unlike authentic artistic performances that try to dramatize and reveal the underlying human reality beneath the culture's surface, and that utilize the same practical ensemble of actors, directors, and technical staff to manifest the contingency and poignancy of the struggle to liberate desire from the alienated constraints we have entrapped ourselves in, the commercial aims to utilize that ensemble's talents to "reify" the alienated surface itself, to claim at a meta-level that there is no human reality behind it. Everyone involved in making the Maalox commercial understands that they do not want a great actress playing that hyperconfident woman professional; what's needed is someone who can be at one with the artificiality of the role, a graduate not of the Actors Studio but of *Invasion of the Body Snatchers.*

Does this mean that the actual actress, who plays the part because she needs the job, and the rest of the crew as well are somehow culpable co-conspirators on the side of alienation, working to seal us in our detachment and isolation and reinforce the denial of our desire for authentic community? It does—but only in the sense that the entire structure of the media is an alienated conspiracy of society talking to itself, as we try to convince ourselves that we do not desire the authenticity of mutual recognition and presence that in fact we most long for.

What keeps this vast, alienated wheel turning is the collective fear that the revelation of this common longing would be met with cynical rejection and lead to a devastating humiliation. By vigilantly keeping the wheel in spin, we evade becoming present to each other—the only route to salvation—because the transparency required for such a becoming present requires a deep trust of the very other we've learned to perceive as a mortal threat. Paradoxically, it is the wheel, the continual evasion, that keeps creating the expectation of humiliation that it supposedly means to protect us from. The warning that we are the source of each other's annihilation is exactly what the wheel of alienated images intends to transmit.

That's why we need Maalox.

MEDIA CONSCIOUSNESS (II)

Press Cynicism as Revealed by Coverage of a Political Convention

IT IS A MISTAKE TO THINK OF THE MEDIA as an "entity" of some kind because it is really a form of consciousness, a way of looking at reality, embodied in tens of thousands of media practitioners and millions of readers or viewers—"the audience." Spending several days covering the 1988 Democratic convention in Atlanta for *Tikkun* helped me to grasp the nature of media consciousness as I never had before.

The physical setup of the convention was a graphic representation of a deeper reality. There was the Omni, the building in which the convention actually took place. Almost surrounding the Omni was a huge complex, the Georgia World Congress Center (GWCC), in which ten to fifteen thousand media people, many times the number who were actual political actors in the Omni, assembled to observe and report on the events in the Omni.

The consciousness in the GWCC was one of constant observation. There were no visible discussions among the thousands of media people about their own relationship to the outcome of anything happening at the convention.

Such discussions would have seemed to be "inappropriate": members of the media were there as observers.

This observer mentality is the central characteristic of media consciousness. It enables people in the media to experience, in a voyeuristic way, being part of a political community and yet, at the same time, to insulate themselves from the risk that normally comes with being part of such a community.

Underlying media consciousness, then, is a destructive compromise between two conflicting impulses: both the desire to be and the fear of being connected to a community. The compromise is to watch it—with all the excitement that "watching it" implies—in a voyeuristic way.

This inner struggle leads to the negative tone that we hear from many members of the media, as well as the posturing and grandiose speech-making characteristic of politicians. Journalists are profoundly affected by the excitement that they experience safely outside themselves. They are both attracted to the political actors, seeing in them the locus of meaning that they want, and contemptuous of them because of the journalists' own pain and anger at being isolated from a community of meaning. Their "role" as journalists makes this split legitimate because it "officially" tells them that it is appropriate for them to insulate themselves from their own desire, and it legitimates their unwillingness to take the risks that being part of the political community would require.

As a result, journalists inevitably are hostile toward the very things that they adore. For me, this point was clearest in much of the press's reaction to Jesse Jackson's powerful, moving address. Several commentators distanced themselves from their feelings, suggesting that Jackson's speech would alienate a lot of whites. The degree of passion and emotional pull that Jackson actually communicated threatened and almost contradicted the smooth defensive neutrality of the official commentators, leading them angrily to reject their own longing that was elicited by the speech.

At the same time, the insistence on distance, the denial that something could have personal meaning is happening, makes members of the press most responsive to the politician who acts as a "public figure" rather than as a human being. This message, subtly but constantly conveyed to political actors, encourages the dominant form of political speech: a bombastic and silly exercise in words that emphasizes the distance between the speaker and the listener.

The absurdity of such speech making was vivid in Atlanta. The speakers orated as if they were addressing "mankind" about the "great issues of the day." In reality, however, many of the speeches were not televised and most of the people in the Omni coliseum were not listening anyway—engaged instead in endless conversations and interviews with the media. The content of the speeches was defined by the "public" or media-oriented nature of the reality: no one would have dared say something like, "Look, folks, we are faced with the problem of Lloyd Bentsen's not really being what most of us wanted or liked, but on the other hand he might bring in Texas, so it's probably worth [or, someone else might have said, not worth] taking this move." Nobody could talk *to* anyone else because everyone was directing their speeches toward a media that required a level of bombast and distance—which, in turn, made almost all the speeches incredibly boring and irrelevant.

The distancing function of the media reflects a type of social consciousness that most of us share—ambivalence about genuine committed action. The way that the media presents reality is relieving to us because it allows us to remain cynically detached, protected from our deeper desires for connectedness as well as from our fears of being disappointed were we to let those desires guide our conduct.

Ironically, though, we resent the media for precisely the same reason that we appreciate it. The media breaks down community and discourages passionate involvement. On some level of consciousness, most of us know that the media helps to create a world that we really don't want. This hostility toward the media is what Spiro Agnew, in the early seventies, and Ronald Reagan, in the eighties, were able to appeal to when they engaged in media bashing. Yet the American people, though attracted by this attack, would not let it go too far, knowing simultaneously that precisely what angers them about the media also protects them from their own all-too-scary desires.

The split described here helps to account for the schizoid nature of the convention and the election campaign. There exist two versions of reality—the media version, on the one hand, and the real convention or real election with politically significant meetings, exchanges of ideas, even changes in emotions undetectable by polls, on the other. If members of the media hope ever to capture this other reality, they can do so only by overcoming media consciousness and recognizing that they are real people with a great deal at stake in the outcome of political affairs. Journalists must be morally alive and emotionally connected human beings; otherwise their neutrality mirrors and reinforces the isolation of the reader or viewer.

But you, the reader of this essay, can help in the process of undermining the media consciousness I describe. You can talk with your friends and coworkers about the issues and about how they are being "framed" by the media. You can invite people over to watch and discuss the debates and news coverage. And you can become actively involved in supporting positions, candidates, and political movements that seem to articulate your own views. Most important, you (we) can overcome the tendency to be observers, resisting the inner voices that push for caution, self-protection, and cynicism.

Our political activity should be directed at creating a climate in which other political candidates can become more real human beings, freed from the detachment and technocratic mentality that has been created in them and to some extent in all of us.

An example of just such a transformation occurred when eventual nominee Michael Dukakis—otherwise known for a woodenness, a not-being-fully-present to the listener, that is in part the result precisely of his unconscious anticipation of the cynicism of the press—gave a powerful, moving, human acceptance speech. To the many of us who feared Dukakis incapable of such passion and authenticity of presence, the acceptance speech was a remarkable moment. That moment happened not, as the media described it, because Dukakis "rose to the occasion," but rather because of the real experiences that he underwent at the convention: he encountered his own constituency and Jackson's constituency in ways that pierced the manipulated media consciousness and his need to pander to it. For a moment, the experts from the Kennedy School of Government and from Georgetown, as well as the media consultants, were no longer able to protect him from the hopes of his constituency, and therefore he was able to be more of who he really is—and we, too, were able to be more of who we really are. If we can support Dukakis and other politicians in making these kinds of breakthroughs, if we can build the kind of confidence among them and among ourselves that makes media consciousness less dominant, there is a greater chance that elections could help recapture the underlying desire for mutual connection, the hidden energy behind our commitment to democracy.

LEFT MEETS EAST

The Necessity of Cross-Cultural Empathy in Foreign Policy as Revealed by an Official Visit to Eastern Europe after the Revolutions

ON MARCH 27, 1990, I RETURNED FROM A SERIES of meetings with Polish and Czech intellectuals and activists who were in the process of rewriting their countries' constitutions. Their aim had been to create, more or less from scratch, political and legal systems that would enable them to realize the democratic aspirations of their revolutions. I was invited to be an "interlocutor" in this process, along with nine other law professors and lawyers associated with the Critical Legal Studies (CLS) movement in the United States.

CLS is an influential left-wing movement of legal thought in this country, but it is completely opposed to the conventional Marxist notion that "bourgeois law" is simply a tool used by ruling elites in capitalist countries to maintain their own power. CLS rejects the whole idea that law is a "tool" at all. Instead, it conceives of law as a culture—a fabric of ideas, images, and rituals that helps to sustain a genuine cultural commitment to democracy *and,* at the same time, serves to subvert these very ideals by justifying the alienated reality of contemporary American life in their name. In the American context, CLS has been critical of legal strategies for achieving social change based exclusively on the pursuit of rights. It has analyzed the ways in which supporters of the status quo have been able to associate the psychic power of authoritarian symbols such as robed judges or "the will of the Founding Fathers" with the manipulable logic of legal reasoning—so as to grant social movements new rights and yet simultaneously drain these rights of their potentially transformative meaning. Not only does this process limit the degree of real change produced by legal victories; it also tends to warp the movement's perception of its own aims, gradually undermining its initial profound ethical and evocative appeal and replacing it with sterile rights debates among warring interest groups, debates that often have little to do with what moved people to take political action in the first place.

I think it is partly for this reason, for example, that many labor unions today retain little political meaning even for their own members—after fifty years of labor laws for which so many workers in the twenties and thirties gave their lives, many unions have come to be seen as impersonal entities fighting over wage levels and benefit packages rather than as visionary associations of human beings striving for workplace democracy and self-realization through cooperative activity. The long struggle to improve the economic condition of working people has of course been extremely important, but the inherent justice of these economic demands was originally linked to a political vision of true social equality. That vision, at least in part, shaped the original effort of the workers to gain the right to form unions and engage in various forms of collective action. Writers associated with CLS have argued that the dissolution of the labor movement's political appeal has in part resulted from decades of labor-law interpretation that has deradicalized the goals of the movement and disassociated its economic demands from their original transformative political foundations.

The message of CLS is therefore not that social movements shouldn't struggle for rights, but that they should do so in a way that carries into the legal arena the authentic ethical and social meaning that they want these rights to impart. This requires the creation of a new kind of progressive lawyer who is less a technician using law as a "tool" to help the less powerful, than an ethical advocate capable of challenging the symbolic and discursive terrain that limits the vision of existing liberal legal culture.

Traveling to Eastern Europe with this perspective placed us in an odd position. We were leftists armed with a critique of rights going to talk with people who had heroically overthrown leftist regimes in order to win rights that we have always had. Although our critique applied with equal force to the kind of socialist law that had utterly corrupted the meaning of socialist ideals and subjected the Poles and the Czechs to forty years of brutal repression, we knew that we would be looked upon with some skepticism and that we would have to work hard to convince our hosts that we were all on the same side. Our expectations were borne out by our Polish sponsor's initial remarks on the night we arrived in Warsaw: "We like to argue with the people on the Left," he said, "but unfortunately there are no leftists remaining in Poland. Therefore, we have invited you."

By the second day of our conference, I felt that perhaps we were getting somewhere when another participant, a Solidarity activist, said that he was relieved by our exchange about rights because "the last thing we need to listen to is a bunch of radical Marxists." Actually, most of us had probably considered ourselves radical Marxists of some kind at various times in our lives, and perhaps some of us still did. But after a few days in Poland we learned that it was easy enough to understand how the ideals of Marxism had become even more repugnant to them than President George Bush's rhapsodic descriptions of the "free market" had become to us.

In fact, I constantly experienced a sense of shock at how miraculously opposite, or mirror image, the assumptions of the people we visited were when compared with our own. Before the revolutions in both Poland and Czechoslovakia, there were state-based women's organizations to support the struggle for women's rights and workers' councils to support the struggle for workers' rights. Basically every goal that we on the Left in America struggled for had been incorporated, though in a distorted form, into the state mechanisms of the Stalinist bureaucracy. And so these goals, for workers' rights or women's rights, had been completely discredited by virtue of having been part of the existing system of domination. When we raised the issue of women's rights, for example, our Czech colleagues informed us that the women's organization in Czechoslovakia occupied the largest palace in Prague. For them the women's movement consisted of this "palace organization" composed entirely of well-paid bureaucrats who did nothing for the people.

Every image that we could put forward that had a progressive connotation came reflected back to us in terms of a phony community legitimizing the bureaucratic state. When we raised the issue of workers' participation, or workers' control, this issue had a similarly negative spin for those who had struggled for freedom: the deputy attorney general and the attorney general of Czecho-slovakia responded by talking about how the workers' councils had been responsible for firing human rights activists around the time of the 1968 revo-lution and the human rights proclamation of 1977. The workers' councils had supported these firings because they were putting out the line of the Commu-nist Party and carrying out discipline within the labor force.

We were equally stunned when women's issues were discussed. Many of us were shocked to find two huge pictures of nude women in the office of the head of the conference, obviously centerfolds from an American magazine. But when one of the women in our group raised the issue, Margaret, a Polish woman who had been profoundly affected by the women's consciousness issues raised earlier by some of the women in our delegation, told us that we simply didn't understand the meaning of those posters in the Polish context. The col-lapse of communism had created an opportunity for people to do outrageous, sexually expressive things, in most cases for the first time. During the Stalinist regime this kind of expression would not have been allowed. This was the explanation for the abundance of *Playboy*-style calendars in all the bookstores in Warsaw and Prague. It represented a symbol of liberation for both women and men in this cultural frame, we were told. Those of us who had seen a simi-lar form of sexual liberation used as a vehicle against the oppressive mores of American society wanted to warn about the potential exploitative and sexist dangers involved; yet we had to acknowledge also that the meaning of the sym-bols needed to be understood in terms of the historical experience of the people we were meeting.

Having always been opposed to the version of socialism that had been put into practice in Eastern Europe—a bureaucratic and Stalinist reality far from the ideals that animated those of us in the New Left—and hence holding no illusions and considerable antagonism toward the communist regimes, it was nonetheless a transformative experience for me to come face to face with those who understood the language and symbols of change that meant so much to us in the West as indicators precisely of the communist bureaucracy we too rejected.

I had gone to Eastern Europe hostile to the language of the "free market-place" that was springing up in Eastern Europe—a language I feared was rooted simply in the naïveté of Eastern European progressives about the dangers of capitalism. But I quickly came to understand that for them the language of the free market was not reducible to economic content alone. Rather, it included a metaphorical meaning that was antistate and anarchist ("we can do what we want without supervision"). For them, the language of the free market represented the opposite of the statism that they had experienced in the past.

There were three economic sociologists in our group, all of whom argued that the importation of markets did not imply, and should not necessarily imply, a particular form of worker organization or labor-management relationship. One argued very strongly that there was nothing inconsistent about trying to develop efficient forms of production in the economy and having some forms of workplace democracy (and worker participation) within the new companies they hoped to start. The Solidarity Movement could, he argued, determine the way foreign capital was brought into the country by developing a theory of its own about the way that it wanted workers' rights and workplace organization to be related to capitalist countries. Further, the movement could develop a theory for its own industry that would allow success in the world market without modeling itself after classic industrial plans of capitalist societies, in which workers perform in largely uncreative, atomized, or divided ways (the classic assembly-line model for work in steel or mining plants). Instead, it could better participate in a postindustrial world by retraining the workforce so that workers could participate in problem-solving modes of worker organization that tend to foster workplace democracy and to reinforce the political aims of Solidarity. This argument was meant to address what we felt was a central problem with the way the Poles were putting forward their own line. Their tremendous desire to open up the country to markets and to foreign capital lacked adequate attention to what the new market systems might do to their own working-class constituency.

Although the Solidarity activists wanted to establish both political rights and social democratic objectives, many felt that Poland was too poor at the moment to afford social democratic entitlements. Therefore, the Poles would have to divide their constitution to include on the one hand political rights based on the Western model and on the other a declaration of intent with respect to future social democratic rights (providing adequate social security, unemployment insurance, worker benefits, health benefits, education, and child care). These, presumably, would be delivered once the society's economic base expanded adequately.

We questioned this division. If you allow market mechanisms to create enormous short-term dislocation and forms of labor-management relations that essentially squeeze the workers for all they're worth in order to generate profits in a factory, you will create a problem we are familiar with in the United States. By the time an economy can afford social rights, it will have produced a political elite so entrenched in the current economic system that it will no longer want to deliver the long-awaited social democratic entitlements. In other words, substituting a capitalist elite for a communist elite may not be the answer.

Moreover, the introduction of uncontrolled market mechanisms, with the likely consequence of dramatic unemployment and escalation of prices, would drive a wedge among intellectuals. Workers would eventually find themselves opposing the very system that they are currently being asked to support as supposedly in their own interests. This could lead either to the Solidarity people being voted out of power or to the creation of a nationalist-based authoritarian regime with some dictatorial dimension.

A third reason we argued for insisting on workers' power at the point of production and various social democratic entitlements is that these things are simply good in themselves. Workplace democracy, for example, is a basic part of the aspirations of our professional group and a basic component of the vision of society we are trying to bring into being.

I was surprised to find that in the discussions about alternative ways to introduce markets, alternatives that might allow for the benefits of efficiency without totally eliminating workers' power at the point of production, there was an undertone to statements by these Polish activists that seemed to be dismissive of the Polish workers. One Solidarity activist summed it up this way: The large masses of our people, through hundreds of years of dependency on feudal governments and now more recently on state communist governments, have learned to rely on the state. They have not developed a sense of individual responsibility or a notion that the individual could be responsible for the outcome of his or her life. You Americans just take that for granted, because you have faced "the fear of death" (as he put it) that is implicit in the workings of the capitalist marketplace, and that has led you to develop a sense of personal responsibility that the large masses of our people don't have. Our people are chronically dependent on the state and therefore have no motivation to work for a living. Leninism has this bullshit ideology about "social man" that is nothing more than a mechanism for maintaining the dependency of the masses on a state bureaucracy, and this blocks the individual's desire for self-determination.

This was quite striking and forced me to recognize the fact that all of us from America, though thinking of ourselves as either democratic socialists or communitarians, took for granted our responsibility for the outcomes of our lives, in part because we felt and had always felt rather isolated and unable to depend on others. It is precisely this aspect of individualism, built into our own personal histories, that has animated us and strengthened our desire to become social activists. We want to build a community that could help us overcome the isolation that we often experience in our lives as this individualism works itself out in destructive dynamics. Yet at the same time, the sweeping nature of the Eastern Europeans' dismissal of the project of building humane communities, the overidentification with their need to foster individualism, blocked our ability to respond. It made little sense for us to explain why it would be important to build emancipatory communities based on genuine reciprocity and genuine social solidarity. This would have sounded so much like Lenin's theory of "social man" that they would have assimilated what we were saying to this deeply hated set of social structures. So, although we felt affiliated, on the same side, every time we neared a discussion of the crucial elements in our vision of humanity there was this dissonance that prevented us from getting any further.

Nevertheless, in both Poland and Czechoslovakia people take for granted a much higher level of social responsibility and social connection than do people in the United States. For example, everyone simply assumes that workers have the right to decent health care and education, to fundamental economic security. These are societies that presuppose in their cultural nature a lot of what ours presupposes in its emphasis on the individual. Thus, even though the people we saw were hostile to the things in which I most deeply believe, they were speaking from the context of a culture that for the most part already takes care of these things. To some extent these countries may already have a built-in cultural resistance to the worse forces of capitalism, and hence they take for granted that they will never allow to happen what *has* happened in the United States, where millions of people are homeless and millions more deprived of basic minimum health care and adequate food.

Yet we argued that if they don't establish a self-conscious cultural plan to resist what is likely to occur when large-scale capitalist companies come into these countries, their residual cultural traditions may not be able to withstand the new pressures. Over the course of the next several decades, we said, they may well face an erosion of the most humane aspects of their society. It seemed to us over and over again in these discussions that many of these Eastern European activists did not have a particularly clear awareness of the interrelationship between the market freedoms they were seeking and the potential erosion of the political rights that they have been fighting for.

I found little indication that people in the social movements understood that the current revolutionary consciousness that animated political life might prove transitory when faced with the passivizing aspects of consumer society. There was at the concrete, cultural level no discussion about how to maintain the solidarity that had enabled the revolution to occur. I understood and of course sympathized with their desire to rebuild their economic life in ways that would alleviate the material hardships people had been forced to endure. Nonetheless, I felt that we had an obligation to alert people to the problems they would face if they mechanically adopted Western economic models without simultaneously trying to learn from the experience of those of us who had lived under them.

I had one really interesting conversation with an architect in Prague, a woman in her mid-thirties, about how McDonald's would conduct a use-permit campaign in Prague to put a McDonald's in the central square under the ancient Czech clock. The Czech version of the McDonald's campaign would send assurances that the appearance of the new structure would conform to the most hallowed traditions of Czech culture. It would play on the appeal of fast food itself as a democratic choice that people might wish to make, and of course it would talk about how the Czech McDonald's would certainly help the economy. It would also warn that failure to allow this enterprise would send a negative signal to others who might be willing to invest in Czechoslovakia (denial of the use permit might convey that there was a bad climate being created for business). That would discourage further investment and create needless unemployment. I told this whole story in a way that she had not heard before. In other words, I tried to make clear to her that the entry of a capitalist enterprise into their local cultural setting was something with which they don't have experience, something that perhaps they hadn't fully thought through, and hence something they might be ill-equipped to fight.

We were, of course, well aware of the potential dangers involved in coming into this situation from abroad. We didn't fully understand the situation, and we were bringing concepts that had been developed in another situation and trying to apply them to Eastern Europe. So, naturally, we approached these discussions with a sense of modesty and a deep respect for the actual experiences of our hosts. On the other hand, they made it clear that they had invited us and wanted to hear from the American Left precisely because we have lived in a society that embodies many of the formal democratic and human rights mechanisms that they valiantly fought for. They wanted to learn from us about some of its pitfalls so that they might benefit from our experience.

What we tried to get across to them was the importance of developing a social reality based on *real* participation, a democratic political culture that could sustain the achievements of the Eastern European revolutions. Although we have democratic forms in the United States, the experience of most people in our society is one of isolation and disconnection from the political process—in part a product of the consequences of the marketplace.

Clearly it is problematic for people who didn't suffer under Stalinism to be criticizing post-revolutionary developments in societies that did experience Stalinist terror and oppression. But real solidarity with our friends in Eastern Europe required that we share our perspective. They didn't have to take our advice, but it would have been wrong for us to keep silent about what we have learned from our own experience.

The notion that we should have restrained our criticism because we were imposing Western experience or Western categories on somebody else's reality, or that it was not for us to criticize the revolutionary choices of the Eastern Europeans, simply resurrects in modern dress the very argument that apologists for the Soviet Union made in defense of Stalinism in the 1930s. While we need to keep in mind that we can't fully understand the situation of our colleagues in Eastern Europe, we also need to watch out for mechanisms that the American Left has fallen into with regard to so many revolutions around the world—namely, to feel that since these other revolutionaries made it and we did not, we should just identify with them as the embodiment of "true" consciousness and admire their achievement, in the process denying what we actually do know about the world.

It's the role of the democratic Left in the West to engage with people of emerging democracies who are in fact inspired by the same positive utopian visions of a democratic society that have animated us in the West—and to try to discuss the potential problems that they will face if they do not engage in efforts to build a democratic culture that goes beyond the institutionalization of periodic elections to a distant parliament that makes laws. A democratic political system is an essential first step. But unless there is equal attention given to nurturing a democratic culture, allowing people to participate in helping to create and shape their own lives, activists in countries undergoing these transformations will eventually witness the erosion of social relatedness, mutuality, and community that gave rise to their movements and allowed people to experience the mutual recognition and confirmation that made this political activity meaningful and fulfilling.

This was a difficult message to convey because in no way did we want to downplay the historic significance of what these revolutions have achieved. Solidarity and Czechoslovakia's Civic Forum still have a remarkable opportunity to create a new kind of nonbureaucratic communitarian civil society. They have collectively engaged in actions that have brought together a community infused with the kind of social connectedness that is a precondition for real democracy. But the peril that these movements still face is that in their legitimate desire to institutionalize democratic forms and hurriedly establish a market economy, they may undermine the social solidarity that inspired their victory over totalitarianism, one of the great transformations of our century.

Our visit—with all its paradoxes and contradictions—revealed with great clarity and also real humor the necessity of being able to put oneself in the place of the other in a cross-cultural encounter of this kind. And this particular cross-cultural encounter was a dialogue among friends who at least wanted to understand each other, however challenging this proved to be when our respective cultural experiences led us to consistently attribute opposing meanings to the same words and ideas. How much more critical it is for a politics-of-meaning foreign policy to find mediative ways of fostering cross-cultural empathy among enemies, whose inclination in light of their history of mistrust is to misunderstand each other and then, often, kill each other on the basis of that misunderstanding.

LOOKING AT THE GULF WAR
BEFORE IT BEGAN

How a Healing-Centered Foreign Policy Might Have Saved
100,000 Iraqi Lives and Spared the Children of American Soldiers
the Continuing Suffering of Birth Defects

I HAVE BEEN IN AT LEAST A DOZEN CONVERSATIONS in which people have tried to talk about Iraq, only to fall, after a few vague attempts at taking a position, into an awkward silence. In part, the silence results from our not really knowing much about the history or meaning of inter-Arab conflicts in the Middle East. But at a deeper level, I sense in myself and almost everyone else a feeling that we just cannot bear to get into an old-style, rationalistic, geopolitical discussion about yet another crazy, dangerous world situation no matter how serious it actually is. For most ordinary people, especially for those of us who think of ourselves as "political," it's slightly embarrassing and even shameful not to want to think about something that could involve the death of thousands of people. For Jews, the situation is even worse, since we know for a fact that Israel and Israelis are facing an extreme and real danger. Yet I believe there is something profoundly right and even hopeful about the paralysis that surrounds this issue.

What is right and hopeful is that many people simply no longer believe that any complex, human situation involving complex cultural and historical distortions in the consciousness of millions of people can be analyzed or solved or even "reached" by thinking about it in *any* of the ways we are familiar with. From military intervention (a lot of people killed; increased fanaticism among Islamic fundamentalists; the "emir" restored to power), to principled nonintervention (Saddam Hussein, poisoner of thirty thousand Kurds in his own country, becomes some kind of hero for standing up for God against Satan; refugees wander around the desert starving to death; Israel finds itself in still graver danger, which in turn strengthens the Israeli Right, increases the severity of the occupation, and drives Palestinians further toward fantasies of a resurgent and violent pan-Arab nationalism), to a long series of other variations that assume there is some discrete set of acts that will produce some discrete set of effects—none of these so-called "options" advanced by rationalistic policy analysts addresses the essential craziness and alienation and distortion in human interrelatedness that is the problem in the first place. I think more and more people are beginning to feel (maybe more women than men, but many men too) that you just can't get there from here and that it's actually better for their own souls and for the world to refuse to participate in Iraq analysis until some new and more emotionally plausible way of thinking comes into being.

My own feeling is that this new way of thinking must be intuitive and aimed at creating cultural change rather than strategic (or "analytical") change and aimed at directly reorganizing power relations. In the case of Iraq and the Middle East generally, this means that we should try to intuitively grasp the directions and intensity of both positive and negative tendencies in world-historical consciousness at this precise moment as these tendencies weigh upon and embody the present crisis. We then need to take practical and symbolic steps that might contain the drift toward craziness and war while accentuating the drift toward sanity and peace. I use the word "drift" to describe these tendencies because they are diffuse and contradictory movements of consciousness that exist both within and across all the cultures implicated in the conflict. They are also drifts in that they move slowly, precisely because they are in contradiction—opposing forces joining in the cultural DNA of each person and rotating, via reciprocal internalization, through small and large groups, through each subculture and (owing to institutions like the United Nations and television) increasingly through the world itself as a single community.

Intervention that takes this form of cultural containment and accentuation cannot proceed by a thought process that engages obsessively with some discrete objective ("Saddam Hussein must withdraw from Kuwait!"). For this kind of instrumental thinking fuses our being to an idea in a way that suppresses our ability to comprehend and alleviate the "stress" produced by the contradictory tendencies I have outlined here. It may be true that Hussein must withdraw from Kuwait, but this objective must, if possible, be achieved by steps designed to "thaw out" rather than intensify the distorted nationalism, ethnic hatred, and religious fanaticism that constitute Hussein's symbolic power. We need to cultivate a way of thinking that is distanced enough to allow us to encompass, through a kind of perpetual double awareness, the contradictory tendencies that shape the meaning of every aspect of the situation in the Middle East, but that still allows us enough direct engagement to intuit action steps that "lean in" to the situation so as to foster the tendency toward sanity and peace.

My sense is that the single most powerful symbolic source of peace consciousness is the patient attitude Mikhail Gorbachev has demonstrated in world politics over what is now a very long period of time. For this reason, I think Michael Lerner is right to call for an immediate acceptance of Gorbachev's proposal for an international conference aimed at resolving the problems of the Middle East as a whole. From the perspective that I have outlined, the principal virtue of immediate acceptance of the Gorbachev proposal is that it would instantly, long before any conference actually takes place, shift world consciousness to a level of reflection on the Middle East that can encompass the contradictory historical forces that have produced the current crisis. Sustaining this level of reflection means comprehending (among other things) the historical reality of colonialism; the partial legitimacy of existing national boundaries irrespective of their origins; the practical reality of the West's dependence on oil from the Persian Gulf, the legitimate need of all the peoples of the Middle East—including Israeli Jews, the Palestinians, and the Arab masses—for a sense of cultural dignity and economic security. In this sense, movement toward an international conference might succeed in disengaging world thought from the dangerous "heat" of such images as violent rocket attacks on Iraqi military installations, the devastation of Israel, the threat of poison gas, the mass murder of American and Iraqi nineteen-year-olds—and Kuwait itself as the mythological location for the latest hallucination of Armageddon, whether the Western version (a secular fantasy based on the protection of "our" interests against the new Hitler) or the Arab version (a religious fantasy of God versus Satan). In addition, by rallying to a true internationalist initiative such as Gorbachev's conference, we would symbolically identify the United Nations with the hope of bringing into being a compassionate, transnational conscience that seeks to confirm and rectify the historical pain felt by all the peoples of the Middle East. This is a very different image of the United Nations from its current one as (at worst) a hopelessly pluralist battleground for every conceivable national interest, and (at best) a potential peacekeeping force that works solely to contain existing international antagonisms.

But to emphasize what is different about the kind of cultural or consciousness-based approach I am proposing, I would say that such a conference should not be proposed jointly by Bush and Gorbachev, nor by the United Nations as such, but rather by Western, Arab, and, ideally, Israeli leaders (most likely leaders of the Labor Party or the Israeli peace movement) who would do so explicitly in Gorbachev's name and follow Gorbachev's lead. A Bush-Gorbachev initiative would reinforce the image of "the superpowers dictating the resolution of inter-Arab affairs," which is precisely an image that must be contained and gradually dissolved. A UN initiative, while it makes symbolic sense in the abstract, would at this point be too disembodied to prevent sectarian squabbles among nation-states over the real, underlying motives of such a conference, and over which representatives would play what role. What is needed is an antiwar, cross-cultural deference to a suggestion made by the person whose presence and perspective have done more to improve the prospect for world peace than virtually any leader of this century. Such a common act of deference, in spite of appearing to "lower" Bush's world status in relation to Gorbachev and to "level" his hierarchical position in relation to Arab leaders or the leaders of the Israeli peace movement, would almost certainly strengthen the moral credibility of the United States, strengthen Gorbachev's antinationalist influence within the USSR, and perhaps provide some opening for the Israeli peace movement to pose an effective moral challenge to the present, seemingly invincible realism of the Israeli Right.

Perhaps this whole approach seems too much like new age utopianism, with its emphasis on trying to link real-world actions to drifts in world consciousness. As of the date of this teach-in [September 30, 1990], my words certainly do not seem relevant to what is actually happening in the Middle East, as "Washington Begins Talking of Early War with Iraq" (to quote today's *San Francisco Chronicle* headline) and Iraq continues to construct poison gas facilities in southern Kuwait. But as you think about what has actually happened if a war does occur, consider the frankly absurd nature of the postmodern cultural diplomacy that went on during August and September. Bush appeared on Iraqi TV; Hussein appeared on American TV; each denounced the other in apocalyptic terms. All this posturing seemed to generate nothing more than increased cookie shipments to young and confused boys in Saudi Arabia on the American side and increasingly frenzied, anti-Satan rallies among the Arab masses on the Iraqi side. Think of how baffled and detached you felt from the entire situation at that time. Bush and Hussein evidently thought that influencing "world consciousness" was very important, judging from the means they used to try to shape public perception of whatever was about to occur. Yet they and other international leaders were incapable of thinking about the situation in the Middle East in a way that might have moved you and millions of other people to try to prevent the violence that you are watching unfold and the long-term suffering that this violence is certain to inflict on countless Iraqi and American families. If the forces of peace and sanity had been able to grasp the situation with true cultural and psychological depth, isn't it possible or even probable that things could have been otherwise? Might not a new way of thinking and intervening right now make such a tragedy less likely and make hope for a slowly developing Middle Eastern *tikkun* more realistic?

PART SIX

How Can We Build a Parallel Universe?

A Practical Prototype

I N ALL THE PREVIOUS ESSAYS, I HAVE BEEN TRYING TO SHOW that understanding and changing our collective life requires a new way of apprehending virtually everything around us. Our conventional ways of seeing reality make the *meaning* of everything invisible to our reflective minds, which then leads us to think and act in ways that cannot move us toward the world we aspire to in our hearts. Because we have been conditioned, through what I have called "the circle of collective denial," to think about society as a kind of "entity" outside our lived experience, as an "It" that we observe cautiously from a distance, we have disabled our reflective minds from illuminating the immediate shared lived experience of social connection that is all that society actually is. Thus in "The Bank Teller" I showed that our common way of thinking about a hierarchy, as if it were a top-down "entity" of some kind, completely misses its imaginary character in which no one is actually above or below anyone else but everyone pretends that everyone is. Apprehending the hierarchy as it really is as a kind of hallucination borne from a living group's conflicted connection is a prerequisite to thinking into reflective visibility what this type of connection (a very, very common one) actually means. And it is only by illuminating the meaning of this pulsing, conflicted "between" (to again use Martin Buber's word for the experiential space where our lived experience of connection actually happens) that we can come to think and then know the true spiritual direction of our efforts to change things.

As we come to see the meaning dimension of everything and move beyond the entity-thinking that analyzes everything as if the world were an "It-whole" made up of "It-parts," we increasingly come to see the necessity of changing all our ideas about politics, about how the world can be transformed. Both the radical idea of revolution and the liberal idea of gradual progressive change through social reforms are vestiges of entity-thinking; each imagines "society" to be an entity outside the living connection of "the between" and so conceives of social change as a kind of external reorganization of the entity. When we come to see society not as an entity but as a lived experience of connection emanating out of each of us and all of us, and when we then work our way through the meaning(s) of this connection as we ourselves experience it and live it, it becomes absurd to think either that we could instantly "fix" the distortions in our connection by revolutionizing power relations as seen from the outside, or that we could gradually do so by discrete and factlike reforms to a "system" that is imagined to exist outside the conflicted intersubjective flow that is all that this "system" is.

What we need instead is a new politics aimed at eliciting and fostering the desire for mutual recognition, that seeks to thaw out the mutual paranoia born of the mutual fear of humiliation by finding sustained ways of both creating and spreading the experience of I and Thou as well as confidence in the reality of this experience. As the gradual vanishing of the sixties and the movements that gave rise to them make clear, the element of confidence in the reality of the disalienating experience and in the becoming-present-to-each-other that is its hallmark is an essential meta-component of sustaining the experience itself, and this confidence depends on spreading a shared reflective understanding of the nature of the alienation that our spirit, our desire, cannot but aspire to overcome. Only by supplementing the experience of disalienation with reflective intuitive and cognitive knowledge of the truth of that very experience can the experience survive the terror of humiliation that inevitably accompanies it—a terror that is both the legacy and the cause of the centuries of alienation that we carry within us and that uses the *claim to reality* of the artificial roles and external personae that envelop us as a defense against our unending desire to transcend this alienating envelopment, this culture of "misrecognition."

Such a politics must be a healing politics that simultaneously knows what it is healing. If it is terror of humiliation that underlies the conspiratorial blockage of our deepest longing for a social experience of transparent presence to the other as reciprocally created in the image of God and as the source of each other's completion, we can only alleviate this terror through efforts imbued with wisdom regarding the complexity of the alientation we are seeking to heal and patience toward the mistakes that will inevitably impede our progress (for as Michael Lerner says, we are all "wounded healers").

What follows in this final section is one such effort, a "Manifesto for a new New College," where I have worked for twenty-five years, that tries to implement the insights in this book in seeking to transform one institution—or as I would prefer to put it, one community. The strategy implicit in this approach is that large-scale change must emerge in something like a cellular fashion, in which practical successes in beginning to create less alienated communities, characterized by a greater degree of mutual recognition, serve as models (or "embodiments") that teach and then spread by example. It is this concentric, horizontal, and initially tentative process of "spreading" that is the appropriate strategy for healing a traumatized culture, for encouraging each other to risk affirming our desire for mutual recognition while gently attending to the fear of humiliation with which that desire is associated. That is the paradox facing a politics of social transformation that sees the overcoming of alienation as the key to our spiritual development as a species and to the consequent realization of our social being.

The particular document that follows is an unedited political document hurled manesfestolike into the middle of an as yet unresolved struggle over the fate of a beautiful workplace community that emerged thirty years ago from the social movements of the sixties. But the ideas in it are relevant not only to the alternative experiments that emerged from the New Left. The core ideas proposed in the Articles of Faith are adaptable to more traditional settings (think, for example, of Article Seven's proposal for an annual day of remembrance for community members and those in their families who have died during the preceding year). Of course it is important to tailor the introduction of these or similar ideas to the preexisting culture of a workplace, but two or more people (remember the structural lesson in "The Bank Teller" about the difficulties confronting one person acting in isolation) can have an effect on even quite traditional workplaces if they have the confidence that the desire existing within themselves to be liberated from the stultifying artificiality of the official system of roles and personae also exists in everyone around them, no matter how much they deny or conceal. This confidence plus intuitive wisdom gained from study and experience regarding the fear that drives our alienation to preserve itself and to marginalize and suppress elicitations of hopeful change, will allow you to find your own best path to potentially successful interventions.

GENERATING MEANING AND CONNECTION IN WORKPLACE CULTURE

The New College Manifesto

Preamble

FOR MANY YEARS, PERHAPS SINCE THE VERY BEGINNING, New College has been trapped between two paradigms. One is the paradigm of a community based on direct personal comradeship among particular people who relate to each other out of affection and informal solidarity. That is the revolutionary New College, the one that sprang up out of the idealism and hope of the sixties and that sought to repudiate the artificiality and robotlike character of the larger market-based society in which people treat each other in a functional, role-based fashion. The other paradigm is that of an organization or "institution," which purports to be on the Left and to be for social change but which is still organized like most other organizations, with a board and a president and people dividing themselves into managers and employees and one or another narrow functional role. This second paradigm should rightly be called the education-and-social-change machine, because it involves conceiving of ourselves as people-machines organized into roles and functions to turn out a product (the graduate of New College who will supposedly work for social change) while not actually engaging in the social change ourselves. Of course, we have done our best to reconcile these two paradigms, so that even when we are in the second paradigm we try to treat each other as humanely as possible. . . . But the fact is that the two paradigms contradict each other and the contradiction paralyzes us from really making our social point. It leads to people saying things like, "Well, the inner circle talks about community, but it's just a cover for wanting power in the organization" or "why won't X faculty member take on more advisees . . . doesn't he or she realize we're a community?"

No area of our life in the college is unaffected by this contradiction. Should someone in the role of "law professor" be expected to answer the phones if necessary? It depends on your paradigm. Should you want to answer the phones if necessary? It depends on your paradigm. Should salaries be allocated according to marketplace criteria? It depends on your paradigm. Should some people be "accruing vacation days" while others never even think about taking vacations except when the time's freed up and don't want to stop others from taking whatever time off they actually need just because they've "used up" their vacation days? Should we follow procedures designed to protect us at all costs from legal liability, or should we reject the paranoid precautions generated by concern about legal liability on the grounds that that whole way of relating to each other is a paranoia-inducing, self-fulfilling prophecy? The answers to all such questions depend on the paradigm one is relating to the world through. For perhaps the whole of its his/herstory, but certainly in the last five years or so, New College has been relating to the world through both paradigms at once.

So we the undersigned sign this manifesto to say—New College should be a radical community. What we mean by this is that we want to stand against the alienation and isolation that characterizes human relationships in the larger society. We believe that all people are motivated fundamentally by the longing for mutual recognition and affirmation—by the need for social connection—and that this need is as central as the need for food or shelter. We believe that the larger society is characterized by a hyperindividualism that is actually a denial of this need and that people guard themselves against the vulnerability associated with this need by hiding behind artificial hierarchical roles through which they can keep each other at "arm's length," at an infinite and anonymous distance. All longings for physical and emotional intimacy are channeled into the nuclear, biological family, with all the distortions that inevitably result from impaction, from trying to channel all our needs for love and connection into an underground bunker located underneath the anonymity of the work world and the larger culture.

We believe that many of the problems in the larger society—problems of domination, discrimination, and abuse—result from the denial of this basic need for loving community and the twisting of this need into pathological, fantasy-based forms of group identity (excessive patriotism, for example) and corresponding fantasy-based phobic stereotyping (xenophobia, for example). We do not say this with a holier-than-thou attitude . . . as if we know how to create good community and everybody else is hopelessly screwed up. On the contrary, we have compassion for all of us suffering from the alienation of the larger society, and we feel we ought to try to do something about it in our lifetimes by showing that people can live in a different way, that they (we) can be friends, work cooperatively, and trust each other not to hurt or abuse each other.

For those of us who have been here long enough to remember our origins, New College arose precisely as an antidote to the alienation, isolation, and individualism that we are criticizing. But twenty-five years ago, it was much easier to share this perspective because it was shared instinctively by the entire counterculture of which New College was a part. Now, the former members of this counterculture, millions strong and scattered all over the world, are largely invisible to each other, carrying around in secret the memory of what was once collectively intuitively clear and obvious.

The counterculture largely abandoned itself because the Left found itself to be as crazy as the Right, bashing each other in public spaces and reinforcing our doubts that we could live in community beyond the family rather than strengthening our confidence that we could do so. The unsafety of the Left destroyed the Left, in forms as diverse as Stalinism and the crazy dynamics of many, many smaller efforts similar to New College, leaving New College as one of the last survivors. This manifesto is based in part on the fact that we see New College as in danger of going the way of the rest of the counterculture . . . in much the same way that Bill Clinton unconsciously decided he would rather be on Mount Rushmore than admit that he smoked marijuana. The communitarian ideals that gave birth to New College were not abolished by corporations or the State . . . they ebbed away as people lost confidence in their original intuition that human relationships could be radically more affirming, trusting, and caring than appears to be the case in the larger culture. This manifesto is a call to prevent these ideals from continuing to ebb away at New College, so that we don't one day find that the New College some of us have devoted much of our lives to has suddenly vanished from too much ebbing away.

One reason that there has been a distinct turn in progressive politics and even in the larger society toward spirituality is precisely this destructive his/herstory of the twentieth century Left. People have rightly lost the ability to believe in any form of political change that does not pay real attention to the rhythms of socially expressed emotion that bind people together. The idea that we could overcome centuries of alienation and paranoia without very delicately and carefully stitching ourselves back together through spirit-enhancing processes . . . well, the his/herstory on the Left of crazy public meetings, accusations, gossip, denunciations, and even physical violence demonstrates the impossibility of that idea. These very same dynamics have all but torn New College apart during its whole his/herstory, as joyful as the experience has also been in spite of these dynamics. But to say that spirituality is important does not necessarily have anything to do with organized religion or even explicitly spiritual rituals. The sixties was libidinally constituted by music, drugs, dancing, and other forms of hanging out together that enabled people to feel their instinctive connection to each other through embodied community—as opposed to ideologically rancorous public meetings or bureaucratic forms of representative democracy. This isn't to say we need only spirit-enlivening experiences with music, dancing, and so on; nor does it mean we shouldn't have ideological debates or representative forms of governance. But it does mean that we should think about New College in spiritual/emotional terms—in terms of what our being together feels like rather than some model of how we are organized. The last thing we are calling for is some new "model of organization" based on community instead of something else. We are calling for the creation of the experience of community and of paying attention to how to sustain it as our way of life.

This means that the process of how this manifesto gains the allegiance of a critical mass of us is as important as the content of the words. We are not asking for people to passively "sign on" to something they don't really agree with, but rather to work and rework the document, addressing people's skepticism and doubt until people really decide they are for it, in settings as free as possible from denunciation, accusation, gossip, and so on, which make the actual creation of community impossible. If we can't gain a critical mass of support for the vision we are advocating for, then it won't happen. The marketplace will then probably dictate that the second paradigm—the liberal-organizational paradigm—will have to be adopted more wholeheartedly, and there is no reason that this couldn't be done in a somewhat humanistic fashion, as it has been in the current contradictory New College over the last few years. But people must realize that the "bottom line"—if the organizational paradigm is adopted as opposed to the communal paradigm—will be operating for profit in an individualistic environment rather than maximizing connection and taking care of each other, which is the bottom line in a communal paradigm. It's Either/Or.

For reasons that we will soon explain, we believe that economic security for each person in New College and for the college as a whole goes hand in hand with adoption of the communal paradigm . . . but it's possible that it could coexist with the second paradigm also.

Articles of Faith

We now set forth these initial articles of faith that express our core convictions about what New College is and should be, and about how our vision should be embodied in the life of the community, in our economy, in our governance, and in our academic programs. These are meant to be subjects of serious discussion—meaning subjects of serious thought and feeling—rather than final positions that have to be accepted or rejected as is.

FIRST ARTICLE: We here repeat our basic tenet about what New College *is*. New College *is* a historical community of particular persons whose aim is to more fully recognize and affirm one another as human beings than is currently possible in the larger society, that emerged as such a community through the consciousness-transforming force of real social movements that themselves embodied this experience of mutual recognition, and that is founded on informal, felt bonds of affection and solidarity. Only secondarily to this fundamental understanding do we refer to ourselves as "a college," "an educational institution," a nonprofit corporation, an organization—we see these secondary terms as clunky metaphors that we have to use occasionally for various purposes because of the predominance of those terms in the larger society, but the meaning of those metaphors is subordinated to and informed by the communal meaning that we ourselves hold dear.

We emphasize the phrase "historical community of particular persons" because we are talking about Jack Leary, Milly Henry, Dale Soules, and others, a latticework of actual relationships that together embodies an ethos of common understanding emerging from a particular lived experience, rather than an interchangeable "workforce" organized according to role and function. What this means is that no person in our community is interchangeable, in contradiction to and repudiation of the dominant capitalist ethos in which all persons are interchangeable depending upon what is most efficient for the organization's roles and functions. We reject this machine concept of human relations that has destroyed so much meaningful culture throughout the world and is rapidly leading to the destruction of other species and the natural environment.

We believe that the closest metaphor that captures what we are striving for is The Village. Although we do not currently live together in a physical village, the idea of the village captures the rhythm of a historical community of particular persons far better than does the idea of an "organization," which inevitably conjures up machinelike, functional notions that have reached their pinnacle in the military and the modern corporation. In a village, for example, people spontaneously take care of each other's families when necessary, and they do not replace each other by more efficient neighbors.

SECOND ARTICLE: The two key principles that should guide New College are "All for one and one for all" and "Act from the heart." The former conveys the idea of seeing each other as we see ourselves or as we would like ourselves to be seen—that is, caring for others as we would like ourselves to be cared for. The second conveys the idea that the way to guide the realization of the first principle is out of the intuitive knowledge revealed by empathy and compassion—the knowledge that emerges from the chakra of the heart rather than, say, such mentally driven precepts as "equal pay for equal work" or other recent inventions of the capitalist era that lead to the unanchored squabbles over interpretation that result from the lack of a heartfelt intuitive center. Both of our key principles are expressions of the fundamental need for mutual recognition and social connection that we exist to affirm.

THIRD ARTICLE: The third article is borrowed from the more utopian thinking of Karl Marx: New College stands for the abolition of wage labor. Although we reject the antispiritualism that ultimately got Marxism into so much trouble—leading to the mistaken belief that if workers seized control of the factories or the land or the State, something good would happen without taking into account the psychological/spiritual need to heal the distortions of centuries of alienation internalized by each person, including each worker, in the course of his or her conditioning—we agree with Marx's point that work is a sensuous, emotional/intellectual, meaningful social activity rather than mere "functioning" that can be measured by "number of hours (or days) worked." "Wage labor" is a capitalist concept associated with the organizational model that we reject. It suggests that in exchange for a definite salary based on quantified work hours (or, to use Marx's phrase "abstract labor-time"), we each receive a specified amount of money that limits each of our obligations to the community and limits the community's obligations to each of us. This way of thinking sees each person as basically a cog in a machine that unites the cogs (the "education-and-social-change machine"), in which each person is a passive functionary and the machine is a phantasmagoric external entity managed by administrators responsible for each passive functionary's fate.

In place of this wage labor idea, we assert that work at New College should be fun and creative and imbued with social meaning—that is, it should feel meaningful, rather than a way to "get money" so that we can do something else, like go skiing, that will allow us to briefly escape the meaninglessness of capitalist culture and the functional workplace. This doesn't mean that some or most of us don't have to work regular hours—people on the phones and doing security, for example, have to do their time more or less exactly or find someone to cover for them. But it does mean that the motive for working in our community is the meaning of our work in relation to the community; it's feeling part of a spiritually grounded community of recognition, a great place. And in this way of looking at things, people should want to cover for each other when necessary because that's part of the fun of it and an expression of our common responsibility, an expression of the meaning of belonging to a community in a world that is mainly individualistic and heartless.

FOURTH ARTICLE: At New College, no one should be involuntarily laid off or terminated. Both layoffs and termination are products of the marketplace conception of the organization, in which persons are perceived as means rather than ends and judged by their utility, their capacity to contribute to the bottom-line efficiency of the organization as defined by marketplace profitability. Persons at New College should be perceived as ends in themselves, as not interchangeable or replaceable any more than family members are perceived as interchangeable or replaceable.

This of course does not mean we should ignore our respective abilities, talents, and experience in figuring out what work each of us does. It means that it is our common humanity and our equal worthiness to be treated with affection and respect that determines the basis of membership in our community. We reject the capitalist principle that subordinates this common humanity to one's usefulness to organizational functioning in a money-driven, competitive economy.

Nor does this mean that no one should be asked in some way to leave the community, no matter how dysfunctional or bizarre his or her conduct has been. Until very recently, there were no layoffs or terminations at New College (except one, which was a mistake that resulted from allowing a single program to develop its own criteria of membership that contradicted the criteria we set forth here). But some people were asked to leave when their coexistence with the rest of us became untenable, or they left voluntarily after sharp disagreements that simply could not be worked out through discussion. In those cases, those who left normally received financial support far in excess of their legal rights as defined by the marketplace, and in more than twenty-five years, there were very, very few such occasions.

FIFTH ARTICLE: The reason we can afford to abolish layoffs is contained in this important fifth article: All members of the community shall divide the college's revenue equally on an annual basis, in a manner that assures the college has no debts. This means that revenue must exceed expenses every year, and that the salary each person receives will fluctuate up or down according to the amount of money we have.

This proposal may lead some at first to think that this will make their personal lives too financially unpredictable, but in fact the opposite is the case. It actually guarantees long-term financial stability for each person by guaranteeing long-term financial stability for the community as a whole. It also strongly motivates each person to behave in a way that maximizes our enrollments and our revenue. Thus in addition to guaranteeing long-term stability, it is likely to increase rather than decrease our annual revenue, and it assures that the impact of passing downturns in enrollment will be minimized by spreading them through the entire community.

In answer to those who are concerned that some will not work their fair share while others will work more than they should, we say the following: If most of us behave in accordance with our collective financial self-interest, those who do not will eventually become ashamed of themselves. This is a more spiritually advanced way to motivate people than threatening them with discipline or termination, a method that relies on power and actually tends to relieve people of moral responsibility for our collective welfare.

Sharing the revenue equally does not necessarily mean that everyone receives the same salary. Giving the same share of revenue to a newcomer with an undemonstrated commitment to the college as we give to someone who has given much to the community for a long time is not true equality, especially when the choice of being at New College for a long period of time means sacrificing (with pleasure!) the chance to "make it" in the capitalist marketplace. So we favor a base salary for all of us, with increments being added on for each five years of membership in the community.

Reconciling this revenue-sharing plan with the mishmash of salaries we have now and the legitimate expectations people have built up based on them will take some time. But we believe this plan is a just economic embodiment of the vision of New College set forth in this manifesto. It rejects the hierarchical role system that values certain roles more than others (administrators more than faculty, faculty more than staff) by rejecting the idea of identity based on role altogether. According to our vision, we're all in it together and equally valuable irrespective of what we do.

In the last few years we have lost a million dollars in revenue, much of it because of unforeseeable losses in our science program but some of it, in the opinion of some of us, because we have been lurching around in contradictory paradigms that have impeded our ability to act in our collective self-interest.

This Article offers a long-term solution to the financial problems we have encountered through communal revenue sharing that prevents the accumulation of debt and eliminates the finger-pointing and political turmoil that always result when declines in revenue make it difficult to meet fixed expenses in an individualistic environment. It is possible that the college can achieve the same long-term stability by wholeheartedly adopting the liberal-corporate paradigm, but this will require (a) very substantial fund-raising from the liberal corporate elite; (b) accommodating the pressure to raise individual fixed salaries in order to be even marginally competitive with marketplace alternatives; (c) more or less continual tuition-raises even with substantial fundraising from the liberal corporate elite; and (d) layoffs as needed to avoid any future deficits. We believe that this path is unlikely to be successful without essentially selling the college to a board and a president with the ability to pay for it (this has been the real historical fate of most alternative projects like New College, which are initially supported by the social movements that give rise to them and then— because they fail to grasp the need to adopt the communal paradigm we are calling for—have no choice but to give up their highest ideals to survive in the postmovement marketplace or go bankrupt). We also believe that it is the wrong path from a moral, spiritual, emotional, and social-change viewpoint even if it is successful. And we believe that the fund-raising efforts of our new Development Office (do we believe in that term?) are more likely to be both successful and consistent with our radical vision if we appeal to our alumni and the progressive community generally by clearly standing for a radical vision of human community that offers a hopeful alternative to the capitalist marketplace that our graduates and friends themselves have inevitably had to compromise with.

SIXTH ARTICLE: New College should have an approach to governance that links community and democracy—or more exactly, that extends the college as a historical community of particular persons bonded by informal affection and solidarity to provide for the continual inclusion of all community members. We reject approaches to governance that separate community and democracy—that is, we reject approaches that rely on purely spontaneous communal governance that fails to consciously reach out to and include all community members (this is community without democracy and leads to the perception of or even the reality of an elite and inaccessible inner circle). But we also reject approaches to governance that rely on formal democratic processes of inclusion that fail to incorporate the wisdom and the feel for what connects us that is provided by, or more accurately "carried by," the historical community. This is democracy without community and leads to what we now have in American society—namely, manipulative power politics among relative strangers who lack any communal anchor and who therefore mirror the disconnection and alienation of the larger society.

Linking community and democracy requires the elimination of the association of governance with power, with who gets to "make decisions" and "run things." The idea that governance is about "power" and "decision making" is almost universally accepted as true but is actually a product of distortions in past human societies and in our own. The idea that governance is about power is a result of the separation of the political and the day-to-day aspects of existence (or in more theoretical language, the separation of the State from civil society). To the extent that day-to-day life is characterized by alienation and isolation and by a sense of passive disconnection from any shared, active communal existence, which is the fate of all of us adrift in the current individualistic and competitive marketplace, governing bodies from the government to corporate boards to really anyone who seems to have socially legitimated authority (Peter, Martin, and Milly!) appear to be the active force in society, using power to "make decisions" that shape our fate as we look for jobs or blankly pass each other on the street or grab a beer before taking the subway home and spacing out in front of the TV. We imagine ourselves to be passively trapped "underneath" governing bodies run by the "people in power" whom we imagine to be "above" us. The strength of this belief affects all of us—it is routinely revealed by our common tendency to feel in awe of "authority figures" in public even as we want to "bring them down" when we gossip about them in private. But in fact, we are suffering from a psychological hallucination supported by the real helplessness of alienated social life—in fact, no one is actually "above" anyone else, and no one is "underneath" anyone else. We are all just here on the same ground together, estranged and unable to connect with each other in real life and therefore spectators of a pseudodemocratic government (how can you have a "government by the people" when there is no "people"?) in political life.

Governance at New College should be understood as the process of building common understanding through gatherings, the specificity of which should depend on the understanding that needs to be built. Or to put this slightly differently, we see governance as simply the reflective part—the thinking and discussing part—of building and shepherding the development of the common understanding of the community. We say this should happen through regular "gatherings" rather than "meetings" because meetings lack any feeling—they connote a way of being together that is too "hard" to advance the rhythm of connectedness. There can of course be administrative meetings aimed at rationally solving administrative problems, but governance should be something quite different: thinking and talking and feeling our way toward our highest aspirations, the reflective part of the life of the community of which it is a part.

At the most general level, there should be monthly community gatherings on the first Monday of each month open to the whole community, including students. The location of these gatherings should alternate between the Valencia Street and Fell Street campuses and should primarily aspire to building the community of the college through the elaboration of our vision in concrete areas—from brainstorming the creation of cultural events to sharing information about and discussing practical problems (say, the parking lot or the state of our revenues and expenses). There should be food and music (say, a guitar player among us), and the gathering should last no less than two hours.

These gatherings should be inclusive of all members of the community, with more specific groupings like academic planning, for example, ideally inclusive (in some way) of all those whose work suggests they ought to be thinking about and discussing the college-wide teaching-learning process. But inclusion cannot mean creating ahistorical organizational entities defined according to functional role with each person being assigned to the entity that fits his or her functional role. This way of thinking about inclusion slips back into the organizational paradigm without attention to maintaining and expanding New College as a historical community of actual persons. Seeing governance as the way to reflect on and strengthen such an actual historical community requires leadership and wisdom from the long-term members and the conscious building up of a communal fabric through the appropriate, somewhat gradual integration of all newer community members into the governance process. The idea of leadership here has nothing to do with exercising power; it has to do with the indispensable responsibility of longtime carriers of the communal memory to gradually enable newcomers to grasp the college's ethos and culture.

This means that these governance gatherings should be seen as synthesizing community and democracy through the widening of a concentric circle, from the center outward, from the elders outward toward the newcomers. From a communal point of view, this is the only way to democratize the fostering and enrichment of the common understanding that actually constitutes the community's essential integrity. Lumping together a group of disconnected strangers who are called "faculty" and giving them an equal vote in an ahistorical, depersonalized "Academic Senate"—that is role-democracy within the liberal, organizational paradigm, but it is contradictory to the communal paradigm. It always produces interest-group politics without a moral or spiritual center.

In more concrete terms, what we mean by linking community and democracy is that all community members should be part of groups that appropriately connect old-timers and newcomers, that these groups be associated in such a way that prevents disconnection of any group from the community as a whole, and that the ethos and goal of such groups is to deepen our common understanding—through the organized reflection that these groups provide for—of our own moral direction in areas as diverse as curriculum, budget, technology, and so forth. In the most general terms, that moral direction is creating a world, beginning with our own college (for you always begin with the current moment), that overcomes the alienation and isolation of the wider society. The wisdom of the old-timers regarding how to do this should be respected, and the inspiration of the newcomers should be welcomed, including their vital role in preventing sclerosis of the communal arteries.

Governance, in this conception, simply dissolves back into the life of the community as its reflective component. It has nothing to do with wielding power over others, little to do with "making decisions" (although it should help shape all arenas of college life), and because of its link to our high aspirations, it should be stimulating and deepening of our friendship and common understanding.

SEVENTH ARTICLE: The cultural life of the college should be consciously shaped to strengthen our spiritual/emotional/intellectual mission of embodying a communal vision that stands against the alienated and bureaucratic character of work life in the larger culture. Among the experiences that should be an essential part of our college life are:

❖ An annual retelling of the story of New College, of the his/herstory of where we came from and why we exist, should take place at the beginning of every academic year. We all should take part in it, and all new students should hear it and get a chance to ask questions about it. To the extent that we ultimately agree on them, the articles of faith in this manifesto and others yet to be developed should be publicly articulated and explained.

❖ All new members of the community (i.e., new faculty and staff) should participate in an orientation regarding our values and the meaning and purpose of New College, and they should be hired only if, broadly speaking, they agree with what we're trying to do. These orientations should be substantial enough to enable newcomers to feel located in the village, and we should look forward to these orientations as important rituals.

❖ As stated in the sixth article on governance, community gatherings should be a regular occurrence, not just for governance purposes, but for culture creation. One possibility is to have get-togethers every Friday afternoon that combine a brief "program" (that might have an interesting and educational public statement about, say, the historical importance of Halloween as a community-constituting pagan ritual as well as minor announcements) with food, drink, and music for us and our families.

❖ At least one day should be set aside each year, preferably in the fall, for evaluations. But our evaluations should not be based on the capitalist model of measuring how "well" each of us has done according to some market-based model of efficient functioning. Instead, they should be drawn from traditions like the Jewish High Holy Days that call for a serious reflection on what we have accomplished in the preceding year in relation to our highest values and the mission of the college. Conducted with one other community member, these evaluations should also encourage the development of aspirations for the coming year and some serious thought about what will be needed, psychologically and from the rest of the community, for these aspirations to be realized.

❖ People should take as much time off as they need consistent with their responsibility to the community. This doesn't mean that people should take more vacation than they currently take. It means what it says, which might mean more, less, or the same as the current practice of twenty days plus the winter break depending on personal circumstances and the needs of the college. If someone abuses this principle, others should let him or her know.

❖ There should be an annual event centered on our alumni, which affirms that their graduation does not mean their excommunication and that we see them as continuing members of the community. We should honor those who have done work that exemplifies our ideal of challenging and seeking to overcome the alienation, isolation, and injustice characteristic of the larger culture. And we should create opportunities for alumni to tell their stories of life after New College, to get help from us about how to extend the college's transformative mission into their current lives, and to serve as mentors for our current students.

❖ On one occasion each year, we should publicly gather to remember community members who have died.

These suggestions are intended as examples of specific ways we can transform our culture so as to deepen the social seriousness of our mission and increase our confidence in the possibility of social transformation by creating it, witnessing it, and marking it together on a regular basis. Some may not be quite right, and there are many other possibilities that we should talk about and consider. But the point of this Article is to call for a conscious reconfiguring of our communal culture to enable us to be the community we aspire to. Without conscious cultural efforts of this type, we will naturally tend to drift back toward the marketplace model of an "educational institution" and devolve back into the gossip and paranoia that is simply an affliction of disconnection. Traditional organizations contain this gossip and paranoia by assigning everyone roles in a flowchart and telling them that's where they belong—that is, people may feel anonymous and disconnected and suffer the real pain of not being recognized and affirmed in their true humanity, but they are provided with an identity-space in an ordered role-hierarchy that has a sort of calming, numbing safety to it. Our rejection of that world means that we must replace the pseudocommunity that it offers people with the real thing.

EIGHTH ARTICLE: Our academic programs should all in some way teach the ideas in this manifesto—we should teach our students the vision of radical community that underlies New College and how it is a challenge to the alienated assumptions that shape the structures of the larger society. To some extent we already do this . . . but without any particular coherence in either theory or practice. Thus, the Weekend College has created a wonderful teaching-learning environment through the cohort model, which provides a unique experience of community for particular groups of students that embodies the disalienating vision that we are calling for. But we have never seriously discussed using the same program-long, small-group model in our other programs, in part because we have never decided explicitly as a community that this kind of transformation of consciousness is what we want to teach and what we want our students to learn.

Our position is that we know a lot about what is wrong with the existing society; we exist in order to challenge the denial of desire that the larger society embodies; we see ourselves as a center for manifesting and spreading a healing understanding of the social world; and we should teach this to our students. This doesn't mean adopting an orthodoxy that must be taught like mantra in every class. It means if we are going to teach property and contract law, or psychoanalysis, or math and science, or Keats's "On First Looking Into Chapman's Homer," we should have some communal discussion and understanding of how these transmissions of knowledge are related to our common purpose for existing. A good example of moving from the center outward through concentric circles would be faculty meetings that were explicitly planned to link our larger vision with the core curriculum of a particular program—where, for example, the individualistic assumptions of property law and contract law were clarified and a teaching strategy developed that would help students understand and go beyond those assumptions. And this point applies to the process of learning as much as to the content: if the Weekend College has developed a process that communicates by example how to create the kind of safe intellectual/emotional space for connecting in a deep way that is blocked in the larger society, perhaps it should be adopted in all of our programs.

This same perspective should shape our development and oversight of internships and apprenticeships. It is good that we aspire to this real-world integration of theory and practice, but we should have a handbook for each program that uses journal-writing and reflection seminars to clarify what the students are supposed to learn in their placements. If what they are supposed to learn is how social-change communities and projects seem to succeed and fail in various ways in bringing about the kind of world we are calling for in this manifesto, there needs to be a consciously created curriculum—a practicum curriculum—for that kind of learning.

In addition, students should themselves participate in the creation of our community while they are here. This means more than giving them a disconnected role in "governance"—it means giving them the opportunity to apprentice in our own daily life—in our business office, program offices, and our community gatherings and cultural events—as part of the curriculum itself. A few other colleges have done this—Berea in Kentucky and Deep Springs in California, as well as the more famous example of Highlander in Tennessee—but not with quite the same communal cultural meaning coming out of the cultural revolution of the sixties that New College could offer. Doing this does require making explicit what that meaning is, and that is why we have produced this manifesto.

NINTH ARTICLE: Finally, we call for a new ethos of compassion for one another and identification with one another that begins to heal and overcome the mistrust that has corroded our sense of community in recent years. We all have doubts that the kind of radical community we are calling for can be brought into being—we all imagine that although each of us longs for this kind of world in the privacy of our own heads, others will probably prevent it from happening and so we had best protect ourselves from opening up to hoping for it again. It is this contradiction between what we desire and what we fear that leads us to keep acting out our doubt through paranoid thoughts about each other, conspiratorial gossip, and more innocently, through failure to support each other in the face of these more destructive dynamics by imagining that we can be safest by remaining in "neutral."

We call for an ethos that leads us to behave in ways that manifest confidence in one another and in the unity of our common humanity and that openly confronts these endless cycles of doubt and demonization. Capitalist culture deals with this doubt by confirming it—it tells everyone that we are all isolated individuals, and provides everyone with little alienated role boxes to live out protected alienated lives in. Our vision of New College is more risky—we say the hell with the alienated role boxes that are meant to help us deny what we most desire, let us try to exist deeply together while we are alive and pass this confidence on to the next generation for them to improve on it after we're gone. But succeeding at this requires a conscious effort to gradually move ourselves toward each other from the position of doubt that we have inherited— that is, a conscious alteration in our objective presence that allows the other to become stronger rather than confirming his or her cynicism and insecurity. It is impossible to actually create this new ethos by our individual efforts alone, but it is also impossible to do so without those efforts, without each of us contributing to the collective confidence in what we are trying to build by leaning in toward the positive through the ambiguity that is inevitably present, for the time being, in so many of our interactions.

INDEX